Warsaw to Wrigley

Warsaw to Wrigley

A Foreign Correspondent's Tale of Coming
Home from Communism to the Cubs

Joseph A. Reaves

Diamond Communications, Inc.
South Bend, Indiana
1997

Warsaw to Wrigley

Copyright © 1997 by Joseph A. Reaves

10 9 8 7 6 5 4 3 2 1

Manufactured in the United States of America

Diamond Communications, Inc.
Post Office Box 88
South Bend, Indiana 46624-0088
Editorial: (219) 299-9278
Orders Only: 1-800-480-3717
Fax: (219) 299-9296

Library of Congress Cataloging-in-Publication Data

Reaves, Joseph A., 1951-
    Warsaw to Wrigley : a foreign correspondent's tale of coming
home from communism to the Cubs / Joseph A. Reaves.
        p. cm.
    ISBN 1-888698-07-1 (alk. paper)
    1. Reaves, Joseph A., 1951- . 2. Foreign correspondent--
United States--Biography. 3. Sportswriters--United States--
Biography.
    I. Title.
PN4874.R347A3 1997
070.4'332'092--dc21   97-9839
    [B]   CIP

Contents

Acknowledgments

Mention the name "Babe" and one image leaps to mind—for baseball disciples and non-believers alike. Babe Ruth was big in life. He became bigger than life in death. But six years before Ruth made his debut with the Boston Red Sox in July 1914, another Babe already was pitching in the big leagues. He was Babe Adams of the Pittsburgh Pirates, who is generally regarded by baseball historians as "The First Babe" in the game. Adams eventually won 194 games in 19 seasons and was among the greatest control pitchers in history. He once walked just 18 batters during an entire season in which he threw 263 innings. I once squirmed through a Sunday afternoon game in Houston when the Cubs and Astros combined to walk 15 batters in eight innings.

The reason Babe Adams came to my attention wasn't because he could throw strikes. It was because he knew how to cover them. Babe Adams became a newspaper reporter when he finished his playing career. At age 70, he covered the Korean War.

Ninety years to the day after Babe Adams was born in Tipton, Indiana, on May 18, 1882, I got my first job in journalism and took the first steps on a weird, wonderful journey that in many ways was a mirror of the Babe's. I'm never going to win 194 games for the Pirates. But I did get paid to watch and write about more big league games than the Babe ever appeared in. And I didn't make my debut in the majors until I'd already put in 13 seasons as a foreign correspondent.

My journey from *Warsaw to Wrigley* started as a gamble and grew into a gambol. For that, I have many to thank. Most I mention in the text, where I hope my admiration and respect are apparent. But a few deserve special thanks. Dick Ciccone is one. Jerome Holtzman is another. They are more than mentors. They are friends. And they are both among the rare breed of superbly talented journalists who, against all odds, remember that people are important—not prizes or profits.

The Filipinos have an expression called *utang na loob*, which means, roughly, a debt of honor, but is far deeper than that. It is a debt that can almost never be repaid. My *utang na loob* belongs to a baseball veteran who encouraged me to write this book and put me in touch with the people who brought it to life, Jill and Jim Langford at Diamond Communications. Besides running a thriving publishing business, Jill and Jim head an organization called "There Are Children Here," which, with the help of volunteer students from nearby colleges, provides care and love for inner-city children. The Langfords have turned the Indiana farmland behind their house into an oasis where kids, who may never have climbed a tree, can fly a kite or sit around a campfire and roast marshmallows. When people learn I once was a baseball writer, they often ask me which is the most beautiful ballpark in America? Invariably, they expect me to say Wrigley or Fenway, Camden Yards or The Ballpark at Arlington. But the most beautiful ballpark I've ever seen is the one Jim and a group of volunteers carved out of a gently sloping wash of land halfway between his house and the enchanted forest where busloads of children come to find hope and love for an afternoon.

It was a privilege working with Jill and Jim Langford.

There are many others who deserve my thanks and have it. Richard Hornik, Edward Gargan, and Jeremy Langford for reading the manuscript and tearing it apart without tearing me down. Ellen Kelly for legal advice and support. Shari Hill of Diamond Communications for capturing green letters out of cyberspace from halfway around the globe and shepherding them onto these pages. Jim Featherston, a grizzled warhorse of a reporter-turned-teacher, for making me want to follow in his footsteps. My father, Joe Jr.; my mother, Shirley, and my two sisters, Patty and Wendy, for their love.

David Lamb, an old friend from the *Los Angeles Times*, shared time with me in the bomb shelters and bars of Beirut before coming home to write a brilliant book in 1991 called *Stolen Season* about his travels through baseball's minor leagues. It wasn't until I finished my manuscript and re-read David's book that I realized how much I owed him.

My colleagues, Joe Goddard of the *Chicago Sun-Times* and Barry Rozner of the *Arlington Heights Daily Herald*, made four years on the road fun. It is incredibly difficult to be friends and competitors in the cut-throat world of Chicago journalism. They were the best at both.

Andy MacPhail, Ed Lynch, and Jim Riggleman of the Cubs were all uncommonly gracious on both a personal and professional level. So was Ron Schueler of the White Sox.

The media relations departments of the Chicago Cubs and Chicago White Sox were terrific. Chuck Wasserstrom and Wanda Taylor of the Cubs, and Scott Reifert and Barb Kozuh of the White Sox, were particularly helpful, efficient, and affable.

Coaches and scouts are the heart and soul of baseball. And they were among the best people in the game to me. Billy Connors, Joe Nossek, José Martinez, Chuck Cottier, Jim Crawford, Hugh Alexander, Bill Harford, Jackie Brown, Jimmy Piersall, Herm Schneider, Dewey Robinson, Dave Trembley, Tom Gamboa, Doug Mansolino, Billy Williams, Fergie Jenkins, Tom Trebelhorn, Dan Radison, Gene Lamont—they all welcomed me into the inner sanctum and shared wit, wisdom, and laughter that will stay with me always.

I mention in the book how traveling secretaries are too-often taken for granted. I tried never to commit that sin. Peter Durso, Glen Rosenbaum, and Jimmy Bank still have my gratitude and admiration. So does Barbara Lang of Phoenix, who found some amazing accommodations for me every spring.

Extraordinary kindness was a gift showered on my by some of the legends of modern Cubs lore: Harry Caray, Ron Santo, Yosh Kawano, Arne Harris, Steve Stone, Thom Brennaman, and Ernie Banks. And whenever I think the worst of the White Sox, which is every time I see a designated hitter come to the plate, all I have to do is remember what a nice, gentle man Ken Harrelson was to me—or how generous and fun-loving clubhouse manager Willie Thompson was—during the solitary year I traveled with the South Siders.

I am forever indebted to Bernie Judge, a former city editor of the *Chicago Tribune*, who got me into the starting lineup. And to my wife, Lynne, who understood and cheered when I finally took myself out of the game.

My son, Kelly, never inherited my passion for baseball. I feel terrible about that because, like any loving father, I want my son to enjoy the best of everything. And, for all its flaws, baseball still is the best of everything. But I owe Kelly a deep bow of thanks. His passions lie elsewhere—in Middle Eastern studies; in the Dead Sea Scrolls, the Koran. And he shares those passions with me. It is all-too-easy to lose perspective in the unreal world of baseball. But not if in the middle of a West Coast road trip your son calls and wants to talk about the paper he's writing on "the relative lack of theological syncretism in the Samaritan 'party' during the pre-exilic period."

My thanks go, too, to a magical group of friends known as "The Swamprats." We have gathered for group vacations at various spots around the globe for 20 years. One of those much-needed soul-purgings came in Arizona during spring training 1996 when I wrote a large chunk of this book. I thank the Swamprats from keeping me from writing more.

Finally, a slow, heartfelt doff of the *chapeau* to Babe Adams, who walked through both worlds—baseball and foreign reporting—long before I ever did. The Babe proved a lifetime ago it was possible to go from *Warsaw to Wrigley*.

Thanks, Babe.

Hong Kong
January 1997

For Lynne

who made it both possible and livable

". . .and there's still so much to be done."

Chapter 1

Heading for Home

██████ first words I remember a major league baseball player saying to me. They weren't the first words I ever exchanged with a big leaguer. They simply were the first worth remembering.

At the time, in the summer of 1991, I was the *Chicago Tribune*'s Eastern European correspondent, based in Warsaw. I had been abroad—first with United Press International, then with the *Trib*—for 10 of the last 13 years. And much of the three years I was back in the States, from 1982-84, I spent traveling out of Chicago to cover the Middle East. So, in effect, I had been exiled from the Fields of Dreams much of my adult life.

With longtime friend and photographer Gary Kemper in the main market in Phnom Penh, Cambodia. A week later, I came down with malaria and had to be medi-vacced to a hospital in Hong Kong.

It had been a great run. I'd lived in London, Vienna, Beijing, Hong Kong, Manila, Rome, and Warsaw. I had all the pedigree and memories of a foreign correspondent. I'd covered wars and revolutions; interviewed presidents and heads of state; dined on 12-course meals in the Great Hall of the People in Beijing; and lived off chocolate bars in Beirut. I caught malaria in Cambodia, meningitis in London and discovered I was allergic to penicillin in Moscow. I was the first Western reporter inside Iraq when the Iran-Iraq war broke out in 1980 and among the last to slip around the Yugoslav army into Llubjana when Slovenia declared independence in '91. I survived the Israeli invasion of Lebanon, Arafat's retreat from Tripoli, the revolution in ███████████ and a half dozen coup attempts.

I stayed around long enough to see a lot of stories come full circle— and to grow weary in the process. I covered the early years of China's opening to the West and the first days after the Tiananmen massacre. I was in Germany when the hostages came home from Iran and in Tehran for Ayatollah Khomeini's funeral. I covered Lech Walesa's arrest under martial law in 1981 and returned a decade later, after watching the Berlin Wall fall, to write about the day he was elected president of a newly democratic Poland.

All of which made me eminently qualified to come home and be a baseball writer. Right? Of course, not. There were dozens, probably hundreds, of writers who were more capable, more deserving, and better prepared for the job. I just happened to be the one who got it.

Oddly enough, in a way my overseas experience was perfect training. There isn't a vast difference between the myopia of pampered professional athletes in the United States and the fanaticism of gun-slinging thugs in Bosnia. Their means and ends, of course, are enormously different; incomparably different. But, for the most part, their self-serving arrogance and narrow-minded views of the world are frighteningly similar.

Nor is there a great gulf in the mentalities of power brokers in a police state and the megalomaniacs who run many sports franchises. Or that of their lieutenants. One thought bothered me repeatedly throughout the 1992 season, my first with the Cubs. I couldn't decide whether Jim Lefebvre reminded me more of Nicolae Ceausescu, the dictator who was executed in the Romanian uprising of 1989, or Ferdinand Marcos, the man who imposed martial law in the Philippines. I finally settled on Marcos, mainly because, like the strongman of Manila, Lefebvre had a brilliant and beautiful wife who probably would have been better at his job—if only the world were a little different.

Admittedly, while the basic reporting skills may be the same, few correspondents get traded from Warsaw to Wrigley in one season. It was, needless to say, a stunning transition—not so much for me as for everyone else in the closed, and highly competitive, worlds of sports and journalism.

When I was in China in the mid-1980s, *The Globe & Mail*, Canada's equivalent of the *New York Times*, made a similar move in reverse. The paper sent its top sports columnist, Allen Abel, to Beijing, where he proved to be one of the best foreign correspondents—in my opinion, *the best*—of his time.

Born in Brooklyn, Abel studied astrophysics at Rensselear Polytechnical Institute in Troy, New York, and worked at several small newspapers in New York state before joining the *Globe*. In 1980, he won Canada's prestigious National Newspaper Award for a series of articles from the Soviet Union. But his real claim to fame was his sports column, which, to this day, remains one of the most popular ever written in Canada. One column I remember in particular was a work of art about nothing more than sitting in the bleachers at Yankee Stadium.

Abel took a columnist's eye and touch to China and wrote a steady stream of essays on everything from a night out at Maxim's, the posh new French restaurant in the heart of Red China, to an afternoon watching bad baseball on a hard-scrabble lot he dubbed "the best little ballpark in Beijing." In the process, Abel did a better job of giving readers a feel for life in a dramatically changing far-off land than any one of the scores of scholarly—and, in my case, not-so-scholarly—correspondents who worked themselves into a frenzy reading tea leaves and writing about the enigma of Chinese politics.

The key, of course, was perspective. Abel brought a new perspective

to China. And his editors at the *Globe* were smart enough, and courageous enough, to let him do it.

Courage—and blind faith—is what the *Trib* needed to take a similar
gamble and put an alien like me on the baseball beat. And the man with
the convictions and thick skin who made it possible was F. Richard
Ciccone, a former Marine who won the Bronze Star in Vietnam and rose
through the ranks of journalism to become one of the most-respected and
longest-serving managing editors of a big-city newspaper in the country.

Ciccone hired me in December 1981. I was working in Vienna at the
time as UPI's Chief Eastern European Correspondent. Martial law had
just been declared in Poland and I was frantically trying to coordinate
UPI's typically outgunned coverage. It was a fascinating time and a truly
wonderful job—one I always regretted giving up. But UPI was in its
death throes. The pay was pathetic. The future was forlorn. Ciccone's
call was like Bobby Thompson's home run—a miracle shot out of the
blue. And I jumped as soon as UPI could ship in a replacement.

I was hired specifically to go back overseas for the *Tribune*, which,
under then-editor Jim Squires, was expanding its international coverage. But since I had never worked for a daily newspaper or lived anywhere in the Midwest—I went to work for the wires straight out of LSU
and lived in New Orleans, Dallas, and Denver before going overseas
with UPI—the *Trib* rightly thought I should spend some time in Chicago, getting to know the paper and its readers. The timing worked out
perfectly. I was in Chicago just six months when Israel invaded Lebanon in June 1982. The *Trib* sent me to Beirut for three months that summer and back the next year when Arafat was holed up in Tripoli. In
between, I worked on several long-term projects in Chicago and inad-
vertently laid the groundwork for covering baseball a decade later.

In early 1984, Squires prepared me to go back overseas by arrang-
ing a three-month fellowship at the East-West Center in Hawaii to study
Asian affairs. The fellowship ended in the spring and I wasn't due to
move to Beijing until Thanksgiving. The unwelcome wait turned into a
godsend, thanks to the Cubs, who came out of nowhere to win the Na-

tional League East and earn their first trip to post-season play since World War II. It was a magical summer. My wife and I owned a condominium on Irving Park Boulevard, a 10-minute walk from Wrigley, and my status as foreign-correspondent-in-waiting left me just unapproachable enough with the mid-level editors that I was free to sneak out almost at will for ballgames. Unfortunately, it also left me conspicuously available for emergency fill-in duty during the glory days at the end of the season when the Cubs were the hottest story in town. Instead of being in a crowded tavern with friends watching the Cubs beat the Pirates, 4-1, to clinch the division on September 23, I was in the newsroom working under the unrelenting whip of a talented young editor named Michael Tackett and his boss, Bill Garrett, who had me taking phone calls from reporters across Chicago and writing about the celebrations. The resulting story ran on Page 1 under the banner headline: "Cubs win! Holy cow!" and made a glimmer of an impact nationally when Bryant Gumbel—like me, a native of New Orleans and longtime Cub fan—opened the "Today" Show on NBC by holding up a copy of the *Chicago Tribune* for the cameras and reading the lede, which said simply: "The suffering is over."

Cub fans, of course, know how unbelievably wrong and naïve those words were. By October 7, the Cubs had become the first NL team to blow a two-game lead and lose a best-of-five playoff series—to the San Diego Padres, no less. The *Trib* sent me to all five games to write newspage stories, as opposed to regular sports coverage, and the assignment planted a seed, in my mind at least, that maybe sports wasn't so different from news reporting after all.

I had covered sports early in my career. As a pup in UPI's New Orleans bureau, I was kicked out of the office, given credentials to watch the Saints practice and told to come back with two features a day—one for morning newspapers and one for afternoon editions. From there, I graduated to covering LSU games in Baton Rouge and, eventually, to writing Saints game stories on the not-so-rare Sundays when my disgruntled and underpaid bureau manager had a few-too-many free beers in the press box to finish the job himself.

In 1975, I transferred to UPI's Dallas bureau where, in addition to my regular news duties, I was put in charge of coordinating Texas high school football coverage, which meant, essentially, getting the telephone number of every Dairy Queen and deputy sheriff's outpost in the state and calling around on Friday nights to gather as many scores as possible and slamming them on the wire. That, too, surprisingly, played a role in my eventually getting the Cubs job. It turned out that Dick Ciccone did the very same job for the Associated Press years earlier. When we discovered this common bond one day in his office, Ciccone and I spent nearly an hour laughing over obscure Texas towns and their high school nicknames. My favorite was the Hutto Hippos, who, I assumed, must have had a great ground game. Ciccone was partial to the Port Lavaca Sand Crabs.

After just one year in Dallas, I was transferred to Denver—this time primarily as a sports reporter to cover the Broncos and Nuggets. I made it through half a season with the Nuggets and was delighted to see Larry Brown was head coach. Brown had been my favorite player when I was paying $1 a game to watch the New Orleans Buccaneers of the old American Basketball Association play on a dangerously elevated court at the Loyola University Fieldhouse. But after the Nuggets' season and before the Broncos could open camp, I was sent back to New Orleans in the summer of 1976 as bureau manager and state editor. That meant I got to assign myself to cover Saints games as well as the New Orleans Jazz, who, like the Saints then, lost a lot, but at least were entertaining with a flashy backcourt of Gale Goodrich and Pete Maravich.

I got my first chance to cover baseball when the St. Louis Cardinals moved their Triple-A franchise to the Superdome for the 1977 season. Those Pelicans only lasted one season, but that was long enough for me to get a real taste of the sport my grandfather loved and taught me to love. That summer I watched—and promptly forgot all about—a young Pelican player named Jim Riggleman, who later would manage the Cubs. But the highlight of that season, and my early years in sports, was meeting the great Satchel Paige, who was "honorary pitching coach" of the Pelicans. Actually, Paige was little more than the salaried companion of A. Ray Smith, the team's owner. Smith, a great baseball man, simply loved having Satchel around. He rented two apartments in suburban New Orleans, named Satchel his honorary pitching coach, and spent the summer talking baseball and drinking bourbon with his good friend.

One night halfway through the season, I got the chance to sit in on one of their sessions. I was dying to meet Paige so I called Smith, told him I worked for UPI, and asked for an interview. He said sure, gave me the address, and told me to drop by about 6:30. I showed up with Pat Benic, then UPI's photographer in New Orleans and later head of Reuters newspictures in Europe, the Middle East, and Africa. Pat and I were, and remain, great friends and longtime baseball fans, who went to every World Series together from 1977 until '86 when I was based in the Philippines and he was working in Hong Kong. We walked into Paige's sparsely furnished apartment in Metairie, Louisiana, that night in the summer of 1977 like two high school kids on our first date. Benic had two bulky bags of camera equipment. I had a pen, a notebook, and a rarely used tape recorder. We shouldn't have bothered. Smith met us at the door with a hearty hello, introduced us to Paige, and promptly cracked the first of two bottles of Jack Daniels he would open that evening. I have an hour's worth of tape that I transcribed and put in my files. Benic swears he has a great picture of Satchel imitating Josh Gibson's batting stance. Somehow, though, neither of us ever got around to writing a story or filing a picture. The hangovers lasted for days. The memories will last two lifetimes.

That was the beginning and end of my baseball writing career until the summer of 1991 when I flew back from Warsaw and walked into Ciccone's office to announce I was leaving the *Trib*. I wasn't happy with some of the recently recycled and rehabbed editors who were running the paper's international coverage. And I was pretty weary. I had been abroad the last eight years and had spent most of that time traveling from one hot spot to another. I needed a break from the frenzied pace of foreign reporting. I had applied for, and been accepted into, a

Ph.D. program at the University of Tennessee. My wife and I were on our way to Knoxville to look at real estate. But I wanted personally to let Ciccone know my decision and to thank him for everything he had done for me. It was strictly a courtesy call. My mind was made up. I had thought long and hard about leaving the *Tribune*. It was a tough decision, but I kept coming to the same conclusion: I'd done everything I could at the paper. Being a foreign correspondent was, for me, the best job in the world. I was simply tired of it and couldn't imagine anything else the paper could offer that would be either as challenging or enjoyable—let alone both. I was wrong. Ciccone listened patiently as I poured out my feelings and talked about Tennessee. Then he started offering alternatives. He suggested Moscow or Tokyo. I was flattered and said thanks, then chuckled and told him he wasn't listening. I needed a break from overseas. "What about Denver?" he said. No, thanks, I told him again. A national bureau would be more of the same. I'd be reporting to the same editors on the foreign/national desk and the work wasn't any different: jumping on airplanes every time the phone rang and never knowing when I'd be home again. If I wanted to keep doing that, I'd certainly choose Tokyo over Denver. I just didn't want that right now. Ciccone finally accepted my mind was made up and changed the subject. We reminisced about a series of things for about a half hour until, at last, I got up, shook Dick's hand, said thanks again, and started to walk away. I had one foot out his office when he said: "What about the Cubs?"

As off-the-wall as that sounded, the possibility had been evolving for years. The seed, as I mentioned, was planted during the 1984 playoffs. But the first time the idea started to sprout was in May 1988. I was making my first trip back to Chicago since moving to Asia for the *Tribune* nearly four years earlier. And, of course, it was customary for foreign correspondents on home leave to come in to the office to kiss the rings. I did and when I got to Ciccone's office, he suggested skipping out the next afternoon to take in a Cubs' game. Needless to say, I didn't need much convincing. The Cubs, as every baseball fan knows, are owned by Tribune Co. And, as managing editor of the *Chicago Tribune,* Ciccone had access to some choice seats—strictly for business purposes, of course.

I didn't know it at the time, but this was to be a business meeting.

We were seated directly behind homeplate on a glorious sunny afternoon mesmerized by the pitching clinic being delivered by Greg Maddux, a skinny 22-year-old with a beguiling impish smile, who came into that season with an 8-18 record and a 5.59 earned-run average in the big leagues. For five innings or so, we talked about little else but the way Maddux was pitching. Up and in with a 90 mile-an-hour fastball. Down and away with a circle change that, from behind homeplate, looked as if it broke a yard and a half from left to right. Ciccone kept saying this kid was going to be great. I exercised uncommonly good sense and kept my predictions to myself.

Somewhere around the sixth inning, Ciccone got down to business. He started by complimenting me on the job I had done in China and the Philippines, then began talking in generalities about the foreign staff. After a while, I realized he kept coming back to the subject of our Africa coverage. It slowly dawned on me—occupied, as I was, with the baseball game in front of me—that Ciccone was trying to convince me to move to Johannesburg and become the Africa correspondent. My wife, who was with us, was all for the idea and not-so-discreetly joined forces with Ciccone when I left briefly to make a run to the restroom. But I was happy in Asia. I wasn't having any part of leaving if I could help it. I tried to make that as tactfully clear as I could to both my bosses.

I knew I finally had prevailed when Ciccone went to the age-old fall-back position and asked where I saw myself going with the *Tribune?* "You want to know?" I said, half-chuckling as I took a sip of beer and looked out at Wrigley Field bathed in the late afternoon shadows. "Here's what I'd like to do: I'd like to spend two or three tours overseas—seven or eight years—and then come back in '91 or '92 and cover the Cubs."

Ciccone and I both laughed. My wife rolled her eyes in frustration. But it was a great way to break off an awkward conversation. I promptly forgot about it until three years later when Ciccone stopped me from walking out of his office with the words: "What about the Cubs?"

The biggest surprise was that I took nearly a month to make up my mind. Covering the Cubs, of course, is one of the dream jobs in journalism. My starry-eyed nephew from Falls City, Texas, once gushed that it had to be "one of the five greatest jobs in the world." He never said what the other four might be, but he isn't alone in his opinion. And I'd have trouble arguing otherwise. Still, covering a major-league team is an incredibly demanding, high-pressure job. Far more so than even most fellow journalists realize. Jerome Holtzman, the dean of Chicago baseball writers, who was inducted into the Hall of Fame in 1989 after two decades of covering the Cubs and White Sox on a daily basis, is fond of saying to anyone who will listen that baseball beat writers are the hardest-working people on any paper. I came to believe Jerome was right about this, as he was about most things he ventured an opinion on regarding baseball. But that, of course, is because we shared many of the same prejudices and passions. Basketball and hockey beat writers have a grueling grind. And prep sportswriters work almost as long and hard and get only a pittance of the recognition from either the public or their editors. They might not agree with Jerome and me about the degree of difficulty of our respective assignments.

Beat writers, for those unfamiliar with the term, are women and men who travel with and write about a team full-time. By the early 1990s, there were only three beat writers covering the Cubs; four covering the White Sox. The *Tribune, Chicago Sun-Times* and the suburban *Arlington Heights Daily Herald* each had beat writers covering both teams. The much-smaller *Daily Southtown*, with its circulation concentrated on Chicago's South Side where the White Sox held sway, staffed all Cubs home games and assigned a beat writer to travel season-round with the Sox. The *Southtown*, which later was purchased by the owners of the *Sun-Times,* was so unabashedly provincial it once ran an advertising campaign with the slogan: "Sox win. Cubs lose. It's a beautiful day!"

The workload, grinding as it is, never was a factor in my hesitation to accept the Cubs' assignment. And never bothered me once I took it. The real reason I wavered in 1991 was simple and sophomoric. I was worried being too close to the game would ruin my love for it. It's one thing to worship anyone or anything from afar; quite another to sustain an infatuation after you've seen the warts and unearthed the skeletons. I remember reflecting for days that, maybe, I should turn down the offer. I could go off to Tennessee and be content the rest of my career in the simple, private realization I could have had one of the best jobs in journalism if I wanted. It was pretty to think so. But not very realistic. In the end, I couldn't resist. I phoned Ciccone when I returned to Warsaw and said I'd take him up on his offer.

I knew, even before I said yes, that I'd be viewed as some kind of freak on the baseball beat. But I never could have imagined the niggling hostility I would face. Or that much of it would come from my colleagues. I could understand the players, with their limited world views, looking askance at a foreign correspondent coming in to write about their beloved game. The same with baseball's senior executives. And I certainly expected the first manager I ripped in print to ask me where I was coming from; what the hell I knew about baseball? But I naïvely figured my fellow writers, at least, would give me a benefit of doubt. The *Chicago Tribune,* after all, isn't running a work-release program for wayward writers. It is one of the top newspapers in the country. And covering the Cubs is one of the highest-profile jobs it has to offer. One of the most delicate, too, since the *Trib* owns the team. I assumed most of my colleagues would appreciate the fact the powers-that-be at the *Tribune* could never risk embarrassing themselves by sloughing off a prestige beat like the Cubs to someone they thought was even the least bit unqualified. Apparently, I assumed too much. I underestimated the nesting instincts of most members of the small community of baseball writers around the country.

The first hint I had of trouble came in early September 1991 toward the end of a 16-day trip I made back to the States from Warsaw. I wasn't due to start the Cubs' beat until spring training 1992. And my replacement wasn't due in Poland until just after Christmas. But Ciccone suggested I fly back and spend a couple weeks traveling with the *Trib*'s two baseball beat writers to see how they went about their jobs. It would give me a chance to see the work load, meet a few players, coaches and managers, and, generally, get my bearings before I jumped in with both feet. It was a great idea and typical of the way the *Tribune* did things right most of the time under Ciccone's leadership.

I spent much of the trip with the Cubs on an eight-day West Coast swing. The writer I was replacing, Andy Bagnato, was terrifically helpful. So were the two competitors traveling with him, Dave Van Dyck of the *Sun-Times*, and Barry Rozner of the *Daily Herald.* The Cubs were in chaos then. Don Zimmer had been fired as manager three months earlier and replaced by Jim Essian, a career minor-league manager who never should have been put in that position. The players openly disdained Essian, whose only sin was taking the greatest job of his life and replacing Zimmer. Essian would be gone, too, in a couple months along with then-general manager Jim Frey and team president Don Grenesko. The organization was unraveling. The team reflected the chaos. The season was deep into the dog days and Bagnato wanted nothing more than to finish his three-year stint on the beat and move on. He had started on a high note, covering the 1989 division-winning team and doing an exceptional job. But things had gone downhill rapidly. Not only did the Cubs revert to their familiar bumbling on the field and anarchy in the front office, but Bagnato's personal life suffered. He lost both his parents in a commercial plane crash. Because of the demands of the job, he never had a chance to cope with the loss and it was beginning to catch up with him. Bagnato had arranged a leave of absence from the *Tribune* and was planning to spend six months in Scotland as soon he could clear the decks and get away.

Considering everything that was going on his life, personally and professionally, the last thing Bagnato probably wanted was to have to hold his successor's hand and show him around. But he never once grumbled. He introduced me to everybody I needed to meet and followed the introductions with helpful background insights. He typed a detailed city-by-city memo of every road stop in the National League, complete with where to eat, where to drink, where to rent a car and where not, the best hotels, and the most-enjoyable diversions. He did all of that and his job, too, which is particularly grinding when the team is on the West Coast because the time difference plays havoc with deadlines—doubling and tripling the amount of stories that have to be written and cutting by one-half or one-third the amount of relevant copy that gets into the paper.

By the time the Cubs wrapped up the road trip in San Diego and headed back to Chicago, I was feeling pretty feisty about the new assignment. The three Chicago writers I had met were friendly, receptive, and encouraging. The players were less so, but that was to be expected. I didn't particularly want to be friendly with them. I always remembered the words of Abe Rosenthal, executive editor of the *New York Times,* when he learned one of his reporters was having an affair with, and accepting gifts from, a politician she was assigned to cover. "It's okay to (sleep with) elephants," Rosenthal said. "Just don't cover the circus." The days when reporters were best buddies with the players they covered were over—or so I thought—and that was just fine with me.

I found an entirely different atmosphere when I flew from San Diego to Dallas to join the *Tribune's* other baseball writer, Alan Solomon, who was covering the White Sox on a road trip that started with a weekend series against the Texas Rangers. Solomon and I would work the two Chicago baseball beats simultaneously for several years until he was taken off the White Sox and re-assigned for a monumentally foolish and laughable act. We never got along and, more importantly, I never came to respect him. In the fall of 1991, though, I was hoping for the best. Solomon and my wife had been colleagues at the *Houston Chronicle* years before. I had attended his going-away party when he left Houston for what turned out to be one of a series of career shifts—this particular one to the copy desk at the *Philadelphia Inquirer.*

When I arrived in Texas, it became immediately apparent Solomon was no Andy Bagnato. He clearly wasn't pleased to have an outsider around. Solomon went through the motions of trying to be polite, but it was obviously such a strain that it set the tone for our relations over the years.

After a few awkward minutes of handshaking and idle chit-chat that first afternoon, Solomon decided to show me around the visitors' locker room. It was three hours before game time and the White Sox players were lounging around in varying states of dress—watching videos, reading newspapers, or flipping through the enormous stacks of hardcore porno magazines for which the visiting clubhouse at old Arlington Stadium was revered around the major leagues.

Solomon was struggling to find a player who would be understanding and patient when he spotted catcher Ron Karkovice, who I later would come to know as one of the nicest and most-decent players with the Sox—a good family man and one of the hardest workers in the big leagues. Karkovice was playing an electronic Game Boy, his face concentrating on the tiny screen while the machine whirred and beeped maddeningly.

Karkovice, obviously, is of Polish descent. And Poland, at the time was going through the exciting transition from Communism to democracy. Solomon figured he was saved. Here was a nice guy who would put up with a minor intrusion and, at the same time, had something in common with this outsider who spent the past two years covering Poland.

"Hey, Ron. This is Joey Reaves. He's going to be covering the Cubs next year."

"Nice to meet ya, Joey," said Karkovice, barely glancing up.

"Joe's spent the past couple years working in Poland. If you wanna know anything about Poland, he's the guy to ask."

This time Karkovice didn't even bother to look up. He waited a couple seconds, flicking the controls of the Game Boy with alternating thumbs, then said, simply:

"Fuck Poland."

Chapter 2

Here's Looking at You, Kids

Just before he mumbles his classic line in *Casablanca* about "all the gin joints of all the towns in all the world," Humphrey Bogart sits hunched over a table in the darkened bowels of Rick's Café Americain in the middle of the night with a half-finished bottle of scotch at his right elbow. His character, Rick Blaine, is wallowing in self-pity. The love of his life, Ilsa, has emerged unthinkably from the past, in tow with a noble, handsome husband Rick never knew she had. All three are trapped in the godforsaken chaos of Casablanca while World War II rages around them.

Sharing the darkness with Rick is his trusted friend, Sam, the piano player, who is tinkling the keys while Rick drinks himself ever-deeper into depression.

"Sam?" Bogart slurs. *"If it's December 1941 in Casablanca, what time is it in New York?"*

Taken aback, Sam starts to ask: *"Wha'?"* then pauses and says simply: *"My watch stopped."*

Half a century later, in December 1991, my watch had stopped, too. The United States I came home to was as different from the one I'd left as Morocco was from Manhattan. When I left, a warehouse was a giant tin shack behind the docks on the Tchoupitoulas Street wharf. When I came home, warehouses were mega-supermarkets where card-carrying club members from the suburbs bought ketchup by the drum and toilet paper by the ton. Tennis shoes had once been easy to buy and easier to wear. Now, I was so intimidated by the wall-to-wall selection and the baffling high-tech options that I couldn't bring myself to step inside a Foot Locker.

In my absence, cable TV had gone from a futuristic fantasy to the hardly noticed ho-hum. And drive-ins had just gone—at least drive-in movies had mostly gone. A whole other bizarre drive-in culture had sprung up and passed me by.

I laughed out loud when my brother-in-law bought a six-pack without leaving his van at the drive-thru liquor barn on Highway 181 outside Falls City, Texas. I embarrassed myself by not knowing what to do when the valet suddenly appeared at the drive-in dry cleaners in Scottsdale, Arizona. And I kept shaking my head in disbelief at the amazing array of drive-thru daiquiri stands on almost every corner near my family home in suburban Metairie, Louisiana. "They can't have booze in those, can they?" I remember asking my youngest sister, Wendy, as she leaned out the window to accept two pineapple daiquiris in foam cups from the gum-smacking teenager working the night shift at Daiquiris 'N Cream. "Sure," she said, pronouncing it with just the proper nasal Noo Awlins accent—*shoooore'-uh*—and turning to look at me with a crinkled brow as if I had just beamed down from Pluto. "Why else would anybody buy 'em?"

I knew Louisiana wasn't exactly on the cutting edge of social enlightment. But my sister works for the state police. Isn't there some kind of law against drinking and driving, I asked? How can you sell cocktails to somebody sitting behind the steering wheel of a car that's running?

"Oh, it's okay as long as you don't drink 'em 'til you get home," she said, punching a straw through the plastic top and taking a long, happy draw of icy rum.

When I came back to the States, I was a stranger in my own land. I had been home to visit a half dozen times since I'd left for London in the summer of '79. And I had spent parts of three years in the early 1980s based out of Chicago. I was delighted and dazzled by America. But I never really had time to study the fabric of the place—the substance of its people. When I packed to go to spring training with the Cubs in 1992, I was, literally, more in touch with the Philippines and Romania than I was with the people of Peoria or Racine. I was trying to find my way back. Fortunately, I had baseball as my road map. For the next four years, I traveled from one end of North America to the other becoming amazed, frustrated, energized, and depressed. After living in eight countries and traveling through, and working from, more than I care to remember, I can truly say the U.S. is the greatest. But it is the greatest with a few giant asterisks.

It was depressing to come home and be greeted with the abiding indifference most Americans have to anything foreign. Ron Karkovice wasn't alone in his contented isolation. On the other hand, the sentiment was understandable. All I had to do was relate to my own feelings. For years, I was accustomed to traveling on Third-World airlines where every flight was an adventure in sanitation and safety. I stayed in hotels on remote islands in the Philippines where running water was a luxury. And I ate meals in the Punjab where I was grateful I couldn't ask what was on the plate. Now, all of a sudden, I was flying first class on charter and commercial airlines, staying in the best hotels in the greatest cities in the United States. My office was the soft green of a baseball field.

For much of my life, when the phone rang, it meant I was off to another far-flung destination, never knowing whether I would be gone three days or three months. Now, all I had to do was look at a pocket baseball schedule and I knew where I would be every day—almost every hour—for the next year. I knew I had my pick of great restaurants and wonderful diversions. And I was getting paid to enjoy it all—The American Dream.

My colleagues used to chuckle when sometimes, without warning in the middle of an inning, looking around the stands at thousands of people basking in the crib-like comfort of one of North America's great ballparks, I would be overcome with the wonder of it all. *"What a country,"* I'd say, out loud and out of the blue—shaking my head and meaning it from the bottom of my heart. I was just a middle-aged, middle-income hack, trying every day, as Jerry Jeff Walker so perfectly described it in one of his songs, *"to slide one by ya once more."* For me, the United States, was a Shangri-la of physical contentment and security. I could only imagine how great it must seem if you were 28 years old and getting paid a million dollars a year to play a game with adoring fans ogling your every move. It didn't take a $500-an-hour psychoanalyst to understand why most baseball players never heard of Bosnia. And why those who did, could give a flying forkball what happened there.

The stereotype of the dumb jock got to be a stereotype with good reason. I didn't expect to be discussing Niebuhr or the disappointments of democratization in the former Soviet Bloc with many players. But I did expect most reporters I'd work with to be interested in what went on in the world outside baseball. Was I ever wrong. I quickly came to believe that a well-rounded baseball beat writer was someone who could also talk about basketball.

There were, of course, some notable exceptions. Jeff Blair of the *Montreal Gazette* and Pedro Gomez of the *Sacramento Bee* immediately leap to mind. So do Fred Mitchell and Andy Bagnato, my two predecessors at the *Tribune*. Another exceptionally intelligent and sophisticated baseball writer was Chris Haft, who moved from the *Houston Post* to the *Cincinnati Enquirer*. But for every Blair, Bagnato, Mitchell, Gomez, and Haft, there were five other "seamheads" sitting in the press box or shuffling across the playing field.

A seamhead is anyone so consumed with baseball and its minutia that he or she can think of nothing else or talk reasonably intelligently about anything else. You can almost see 108 red stitches holding their heads together.

I worked the beat full-time for four years. So I know how all-consuming it can be and what monumental effort it takes to stay on top of the job. There are valid reasons beat writers rarely last more than two years on the job anymore. The pressure is intense. The rewards are fleeting. And the pace is devastating. But you'd think that would be all the more incentive to find other outlets—to read a book about something other than baseball every now and then; to open a paper to somewhere other than the sports pages; to talk with someone about something other than the number of times Steve Trachsel throws over to first when he has runners on base.

Not so. I learned that if I wanted to avoid ridicule, I'd read the front section of the *New York Times* in my hotel room before I got on the team bus. I'd wait until the lights went out on the team plane before pulling out a hardback book. And never, never would I try to start a discussion about current events, particularly international affairs.

My last day at the *Tribune* before I went to Beijing in 1984, I got stopped on my way out the door by Bill Garrett, who, basically, ran the paper from the city desk in those days. He was one of the best journalists I worked with anywhere on the globe. Garrett could no more fathom why I wanted to go to China than I could comprehend why he wanted to run the city desk. To him, being a foreign correspondent was some kind of hazy, nebulous fantasy. Real journalism was down and dirty in the streets of Chicago. It was: get the facts, get 'em straight and get 'em in the paper. Garrett didn't coin it, but he certainly preached the age-old newsroom gospel that says: "If your mother tells you she loves you, check it out."

As I was walking past the city desk that day, Garrett made one last—and, as it turned out, lasting—attempt to put things in perspective for me. "Hey, Joey, what are we gonna do every time you file a story? Call the Chief Chinaman to check it out?"

In the new age of political correctness, Garrett might want to re-phrase his remark. Then, again, knowing Garrett, he might not. But the point he made stuck with me all the while I was in China and long after. I was on my own, but I was responsible to everyone. It often would have been easy, as Garrett hinted, to fake a quote or embellish a scene when I was 7,000 miles from Tribune Tower. And, trust me, it isn't exactly an uncommon occurrence. One of my colleagues at the *Tribune* and another at the *Los Angeles Times* were laughably notorious within the foreign correspondents' community for fine-tuning the facts to fit their stories. But the Fear-of-Garrett kept me in line whenever I was tempted to falter.

The trouble was, when I joined the baseball beat, I wasn't sure of the rules anymore. The basics were the same—get the facts, get 'em straight and get 'em in the paper. But what was this crazy mix of journalism and entertainment? Baseball players are definitely public figures— the same as politicians. But they aren't held to the same standards of accountability. Nor should they be, because they are entertainers, not public servants. So what then, is the role of the beat writer?

I was constantly amazed by the handful of baseball reporters who felt the best way to cover the game was by trying to be part of it. There was a writer for one of the California papers who actually dressed out and shagged flyballs with the team during spring training. Another reporter from Denver constantly walked around like an old-time scout spitting brown blobs of chewing tobacco onto the field or into a foam cup in the press box.

But most amazing to me were the reporters who either for misguided professional reasons, or out of some barely suppressed sense of star-struck giddiness, simply yearned to be buddies with the players they were covering. A shining star in the field was one of my colleagues at the *Tribune* who sometimes sent notes to players, addressing them by their nicknames. One particularly memorable dispatch that made its way into the hands of smirking fellow reporters was written to Randy Myers, the notoriously high-strung ace of the Cubs' bullpen who kept hand grenades in his locker, was fond of camouflage fatigues, and once gleefully punched out a fan who made the drunken mistake of charging the mound during a typical frustrating afternoon at Wrigley. The note carefully, and ridiculously, laid out this writer's version of reality in some insignificant clubhouse crisis *du jour* involving Myers. The note was addressed: "Dear Mellow."

It is easy to figure how that note and others got into public circulation. Many of the players this writer cultivated as bosom buddies liked nothing better than to set him up for ridicule. And he never quite caught on. Several times a year, other writers would laughingly repeat the story about the time their colleague was covering the Cubs and pitcher Al Nipper brought a pair of handcuffs to the clubhouse. Nipper lured this writer to a locker, slapped the cuffs on him, then left him stranded in the clubhouse while the team and other reporters went on the field for pre-game workouts. The players got a tremendous laugh out of it. So did the fawning scribe. He thought it showed he was one of the boys. Given the choice between being a professional or being involved in one of the players' jokes, this guy always chose the joke—even if he was the butt of it.

One of my competitors and friends when I was on the beat had a similar, though considerably less groveling, reputation for courting players. He regularly would be seen drinking with athletes and just as regularly deny it when other reporters mentioned it. One night in St. Louis, however, he found himself in an embarrassing position. Normally a swift writer, he was having trouble that evening. He was so slow, in fact, that two players tired of waiting for him in the clubhouse. They decided to come up to the press box to hustle him along for a pre-arranged post-game pub crawl.

While reporters visit the clubhouse daily, players almost never come to the press box. For one thing, they don't have the occasion. They are usually busy with their own commitments before, during, and after games. For another thing, the press box is supposedly reserved for working media and club officials. Not that there aren't regular exceptions. But those exceptions rarely include players hanging around to go drinking with reporters. This particular night they did. And while it was clearly a source of great embarrassment for the reporter in question, the players seemed oblivious to the discomfort they were causing.

One of the two players involved was pitcher Steve Trachsel, who came into St. Louis that weekend with just one win in his last 14 starts. He had given up 87 hits, 40 walks, and 44 earned runs in his last 76 innings, stretching from mid-May through the end of July. He was, to put it bluntly, stinking up the league. But that same week, my competitor— the one who would drink with the players—wrote a story about how Trachsel really wasn't pitching that badly; how he was just having a run of bad luck. When I read the copy, I thought of the quote from Abe Rosenthal about reporters covering the circus. I could almost smell elephant dung and see peanut shells sprinkled across a set of wrinkled satin sheets. *"It's okay to sleep with elephants. Just don't cover the circus."*

I later spoke with my friend about the Trachsel incident. He was, understandably, bothered that I might consider his behavior unprofessional. His argument about the story was that he never actually defended Trachsel. He merely quoted Trachsel. It was Trachsel who'd said he wasn't pitching badly—not the reporter. My colleague used this rationale often to explain stories that were widely perceived to be "pro-player." Different people see things differently, of course. And, despite our disagreement on this and other issues, I still like and respect my former colleague. But to me, he was being incredibly naïve. It was almost as if he considered his role to be a stenographer instead of a reporter—as if merely giving the players or front office a forum to explain things in their own words absolved a reporter of all responsibility for context, perspective, or insight; as if it were okay to simply write something and never think of the consequences. I didn't believe that was true, even in sports journalism.

The seeming lack of professionalism among some in my new community of baseball writers—or, at least, lack of professionalism as I saw it—was as surprising to me as the sudden proliferation of drive-up daiquiri bars. It was by no means universal. And, by lack of professionalism, I don't mean to imply any lack of effort. To this day, I believe baseball writers are among the hardest-working members of the media—sports or otherwise. But beat writers are, by definition, at the top of their field. Rarely do you see top journalists in other areas going out of their way to cozy up to the people they are covering. Cultivating sources is one thing. But regular social drinking is quite another. And passing notes back and forth with cutesy nicknames was something most people quit doing in the fourth grade.

Easily, the most graphic manifestation of the lack of professionalism—certainly lack of personal pride—among many baseball writers was the way they dressed. Some beat writers looked as if they walked through a car wash on their way to the ballpark every day. Jeans and shabby polo shirts were the unofficial uniform. A natty beat writer might wear a long-sleeve shirt that actually had a collar. Again, there were notable exceptions. John Lowe, an impressively dedicated and talented writer with the *Detroit Free Press*, often wore a tie and sport coat. So did some of the senior baseball writers, such as Jerome Holtzman of the *Tribune*. Marty Noble of *Newsday* sometimes wore ties to the ballpark in the mid-1990s and quite a few other writers who disdained ties at least wore dress slacks and neatly laundered shirts. But far too many writers showed up for work every day looking as if they were on their way to clean out the garage.

I made a point of wearing a dress shirt and tie every day I was on the beat. I never missed a day in four years. Once I left all my ties sitting on my bed at home and had to buy several when I landed in San Diego to get through a week-long road trip. Once all my luggage was lost en route to St. Louis and I had to scramble around the mall in Union Station to find a shirt and tie three hours before game time. But I was determined not to show up at work without looking, and feeling, like a professional. Admittedly, it was a superficial and neurotic idiosyncrasy. And an agonizing one during Sunday afternoon games in St. Louis in August. The only bye I permitted myself was during spring training. It's a wonderful time of year—the best. But spring training isn't really Major League Baseball. The players aren't even drawing their salaries until Opening Day. Besides, if I wore a tie in spring training, I'd have been putting it on and taking it off all day—what with a morning walk around the golf course, the traditional post-practice siesta, and my nightly poolside repose after filing my stories. A tie simply isn't compatible with the workload in Arizona or Florida.

I remember the day clearly. It was Friday, July 30, 1993. I had been covering major league baseball for more than a year and a half—265 games to be precise—when a player finally stopped me and asked me why I wore a tie every day. I was covering the White Sox that year and the team was in Seattle. I was walking through the visitors' clubhouse in the Kingdome, headed for the dugout where I intended to put my feet up for the next hour or so, when pitcher Kirk McCaskill said in a pleasant voice: "Hey, Joey, you got a minute?"

The sheer politeness of the question and the pleasant tone in McCaskill's voice shocked me. Alarm bells went off in my head immediately. This could be the perfect setup for some kind of practical joke. I looked over both shoulders, then turned 90 degrees on my heels and looked around again. Nothing seemed out of the ordinary. Players were lounging lethargically trying each, in his way, to get ready for a game still three and a half hours away. "Yeah, Kirk, whatta ya need?" I said, frantically searching my memory banks to think of anything I had written that might have offended him, his mother, or anyone he ever knew or met. My conscience was clean.

"You mind telling me why you wear a tie every day?" McCaskill said straight out. "I've been around this game a long time and I can't remember another writer who wore a tie all the time. Why do you do it?"

If he had flashed me the hit-and-run sign on a 3-0 count with the bases loaded and nobody out in the bottom of the ninth inning of a tie game, I couldn't have been more surprised. I did a quick double take over both shoulders again to see if I was being set up. Then I said: "You want a real answer or you want a flip response?" He said: "The real answer. I'm curious." I muttered something about sounding corny, then told him the honest—and corny—truth. I considered myself a professional. I considered the players professionals. And I considered Major League Baseball one of the great institutions of American life. I wore a tie out of respect for myself, for the players, and for the game—not necessarily in that order.

"That's nice," McCaskill said, sounding genuine. "I like that."

The particular tie I had on that day was deep red with yellow and black patterns. If you looked closely, the black turned out to be Cyrillic letters and silhouettes of airplanes. The yellow turned out to be Soviet hammers-and-sickles. The tie was one of a collection, each of which illustrated a Beatles' song. This one was "Back in the USSR."

McCaskill pointed to the tie and said something about hearing I'd been a foreign correspondent who worked a lot in Communist countries. He wanted to know what it was like. For the next half hour, McCaskill and I talked about Eastern Europe, about the collapse of Communism, about the breakup of Yugoslavia, the chances for peace there, and about the future of a world without a Cold War. It was the single most-enjoyable and rewarding conversation I had with a major league player. It was one of the most-enjoyable conversations I had with anyone in those years.

Kirk McCaskill is hardly a typical big league baseball player. His father, Ted McCaskill, was a professional hockey player. Born in Ontario, Kirk attended the University of Vermont and was captain of the hockey team. He was runner up for the Hobey Baker Award, college hockey's equivalent of the Heisman Trophy, and was the first college player chosen in the National Hockey League draft in 1981. All of that is enough to make him stand out from the crowd, but what really separated him in the world of baseball was the fact that he was a dean's list student in sociology. He had brains that would outlast his breaking ball and a refreshingly inquiring mind about the world around him.

The only other player in four years on the beat who ever asked me about the way I dressed was one of my favorites: pitcher Jim Bullinger, then with the Cubs. We were years apart, but Bullinger and I went to the same high school—Archbishop Rummel High, an all-male Roman Catholic school in Metairie, Louisiana. The school, embarrassingly, was named for an arch-racist who steadfastly fought integration in New Orleans. The good archbishop lost his battle, but apparently won the war. Nobody remembers his archaic social beliefs and the school that bears his name became one of the best in Louisiana.

Bullinger and I were the only two people around the clubhouse who knew the proper New Orleans way to greet each other. In Austria, when people meet in the morning, they say: *"Gruss Gott,"* which means "God's Greeting." In China, people ask each other: *"Ni chi le fan meiyou?"* which translates to "Have You Eaten?" But in New Orleans, friends simply say: "Where yat?" It is short for "Where You At?" Besides being grammatically grievous, it seems pretty ridiculous since the person you're talking to is right in front of you. Still, whenever I'm in New Orleans, or around anyone from there—especially fellow Rummel grad and lifelong friend Joe Manguno of CNN International—I slip easily back into "Where Yat?" And Bullinger and I would occasionally "yat" each other to keep our heritage alive and our linguistic skills honed.

I was in the visitors' clubhouse at Coors Field in August 1995 when Bullinger stopped me before a game and said: "Hey, Joey. You're looking pretty sharp today. Why are you all dressed up?" I gave Bullinger the frustrated look and roll of my eyes I usually reserve for Dan Rather, when I'm sitting on my sofa and hear him read another particularly sophomoric line on the "CBS Evening News." "What are you talking about? I dress like this every day."

Bullinger was genuinely shocked. "Nawhhhh. Git outta here," he said. I told him I'd worn a tie every day for the past four years and reminded him he'd seen me almost every day from February to October in three of those four years. "Nawhhhh. Git outta here," he said again, turning his back and walking a couple steps away to let me know he didn't appreciate my pulling his chain. He was serious.

I was sadly sure I'd never convince him it was true—that he'd seen me in a tie every day and simply hadn't noticed—when, out of the blue in Chicago a couple weeks later, he walked up to me and said: "I think I got it. You must be wearing a sport coat more this year."

Bingo. Bullinger was right. I had bought a couple new sport coats during the winter. Frankly, they fit me a lot better than the jackets I'd been pretending to ignore were getting snugger by the day the past few seasons. Because the jackets were comfortable again, I was more inclined to keep them on rather than leave them hanging in my hotel closet or on the back of my chair in the press box when I went down to the clubhouse to make my rounds.

Maybe Bullinger wasn't impressed with a tie, but a coat *and* tie was something else. He noticed.

You can't slide much past us Rummel boys.

Fashion consultants may argue otherwise, but clothes don't make the man—or the woman. One of the great strengths of the baseball beat is the intense and prolonged exposure reporters have to the people they are covering. You can dress like the prime minister of France every day and it won't matter if you can't get the job done. Your credibility is on the line, in print and in person, almost every day for 10 months. That was one big difference from many jobs in journalism, including foreign correspondents. Just being far away can hide a multitude of shortcomings.

I was still in Warsaw with another gray, snowy winter about to settle in when the *Tribune* finally announced I would be replaced by a young woman who had been working the police beat in Chicago. She was a driven, personable reporter. I had met her before I went to Beijing for the *Trib* in 1984 and occasionally saw her with mutual friends when I returned on home leave. I liked her a lot and was pleased when she called me one night in Warsaw to ask my advice about the move. We spent some time going over logistics—what the accommodations were like in Warsaw, what was and wasn't available from the food markets, who else was in the press corps, and so on. I told her about our two translators—how one was nice, but barely competent, while the other, Kasia Znaniecka-Vogt, was nothing short of a gift from heaven. And I mentioned we had a nice company car—a forest green BMW purchased by my predecessor shortly before he was summoned home and put into an alcohol treatment center.

My successor, who, until then, had been listening quietly, suddenly chirped up. "I wanted to ask you about that," she said. "My boyfriend's planning on coming with me. *Can we drive to Europe from Poland?"*

I was stunned. I couldn't answer for a several long seconds. I was scrambling to find some logical explanation. Surely, everyone knows Poland is in Europe. Right? It was like asking if you could drive to the U.S. from Chicago. What could she possibly mean? I had a flashback to Marge Schott on national TV at the 1990 World Series, just before the start of the Gulf War, praising our troops in the "Far East" when, of course, she meant the Middle East. She was only half a world off. But, at least, Marge Schott wasn't being sent to the Middle East to cover the war.

After a couple awkward seconds, I said: "Um. What was that?"

My successor said, again: "I was wondering if we could drive to Europe?"

Flabbergasted, I seized on what I hoped would be a face-saving answer. "Sure, you can go to *Western* Europe easy these days," I said emphasizing Western even though, by then, The Wall was long down and Europe was unified. "Central Europe's easy, too. Lynne and I just drove down to Vienna a couple months ago."

Maybe that was what she meant, anyway: Could she get to Western Europe? But from the way she worded the question—*twice*—and from the context of the conversation, it was clear to me she was lost, both geographically and professionally. As soon as I got off the phone, I repeated the conversation to my wife several times and made her grill me about the exact words. I wanted to make certain that as the years rolled by I wouldn't embellish or diminish the story. It was so thoroughly unbelievable, I wanted a witness.

I was both pleased and proud the *Tribune* was making a determined effort to break the mold of white male correspondents that dominated the foreign staff for decades. It was long overdue. But I was astonished and privately embarrassed that such a plum assignment would be given to someone so ill prepared. After all, Chicago, we always claimed, is the world's largest Polish city outside Warsaw.

I needn't have been so pompous. The title of foreign correspondent itself bestows credibility on any reporter. At least, credibility enough to buy time for a determined reporter to grow into the job. I am living proof. When I was named UPI's Chief Eastern European Correspondent in the still-dark days of the Cold War in 1981, I was hopelessly out of my league. Shortly after my appointment, I went to Moscow to pick up a "resident's visa" that allowed me to travel to and from the Soviet Union on a regular basis. While there, the UPI bureau chief arranged dinner at his typically grim apartment in Kuzutowsky Prospekt so I could meet an internationally known Soviet "journalist," who specialized in Eastern European affairs. The "journalist," of course, was a KGB agent and he came to dinner solely to size up the new UPI reporter in his territory. I long ago repressed the details out of sheer embarrassment, but I remember distinctly at one point in the evening trying desperately to recover from the blank stare that came over me when the conversation shifted to events in Tirana. I was so clearly lost that our KGB friend looked at me and said, with a wry grin: "Tirana. You know, the capital of Albania."

I doubt after that dinner the Soviet intelligence community felt

In the Great Hall of the People in Beijing for the opening session of the 13th Communist Party Congress. Joining me in the VIP seats are four hacks who remained close friends through the years: (from left, standing) Edward A. Gargan of the New York Times, *Jaime FlorCruz of* Time *magazine, Stefan Simons of* Der Spiegel, *and Rick Hornik, then* Time *magazine's Beijing bureau chief and later* Time*'s chief of correspondents. (Photo courtesy of Robin Moyer)*

compelled to assign its top agents to keep tabs on me as I bumbled around behind the Iron Curtain. But the mortifying experience of that evening had a positive impact. It instilled in me an eternal fear of being ill-prepared and under-educated. That one night is probably a reason I wound up with a career that spanned Old China and New Comiskey.

I expected, when I came home to the States, to be met with massive indifference toward, if not total ignorance about, Tirana, Tibet, and Timbuktu. Especially since I was coming back to the self-absorbed world of sports. And, my expectations were fully met. But, for some reason, I had deluded myself into believing I would find more people outside baseball who shared at least a passing interest in many of the things that had consumed so much of my life. I met some. They were few and far between. But they were impressive and greatly appreciated. It was, however, frightening and flabbergasting to discover how adamantly most Americans ignored the rest of the world. They had to make a conscious and determined effort to do it. Technology and the staggering resources of the United States meant that a bomb blast in Peshawar could be heard instantly in Peoria. All you had to do was listen. And if you listened long enough, you might learn why it mattered. But hardly anybody wanted to listen. The only things most Americans seemed concerned about were the jobs they hated, the sports teams they loved, and the TV talk shows that titillated their lives.

My wife had the advantage of finding a rewarding job with Golin/Harris, one of the biggest public relations firms in Chicago, where she worked almost exclusively on international affairs for McDonald's restaurants. She was able to come home and stay abroad at the same time. And she helped me. I kept up with international affairs and made new worldly friends through her job. That satisfied one important part of me and made it possible to concentrate on what I set out to do when I accepted the Cubs' job, which was to get back in touch with America through my love of baseball.

Baseball is one of the world's most exclusive and protective societies. It is a lot like the Chinese Communist Party or the Chicago Police Department. You're either part of it or you're an unwelcome outsider. It is tough to get in and tougher to leave. Almost everyone who ever got a glimpse of the inner sanctum of the game wants to stay. That goes for bat boys and owners, clubhouse attendants and beat writers, scouts and umpires, marketing directors and managers. It is an indescribably wonderful game, filled with magic and memories, characters and good cheer. I thought that before Dick Ciccone and the *Trib* gave me the chance to be part of it. I'm happy and proud to say I still think so now.

In 1993, Bob Condor, then sports editor of the *Tribune*, came up with the idea of running a series of essays on baseball by staff writers in the annual "special section" that most papers publish before every sports season to generate extra advertising income. Condor was far and away the best of four sports editors I worked with during four turbulent years in the *Trib* sports section, where turnover was an art form and consistency a sin. Condor's idea was to have a half dozen writers pick something—anything—about the game and describe why it was special; why it endured.

I thought about it for days, then wrote a piece that Condor ran next to a wonderful photograph of Ernie Banks kissing a baseball. The essay was an answer to myself why I had come home to cover baseball—and why I was loving it.

I began with my favorite anecdote about the late Angelo Bartlett Giamatti, who, besides being commissioner of baseball, was a Renaissance scholar, professor at Princeton, president of Yale, and lifelong Boston Red Sox fan. Needless to say, I can't begin to compete with Giamatti's intellectual credentials. My own academic career was summed up pretty succinctly and accurately in a Randy Newman song where he says: *"Good Ole Boys from LSU, went in dumb and come out dumb, too."* But Giamatti and I did share one defining experience. Like me, Giamatti was asked repeatedly by incredulous friends and colleagues how he could abandon seemingly significant pursuits for something so trivial as baseball. Making the transformation, in my case, from foreign correspondent to baseball writer—or, in Giamatti's case, from the upper floors of America's most prestigious Ivory Towers to the office of baseball commissioner—seemed, for many, to be the equivalent of walking away from a White House banquet to sup with truckers at a roadside diner.

"There are a lot of people who know me, who can't for the life of them understand why I would do something as meaningless as baseball," Giamatti once admitted in a speech. He paused briefly, then looked out at the audience with a knowing grin and gave the only answer he could:

"If they only knew."

Giamatti was the son of an Italian professor. He spoke several languages. He was a world-class scholar. Yet, this brilliant, articulate man was lost for words when it came to explaining something so simple and all-consuming as his passion for baseball. I felt the same.

I tried for several paragraphs in my brief essay to paint the beauty of baseball—how I felt when I saw a home run ball streak through the night sky or how magnificent it was to watch something as simple as a lazy flyball to right when the second-baseman rushes into the outfield grass, right hand pointing high over head, to help a teammate make the play. I wrote about the "comforting crescent of gold and emerald where the infield meets the outfield—the border between one world and another, between groundouts and singles."

The word pictures were pretty, but woefully weak. I realized I had slipped into the same tar pit that had swallowed poets and writers forever. I was trying to express the love I felt by writing about the beauty I saw. It couldn't be done so I rousted one final flurry of images and ended the essay with a bow to the simple eloquence of a far-wiser man.

"Words will never convey the profound passions kindled by something as simple as the sound of a fastball nestling comfortably into a mitt, or the sign of a newly chalked batter's box waiting to be trampled," I wrote.

"Giamatti was right.

"If they only knew."

That love of baseball, that passion, could only go so far profession-ally. If anything, it could be a detriment to a beat writer. A columnist can wax poetically about the beauty of the game time and again. A beat writer blessed with a daring editor might get a chance once or twice in a career. My job was to keep the magic and mystery of baseball alive day in and day out, week in and week out, for nearly 10 months a year. I had a couple hundred Polaroids I was trying to paste into one Picasso.

Obviously, I'd like to think I did a good job at it. I certainly have a file drawer full of letters from loyal readers who took time to write to say they thought I did. Then again, I have just as many letters from irate fans who thought—in almost equal numbers—I was either to coddling of the Cubbies or unthinkably harsh on a nice group of well-meaning, hard-working young men.

One of my favorites was a constantly irate reader who sent me huge packages sporadically throughout the season. Each correspondence was crammed with either photocopies or originals of my articles, weeks worth at a time. Every article would be critiqued in mad scribble and each packet would contain a cover letter, scrawled in block letters with a black broad-tip felt marker.

The first few letters the first season started harmlessly enough with phrases like: "Attention Big Time Writer Reaves of the Chicago Tri-bune, who owns the rotten, stinkin, filthy, puke Cubs."

By my fourth season on the beat, this loyal reader had degenerated to threats of physical violence and death. "Take a good look in the mir-ror, Reaves. We don't think you will look the same soon," said one let-ter, followed a few weeks later with a dispatch that ended: "Don't worry about looking over your shoulder. It is coming right at your face. Good Bye Slime Reaves."

I nicknamed that reader the "Marks-A-Lot Madman" and actually looked forward to the letters. They never were signed, but occasionally a return address, written in the same hurried block letters with the same black felt pen, would read: "Cubby Bear Lounge."

My all-time favorite letter came from a reader in Minneapolis, who caught an idiotic mistake I made in a Sunday column about crazy base-ball contracts. I wrote about pitcher Ray "Slim" Caldwell, who once signed a contract that actually called for him to get drunk after every appearance on the mound. Caldwell pitched for the Yankees from 1910-1918. He was traded to Boston at the start of the 1919 and traded again midway through the season to Cleveland, where legendary outfielder Tris Speaker was in his first year as player-manager. Speaker knew Caldwell's reputation all too well and figured there was no way to stop him from drinking. So Speaker drew up a contract that required Caldwell to get drunk as soon as he stepped off the mound. The following day, Caldwell was bound by his contract to stay home. The next day, he would report to the ballpark to run. And the fourth day, he had to be ready to pitch again. Caldwell had gone 34-40 in the previous three seasons with the Yankees and Red Sox, but he came alive again under his new work rules. He went 5-1 for the Indians the second half of the 1919 season and was 20-10 in 1920 before his arm gave out and he finished his career with a 6-6 record in 1921.

In writing the column, though, I made a horrendous blunder. I said Caldwell played with Boston until the All-Star break in 1919, when he was traded to Cleveland. I certainly knew, and almost every baseball fan knows, there weren't All-Star Games back in those days. So, of course, there wasn't an All-Star break. The Brooklyn and New York teams had something akin to an All-Star Game back in the late 1850s, but the first real All-Star Game as we know it was in 1933 when Arch Ward, sports editor of the *Chicago Tribune,* convinced reluctant league owners to stage the event to coincide with the city's Century of Progress Exposition.

Three days after the column appeared, I received a one-page, single-spaced letter typed on lined loose-leaf paper. Without reading a word, it was easy to see the author was incensed. He hadn't paused long enough to provide half the required punctuation or a single paragraph mark. And the keys had been struck so hard that nearly every letter ripped through the paper.

"What a stupid beyond belief Moron I can see that you are," my friend wrote. *"All star game in 1919 don't make me howl in derisive laughter you jerk ... It was ARCH WARD of your own rag that dreamt up that annual nightmare that is named the All Star Game that I refer to*

as the ALL BUMS GAME. They never had the first one you idiot till 1933 so there was absolutely no all star break they kept right on playing the season back there with only day breaks here and there to travel by the vastly superior STEAM TRAINS of yesteryear to other parks. There was absolutely no all star game or break back then you incomprehensible stupid beyond belief jerk. How the hell do they get such unbelievably stupid clowns like you on a stinking rag like that talk about stupidity you are one of the tops."

To add insult to injury, at least as far as this reader was concerned, my column had run on the same page as one by Jerome Holtzman. The fact that Holtzman is in the Baseball Hall of Fame for his work apparently held little sway.

"Phew the stink of idiocy is sure in your column just like with Holtzmann," he continued. *"Maybe thats why they put your two stupid beyond belief articles side by side, because your evidentally two of the most stupid beyond belief ass holes that there are at least for that rag. So do as I told Holtzmann to do would you please and go down to that piss pot Lake Michigan of yours and jump in twice and come up only once, who the hell would miss such idiotic trash as you."*

The letter wasn't signed, but the envelope was postmarked Minneapolis and there was a wonderful closing in all-caps:

"THE GREAT ONE HAS SPOKEN, ALWAYS REMEMBER WHEN YOU WANT THE FACTS ON ANY SUBJECT, ALWAYS ASK THE ALL TIME GENIUS, THE ALL TIME EXPERT, THE WALKING ENCYCLOPEDIA JOHN RICKARD THE GREATEST MINNEAPOLIS MINNESHNOTALANAND MISSPELLED MINNESOTA."

I loved it. I scrawled an A+ across the top of the letter and put in a place of honor in my filing cabinet. What could I say? The walking encyclopedia John Rickard was "absolutally" right.

The mail I got from fans was a staggering and graphic reminder of what a different world I'd stepped into. I got more "hero-grams" in one week on the Cubs' beat than I did in 14 years overseas. I got more hate mail for a day's work in baseball than I did for a summer being shelled in Lebanon.

I learned pretty quickly what the *Tribune*'s readers cared about and it was a rude awakening. If I was going to get killed on the job, I'd be a lot better off getting my head bashed in by a baseball player angry at what I wrote than I would be taking a bullet in the back running away from a coup. At least, I'd get a better obituary.

Newspapers spend unsavory amounts of money on readership surveys that, in one way or another, dictate what gets covered and how. But the truth is, for the working journalist, there really are no accurate barometers of success or failure. There are no stats for errors per story, or beautiful phrases per week. The closest thing to a blown save is a missed deadline—except that in journalism you're usually only allowed one blown deadline a career. Everything is subjective, which is why journalism is so riddled with the "Flavor of the Month"—reporters who come out of nowhere to be labeled the greatest thing since Mencken, then just as quickly get cast aside by the editors who were singing their praises. It all holds true whether you're writing from Warsaw or Wrigley, from city hall or the suburbs. The big difference I found with baseball writing is that things are even more blurred. Is it journalism? Or is it entertainment? Is it some bizarre mix? Or is it neither?

I never honestly found out. I was too busy trying to paste the Polaroids together. All I know is I came home to a country I didn't quite understand, to a career where the rules had changed, and to a game that made it all worthwhile.

My watch had stopped. But I didn't care.

Chapter 3

Basra Bombers, or Why Ask Why?

Jim Lefebvre and I first passed each other in the skies over Europe—appropriately enough, going in opposite directions.

Lefebvre was hired November 22, 1991, to replace Jim Essian, who had the sorry misfortune of becoming a big-league manager earlier that same year. The misfortune was more in Essian's timing than his ability. Essian had been quietly doing a superb job managing the Triple-A Iowa Cubs early in the 1991 season when his bosses at Tribune Co. locked themselves in a paneled room high atop their stone Tower on Michigan Avenue and emerged with yet another of the unfathomable edicts that bolstered their richly deserved reputation in those days as the Keystone Kops of Baseball. They fired Don Zimmer.

Depending upon who you talk to—and where—Zimmer is either one of the most-beloved characters in the game or a mindless gerbil with a tin plate in his head. In Boston, he's a rodent. In Chicago, he's a saint. The big difference is winning.

Boston fans never forgave Zimmer for the collapse in 1978 when he managed the Red Sox to a seven and one-half game lead in August, only to end up in a tie with the Yankees and lose a gut-wrenching, one-game playoff at Fenway. Zimmer was fired in 1980, much to the relief of a sizable slice of the New England population. Years later, time had done little to temper the self-satisfying Puritanical outrage. When another Red Sox manager, Butch Hobson, brought Zimmer back to coach third base, the tabloid *Boston Herald* conveyed the news under a classic screaming headline: "YOUR WORST NIGHTMARE COMES TRUE—HE'S BAAACK."

To be sure, there are those in every major league city who share a less-than-heroic image of Zimmer. But in Chicago, by and large, Zimmer is respected and, sometimes, revered. Not only did he manage the Cubs to the National League playoffs in 1989, but he did it with a fun-loving flair that Chicago fans appreciate. The Boys of Zimmer, as that team came to be known, violated almost every accepted precept of modern baseball. They played hit and run with the bases loaded and one out. They laid down bunts when all logic said they should have been swinging away. They stole more bases than all but two Cubs teams since 1924.

Most of all, though, Zimmer's Cubs had fun. And they *looked* like they were having fun. At least, until the playoffs, when, true to Cubbie form, everything fell apart. Greg Maddux couldn't win a game. Andre Dawson and Ryne Sandberg looked like embarrassed Little Leaguers swinging at big-league curveballs. And the buttons Zimmer had been pushing so successfully all season suddenly started opening trap doors that sucked him and his players into oblivion.

Zimmer was a fan favorite in Chicago long before 1989. He had been a lovable, feisty third-base coach under then-manager Jim Frey when the Cubs won the National League East in 1984 and went to post-season play for the first time since World War II. That alone would have been enough to earn Zimmer a warm, fuzzy place in Cubbie lore— given the dearth of memorable moments in modern franchise history. But when he became manager in 1986 and took the Cubs to another title in 1989, Zimmer joined Mayor Daley, Mike Ditka, and Mrs. O'Leary's cow in the throne room of Chicago deities.

At least, as far as the fans were concerned.

Tribune Co. never bought into the myth of Zimmer as some kind of cuddly, pot-bellied Zeus. More specifically, Don Grenesko didn't buy into it. Grenesko was president of the Cubs, a pencil-pushing bottom-liner plucked from the bowels of Tribune Tower to make sure the smell of money overpowered the sweet bouquet of Smokey Links and fresh-mown grass at Wrigley Field.

Letting Grenesko run the Cubs was the parallel of putting Don

Zimmer in charge of the *Chicago Tribune*. Grenesko knew as much about baseball and player management as a baseball lifer knows about upper-quintile advertising audiences or the nuances of newspaper distribution. While the top officials at Tribune Co. never would have dreamed of putting Zimmer in charge of one of their many lucrative subsidiaries, they had no problem giving suit after suit the power to push the baseball buttons that set the course of one of the highest profile sports franchises in the world.

Grenesko never had a clue about baseball. And, in his defense, he and his bosses knew it. Grenesko was, however, a master at running a business. That always was what the Cubs were—and ever will be—to Tribune Co. Put Grenesko in a bar at midnight with a half dozen pleasantly soused, hard-nosed veteran coaches and he would have an easier time explaining Stephen Hawking's theory of thermodynamic time arrows than he would comprehending the intangibles it takes to transform a group of merely competent baseball players into unbeatable champions.

There usually isn't a tremendous gulf in talent from one major league club to another—with the possible exception of a few of the Cubs' offerings over the years, and, maybe, Casey Stengel's early Mets. Often what separates winners from whiners is the simple feeling they *can* win. Sometimes, the front office spawns the magic. Sometimes, the players themselves create it. More often than not, the manager is the one who kindles a winning spirit and keeps it alive.

Just in from Rome, I'm joined by old friend Pat Benic and a new-found friend in blue as we get primed for Game 1 of the 1989 playoffs.

Zimmer did just that in 1989. Obviously, Andre Dawson, Rick Sutcliffe, Greg Maddux, Shawon Dunston, Ryne Sandberg, Mitch Williams, and the rest of the players made it happen. But Zimmer made it possible. He melded his sway as a baseball lifer with a refreshing "c'mon-let's-have-some-fun-out-there" approach to the game that, quite simply, clicked with the '89 Cubs. They went from being a barely capable gaggle of professional athletes into being a team—a club, in the true sense of the word that everybody else was on the outside wishing they could belong. And that intangible was enough to separate the 1989 Cubs from the rest of the National League East.

Zimmer's reward for making the desert bloom on the North Side of Chicago was massive corporate indifference. He was a hero to the fans, his players, and the always self-congratulatory baseball community in general. But Tribune Co. apparently could care less. Zimmer wasn't even given the courtesy of having a year or two tacked on to his contract—the common gratuity most organizations almost automatically bestow on title-winning managers. Zimmer still had a job, of course, and a contract that ran through 1991. But failing to offer him even a token extension was a graceless snub all-too symptomatic of Tribune Co.'s way of doing business on the corporate level. Then again, faceless corporations like Tribune Co. weren't alone in forgetting the human touch during baseball's Suicidal Stage in the early and mid-1990s. The White Sox were run by real people, not a stone building. They were the very embodiment of two larger-than-life figures—chairman Jerry Reinsdorf and General Manager Ron Schueler. Love them or hate them, at least Sox fans could point to Reinsdorf and Schueler and know who built the team. But the Sox outdid even their cross-town corporate rivals in boorishness by repeatedly refusing to offer a long-term contract to manager Gene Lamont, whose only sin was to win quietly with class. Lamont led the White Sox to three consecutive winning seasons, a 258-210 record, and their first division championship in a decade. He had the sixth-best record of 35 Sox managers this century. His worst season was in 1992, when as a rookie manager, his team finished 86-76—a better record than all but five teams the Cubs fielded since 1938 when Charlie Grimm was still managing. In Lamont's next two seasons, he led the Sox to back-to-back division titles. His record was, quite simply, unbeatable. Yet, Lamont never enjoyed the security of a contract beyond season's end. And he was fired the first time his fickle, moody players went into a slide.

Grenesko's silent snub of Zimmer after the 1989 season was, in fact, a clanging alarm for the future. If Zimmer couldn't get an extension after winning a title, then it hardly seemed likely he could expect much support if things turned sour. He couldn't.

The Cubs picked up in 1990 where they left off in the '89 playoffs. Their woes were compounded by injuries and they finally finished in their more-accustomed fourth place with a 77-85 record. What passed for a honeymoon for Zimmer was over. He, and everybody else, knew 1991 would be a make-or-break season—for him and the team. The Cubs still had a formidable roster led by Maddux, Dawson, Dunston, Sutcliffe, Sandberg, and Mark Grace. They were almost everybody's pre-season pick to rebound and win the NL East. Instead, they unraveled like an old battered batting practice baseball.

The beginning of the end came in April 1991, when Barry Rozner, a skillful, hard-working Cubs' beat writer for the suburban *Arlington Heights Daily Herald*, talked to Grenesko about the club. Zimmer's contract was up at the end of the year and Rozner knew Grenesko had no love lost for his manager. In the interview, Grenesko bluntly refused to give Zimmer a vote of confidence. All Grenesko would say was that Zimmer would be evaluated at the end of the season. Implicit in those seemingly innocuous words was the sentiment that the Cubs had to win at least a division championship, and probably go to the World Series, for Zimmer to keep his job. It was another classic example of how little Grenesko knew—and obstinately refused to learn—about baseball. Zimmer had the respect and admiration of his players. They had won for him once and could do it again. But neither he nor they could control injuries or personnel moves by other teams. It was always possible the Cubs could have a great season under Zimmer, play to the best of their abilities, entertain a lot of people doing it and still come up short. That wouldn't mean the season was a failure. It shouldn't be grounds for firing a winning manager. But Grenesko was plainly and pointedly keeping his options open, just as he had at the end of the '89 season when he refused to give Zimmer a contract extension.

Strictly from a corporate point of view, Grenesko's position made perfect sense. Why force a decision now, when Zimmer already had a contract? Who knows what might happen between April and October? The team could self-destruct. Another, better manager might be available. A million things could change.

The trouble with that thinking, fiscally and analytically sound as it might be, of course, was it underscored the lack of stability that had become Tribune Co.'s trademark in baseball. Under Tribune Co., the Cubs changed managers constantly—never allowing a new skipper to work through an injury-filled year or the cyclical downspins every team goes through. If a manager struggled for a season, he would feel the bosses in the Tower breathing down his neck. He would begin the next season taunted by constant second-guessing until he was fired.

By failing—or refusing—to find a more gracious and sensitive way of dancing around what should have been a non-issue, Grenesko publicly embarrassed Zimmer. And Zimmer was justifiably enraged. He pointed out that he had been in baseball his entire life. If he was going to be evaluated, why not do it now and get it over with? His record spoke for itself. And his record showed he was an integral part of the only two Cubs' teams to win anything in the last two generations.

Zimmer's contract status never should have been an issue in April, nearly an entire baseball season before it expired. But it became an issue as soon as Rozner brought it up. It become a hot story that adversely affected people's lives and careers when Grenesko deigned to comment.

I was working in Warsaw as all this was unfolding. My closest contact with the Cubs was devouring the sports sections of the *Chicago Tribune* that arrived weeks late and piled up like cordwood in my office while I was trying to report and write about the confusing world of a newly democratic Eastern Europe. Andrew Bagnato's superb coverage and the videotapes of two or three Cubs games per week that I paid an outfit in Frankfurt several hundred dollars to record and ship to me enabled me to stay somewhat in touch. That's all I needed because when I joined the baseball beat, the chaos of 1991 would become maddeningly familiar. The number of stories that shook the clubhouses and front offices of major league teams—for, literally, no reason—was amazing. If baseball was such an almighty high-powered business run by supposedly brilliant executives, then how come chaos and controversy were common? How come order and reason were rare? The answer is two-fold. First, not a whole lot of baseball executives are all that brilliant. Does anyone honestly believe Marge Schott can even spell brilliant without cheating off a box of laundry detergent? And second, even the dumbest baseball executive knows how to play the media.

The baseball season is long. I always left for spring training the morning after Valentine's Day and couldn't count on a real break until Halloween. That's 259 days. With rare exception, beat writers are expected to produce a story a day during spring training, then a game story and a package of newsy notes daily once the regular season begins—plus, usually, a Sunday column and sporadic features. On top of that, there is the mindless, but time-consuming drudgery of things such as: How They Scored, the inane agate type recapping every run produced during a game; and On Deck, the pre-series look at every team your club is about to play, complete with pitching rotations, radio and TV times, and updated stats on who's hot and who's not. Some papers, particularly the hungry, up-and-coming suburban journals, expect even more copy from their writers—and devote far more space for every story. It all adds up to a staggering work load. More staggering than anyone but fellow baseball writers can appreciate. I twisted an old phrase I'd heard somewhere along the line and called it: "Feeding the Dragon." The dragon was insatiable. She never slept. And she always needed to be fed. Not every meal could be a feast. Sometimes the dragon had to settle for junk food. More times than not, as a matter of fact.

This voracious appetite for newsprint was a big reason I came to think of sports journalism as an oxymoron—at least so far as it was applied to baseball coverage in most daily newspapers. There were exceptions, of course. Exceptional writers like Jack Curry of the *New York Times*. And exceptional papers like the *Los Angeles Times*. But too much of what passed for news on the baseball pages was little more than gossipy tidbits worthy of *Entertainment Tonight* or non-issues that were made into stories simply to Feed the Dragon. Others were only tangentially relevant to anything that was happening during the current season. There were writers who would go out of their way to talk to players they once covered, who now played for other teams or were retired, and get them to comment on something that was happening with their old club now. Invariably, of course, these were confined to players the writers had been friendly with, so the stories were easy to produce. The dragon got fed. And since somebody, somewhere, is always going to like anything written about baseball, regardless of how trivial or trite, the writer can always argue he or she is producing interesting and informative copy that the competition doesn't have.

Doing a cutesy note about Mark Grace's birthday, or a sidebar on what Andre Dawson thinks of the new Cubs' management three years after he left the team, is harmless enough. And marginally justifiable, I suppose, if the dragon's stomach is growling. But too often the copy grind—and the unquenchable ego-driven lust to scoop the competition—led misguided writers to force stories into existence, either prematurely or irresponsibly. They get away with it because it's baseball. It rarely happens on the city desk, and even less-often in the national and foreign sections, where space and time constraints are less voracious. That's not to say contrived, ill-advised stories don't make it into other sections of the paper. I certainly produced my share from overseas. But it happens more often and more easily on the baseball beat—sometimes with devastating impact because someone in the front office has a vested interested in birthing a story and the reporter is too naïve or self-consumed to wonder why.

The Zimmer story was a classic example. A manager's contract status is a legitimate topic. But, in this case, it should have been a non-issue in April. By letting Rozner open public speculation months early, Grenesko set in motion a chain of events that literally changed the history of the franchise for the worse. Zimmer, Grenesko, and general manager Jim Frey all would be ousted in a matter of months, the team would go into a devastating tailspin, and the entire organization would be so torn apart and disoriented that it would take years to rebound. And it all began because Gresnesko spoke on the record about something that didn't need to be discussed at the time.

Gresnesko, of course, knew exactly what he was doing. He could have refused to speak to Rozner or talked only on background and forced Rozner—if he was going to do a story anyway—to write his own opinions or quote unnamed sources. But Gresnesko, like an amazing number of Tribune Co. executives, couldn't resist seeing or hearing his name mentioned in the media. No matter how much corporate power, stock options, or financial windfalls they had in their lives, the Don Greneskos of the world still got a kick out of seeing their names in the papers. They couldn't help themselves. But because Gresnesko couldn't help himself, he was waylaid by the media into embarrassing Zimmer and, in the process, ruining the Cubs for years to come. Rozner, for his part, could walk away from the mayhem he helped create and say he was only doing his job, which, of course, he was. He beat everybody in town on what turned out to be a big story. That's what he got paid to do. And he was very good at it. But was it good journalism? I don't know. It was definitely sports journalism. And I'm convinced the overwhelming majority of baseball writers in America would say it was a job well done. But, it seems to me the story didn't need to be written then. I wasn't on the beat at the time, so this isn't sour grapes from someone who was beaten on a story. I like and respect Rozner. He and Joe Goddard of the *Sun-Times* managed to keep the potentially volatile mix of competition and friendship in keen perspective and did as much as anyone to make my time in baseball pleasurable. But I believe the Zimmer story and too many others were unduly contrived. And, in the contriving, lives were changed for the worse. People were hurt. And organizations were damaged. Gresnesko, not Rozner, deserved the lion's share of blame for the Zimmer fiasco. He controlled the situation. And, fittingly, he was consumed by the chaos he unleashed. But the entire episode need never have happened the way it did, when it did.

The line between a legitimate, timely story and one that's forced and contrived, usually is just hazy enough to allow convincing argument on both sides. There are, however, rare occasions when even a harried hack can't escape the difference. One such occasion came during the early days of the Iran-Iraq War in 1980. I was working for UPI then and traveling with Charles Cancellare, a gifted but particularly high-strung photographer sent out from Brussels. We were operating out of a shabby, shell-shattered little hotel in Basra, Iraq—a place novelist Graham Greene once described as the asshole of the world. Personally, I'm convinced Mr. Greene must have had a particularly delicious young lover in Basra, else he never would have been so sentimental.

Our routine those days was to rise at dawn and hire a creaky wooden *dhow* to ferry us across the Shatt al Arab, which is the muddy confluence of the ancient Tigris and Euphrates rivers, and the border between Iran and Iraq. We were in what was believed to be the cradle of modern civilization—Mesopotamia, where some scholars insist the Garden of Eden had been. It was paradise as far as I was concerned, because, waiting, like a miracle, on the banks on the Iranian side when we landed every morning was a well-rusted, but surprisingly reliable orange and white 1956 Chevrolet—available for hire, with an absolutely fearless driver named Yousif Hamad, at the going rate of 45 Iraqi Dinar, $150 U.S., per day. The car and driver, of course, were anything but miraculous. They served at the pleasure of the Iraqi Information Ministry, which, for a few weeks anyway, was only too-eager to let a Western wire service record the magnificent deeds of Sadaam Hussein's war machine. Some of the same troops that would be swept easily aside by the U.S. Army a decade later were then advancing on the Iranian port city of Khorramshahr and feeling supremely confident of their invincibility. Cancellare and I were covering their progress and becoming a familiar sight to the field commanders, which helped make my job pretty easy. All I needed was a keen eye, a few quotes from somebody in charge and a working phone line back in Basra at the end of the day and I had my stories. Cancellare, though, needed action pictures—or, as we used to say: he needed *bang-bang*. Trouble was, after the first few days of the war, there was precious little *bang-bang* to be had. The Iraqi army was advancing, but barely. In reality, Khorramshahr was under siege

With photographer Charles Cancellare and some of Saddam Hussein's troops aboard an Iraqi tank east of Shalamcheh, Iran.

and the most dramatic pictures available for long stretches were of Iraqi soldiers resting in the shade of dust-bathed date palms on the banks of the Shatt al Arab. Then one afternoon, after waiting patiently for hours while I sipped endless cups of sweet tea and interviewed a field commander, Cancellare decided something had to be done. As we were preparing to climb back into our Chevy chariot, he looked around at a group of .106-mm artillery pieces lined up in the desert and asked if he could take pictures. The always laborious translation process started and after several minutes, several thousand words and countless games of charades, the answer came back: "Sure. Take as many pictures as you like." Cancellare clicked a few frames, then asked if the guns ever fired on Khorramshahr. Of course, we were told. Cancellare brightened, then asked if he could take pictures when the guns started firing. This set in motion another round of particularly animated gibberish and gesticulation. Cancellare and I figured questions of military security were being breached and we tried to look as much like harmless, doe-eyed puppies as possible to help ensure a favorable response. Suddenly, we both realized something terribly strange was happening. Soldiers were snapping-to all around. Olive green crates were being pried open. Camouflage netting was being pulled back ... *the Iraqis were preparing to dump tons of flying white-hot metal into the streets of Khorramshahr so United Press International could have an action photo!*

For a few scary moments, I thought Cancellare was going to let it happen. He was desperate. He had been putting in 20-hour days in 100-degree heat with precious little to show for it. Covering the war was a big break for him. He was determined not to fail. He needed some *bang-bang*.

In the end, of course, there never was any question what had to be done. We launched into our own panicked game of charades and managed to abort the unscheduled artillery barrage. It is one thing for a journalist to record an event—regardless of how horrific the moment or its consequences. It's quite another thing to have even a fleeting role in initiating that event. They taught us in journalism school at LSU that a good reporter is like a fly on the wall—silent and always watching without intervening. Too often, the temptation in journalism is to be more like a fly on something else.

There is no comparison, of course, between an artillery bombardment on a besieged Iranian city and an interview with the president of the Cubs about his manager's contract status. But every story has its fallout. It is a lot easier to forget that in a ballpark than on a battlefield. I remember once talking to Andy MacPhail, the refreshingly solicitous president and CEO of the Cubs, about baseball writing in general. We had never, and still have never, discussed the Iran-Iraq story or the Zimmer incident. We hadn't mentioned the specific names of any writers or newspapers. We were simply jawing informally about the state of baseball writing in America in the 1990s when MacPhail said: "To me, the best writers are the ones who can see the consequences of what they write before they write it."

The consequences of the Zimmer story were quick to unfold. Zimmer went to Grenesko and let it be known face-to-face he didn't appreciate having his fate handled through the media. He privately demanded his contract status be settled and publicly fussed and fumed. His anger infiltrated the clubhouse and his team went into a funk. A new rash of injuries compounded an already untenable situation and by mid-May things were so ugly that Grenesko had Zimmer where he wanted him. Even Zimmer's lifelong friend, General Manager Jim Frey, could see it.

Frey tried to buy Zimmer a little time, hoping things somehow would turn around. But when the talent-rich club fell to 18-19, Grenesko made his move. He flew to New York and fired Zimmer on May 21, just before the start of a series against the Mets. Zimmer's token slap of revenge was to empty the mini-bar in his suite at the Grand Hyatt and pass out all the beer, booze, and snacks to the beat writers when they finished their final interviews with him. Grenesko and Tribune Co. got stuck with an inconsequential, but, doubtless, unwelcome surcharge.

The Cubs, meanwhile, got stuck with an unwelcome manager. Grenesko saw the good job Essian had done at Triple-A and decided he was the man to succeed Zimmer. Chalk up another one to Grenesko's brilliant baseball insights. In all fairness, Essian did a credible job given the circumstances, managing the club to a 59-63 record. But he was perceived as a disaster—mainly because he never had a prayer. The players, irate at the sacrifice of Zimmer, were ill-disposed to accept anyone Grenesko wanted. And when Grenesko's man turned out to be a minor-league manager, the players simply closed ranks and shut him out. They started skipping batting practice and sitting around playing cards in the clubhouse. They snickered at team meetings and dogged it on the field. Players who liked to puff out their chests and boast how professional they were, began behaving like pouting teen-agers. I wasn't there to see it, but I've heard all the gory details from dozens who were. And I saw the same thing repeated three years later with some of the same players in the same clubhouse. It was nasty and pathetic—so nasty and pathetic that on both occasions even the Tribune Co. suits, isolated in their Tower and fixated on their profit margins, realized something had to be done.

The housecleaning was swift and thorough. On October 17, 1991, Grenesko was reassigned to the Tribune Tower, returning to a financial position he was better equipped to handle and—so it seemed—immediately making the future brighter for the Cubs.

On October 18, Essian was relieved of his managerial duties.

On November 14, 1991, Frey was unceremoniously put to pasture as a special player consultant and told to work out of his home in Baltimore, Maryland.

With the decks cleared after the disaster and all the talent in the world to choose from, Tribune Co., typically, stepped up to the plate and struck out looking. The corporate honchos hired a White Sox reject, Larry Himes, to take over as general manager and rewarded him with sweeping powers by leaving Grenesko's job vacant. Himes would go on to earn a place in baseball trivia as the only general manager ever fired by *both* the Cubs *and* White Sox. But that was three years away. In November 1991, Himes was king of all Cubdom. And one of his first priorities was to find someone to replace the ill-fated Essian as manager. Himes probably would have preferred that job stayed vacant, too, so he could expand his power even more. But that clearly was impossible. So he set out to do the next best thing. He was determined to hire a yes-man as manager. In fact, he hired two yes-men—one as manager and one as *de facto* manager-in-waiting. It was a bizarre and awkward way of running things. But it proved to be an unnerving trend during the Himes regime.

The two managers Himes hired were Jim Lefebvre, who got the title, and Tom Trebelhorn, who would succeed him when Lefebvre proved less pliant than expected. Aside from being white males, which basically was a pre-requisite of baseball, in general, and certainly of Tribune Co., in particular, at the time, Lefebvre and Trebelhorn were drastically different. Trebelhorn was a part-time school teacher with a college degree, a fast-working mind, a passion for Broadway show tunes and a proven record as a winning major league manager despite never playing a day of big-league baseball himself. Lefebvre was a former National League Rookie of the Year with the Los Angeles Dodgers, who had a break-even record as a big-league manager. He somehow promoted himself as a hitting guru, even co-authoring a book entitled *The Making of a Hitter*. This, in spite of the fact he was a .251 career hitter. And the only reason he was that mediocre was because he got off to a hot start. Lefebvre's career spanned parts of eight seasons from 1965-72 and his batting average for the last five of those eight years was .239—much closer to Mario Mendoza than Ty Cobb.

Lefebvre and Trebelhorn both came to the Cubs on the rebound— Lefebvre from Seattle, where he had an ugly personal confrontation with his bosses, and Trebelhorn from Milwaukee, where he was squeezed out because a new regime, typically and understandably, wanted to bring in its own people. Himes knew both Lefebvre and Trebelhorn were eager for fresh starts and were determined to be on their best behavior. He figured he couldn't lose with either. Trebelhorn had the better track record. He was the winningest manager in Brewer franchise history. But Lefebvre had won, too, in his last year at Seattle. In three seasons with the Mariners, his teams finished in sixth place once and fifth place twice. His career record at that point was an uninspiring 233-253. But he had led a so-so Seattle club to an 83-79 record the year before. And Himes had been impressed several seasons earlier when he interviewed Lefebvre for the then-vacant White Sox manager's job. That was enough to tip the scales. On November 22, 1991, Lefebvre signed a two-year deal worth $700,000 to manage the Cubs. Trebelhorn, with Lefebvre's assent, was brought on as bench coach five days later. The Party line, echoed dutifully by Lefebvre, was that you could never have too much talent on your coaching staff. The reality was Himes had a manager and a potential successor in the wings. Maybe that formula worked fine for

Ronald Reagan and George Bush. But it was a recipe for trouble with the Cubs, who seemed to have written the cookbook on disasters.

Perception is as important as reality—usually more important. And the perception in the Cubs' clubhouse was that Trebelhorn was brought on board to be Himes' spy in the clubhouse. I came to know Trebelhorn reasonably well in the next few years and I cannot believe for an instant that he would sink so low as to stab a colleague in the back for personal aggrandizement. Not that I consider Trebelhorn some kind of saint. He is as prone to ego-driven error as any of us. But he is simply too smart, too confident, and too capable to have to resort to such desperate and undisciplined measures—particularly in this case when it seemed obvious it was only a matter of time until Lefebvre wore out his welcome as he had in Seattle.

Still, reality rarely wins against perception. And the almost universal perception among the players in those days was that Trebelhorn was Himes' eyes and ears.

One of Lefebvre's first official duties as manager of the Cubs was to accompany representatives of Major League Baseball International on a winter junket to Europe. Baseball, ever the mirror of the national psyche, had, for years, been blissfully indifferent to the outside world and all its intriguing potential. While baseball owners were busy putting two teams in Seattle and dangling a half-dozen franchises in front of Tampa Bay, football and basketball owners were tapping new markets and winning new fans abroad—particularly in Europe, where political and economic change offered creative opportunities. Major League Baseball, of course, had its patronizing attitude toward Japan and its neo-colonial ties to Puerto Rico and Latin America. But it was light years behind football and basketball in reaching out to new global markets. Now, a few enlightened souls in the game, including Jim Small, then in the commissioner's office, were trying to change things. The junket to Europe two winters after the collapse of Communism, was a small, but important step.

Lefebvre, like a good many major leaguers, finished his career in

Japan. And he grew up in California. So he was no novice to strange and foreign cultures. But he got an eye-opening shock during the 12-day trip through the Netherlands, Czechoslovakia, and Italy. In recounting his adventure to Jerome Holtzman of the *Chicago Tribune,* Lefebvre told how surprised he was when Anthony Kroll, a serviceman from LaGrange Park, Illinois, stopped him at an an Air Force Base outside Amsterdam and proudly pulled a Die-Hard Cubs' Fan Club card from his wallet. Lefebvre was tickled, too, that 100 tourists stopped and gawked when he and Don Rowe, a one-time pitching coach with the White Sox, stood in full uniform in the Colosseum in Rome to have publicity photos taken. But Lefebvre said one of the most amazing moments of his baseball life came when a woman interrupted one of his typical rah-rah pep talks during a town meeting in Prague.

"I was explaining the many ways a manager can make out a lineup," Lefebvre told Holtzman. "I said: 'Ryne Sandberg is such a good hitter, he could bat in the cleanup spot.'"

In the back of the room, an attractive woman in her 30s waved her hand, trying to get Lefebvre's attention.

"Yes, ma'am," Lefebvre said, "do you have a question?"

"No, no," the woman said. "Sandberg is your No. 2 hitter. That's where he belongs, batting second."

I read Holtzman's column with fascination just a couple days before I flew to Arizona for my first spring training with the Cubs in early February 1992. I was going out unusually early because, frankly, I couldn't wait to get started. Conveniently, the Sunday editor at the time, Ken Paxson, assigned me to do a profile on the new manager. So I had a legitimate excuse. Lefebvre lived in Scottsdale, Arizona, the wonderful town where I'd be staying, just 20 minutes from the Cubs' spring training camp in Mesa. I figured after reading Holtzman's column that I was going to meet a worldly man of broad interests—someone, who after having just traveled through Eastern Europe, would, at least, be curious about my experiences, and, at best, would have some interesting insights of his own. *Wrong.* I was looking fastball and Lefebvre froze me with a screwball.

Lefebvre, to his lasting credit, was most gracious that first evening. He invited me to his magnificent mountainside home, complete with swimming pool, gazebo, workout room, a chipping practice area, and a net-draped tunnel that doubled as a home batting cage and driving range. Like virtually every manager and coach in baseball, Lefebvre loved golf. The driving range came in particularly handy since his next-door neighbor was Andrew Magee, then one of the leading money winners on the PGA Tour. Lefebvre was justifiably proud showing me around the place. He was a wonderful host all evening—as generous with his time as his wife and children were with their patience. I left feeling upbeat about Lefebvre. He was nothing, if not personable. His charisma, alone, bode well for his leadership role, I thought, and dashed off to write a glowing, if hardly ground-breaking, profile.

Years later, I reread that piece and was pleasantly surprised to find several telling and accurate insights. But, overall, it was the first of many disappointing failures in my new career. I had too quickly made the transition from journalist to baseball writer by abandoning one of the cardinal rules of journalism, which is to always—*always, always, always*—ask why. Why would Lefebvre be so generous to an outsider with little or no baseball credentials? Why did he leave Seattle? Why did Himes pick him to manage the Cubs? Why? Why? Why?

The answer to why he was so generous with me was obvious and should have been factored heavily into everything I thought or wrote. I was the *Chicago Tribune's* beat writer. I worked for his bosses. I'd be covering the team for the biggest newspaper in the Midwest, one of the biggest in the country. I was far more useful as an ally than an enemy.

As for why he left Seattle, I did, at least, make a few calls. But I had gotten such conflicting and shadowy information that it was easier for me to simply skate around Lefebvre's tenure with the Mariners, which I did. The piece was supposed to deal mainly with Lefebvre as a person, anyway. In truth, though, if I had dug harder and longer—if I had been a journalist instead of a baseball writer—I would have learned more about the long-running feud Lefebvre had with ownership in Seattle and how some of the same players who once wore shirts proclaiming themselves "Lefebvre Believer" eventually became his biggest critics. I could have prepared myself and my readers for what was to come in Chicago. And why.

If I had kept asking long enough, too, I would have gotten to the core of why Himes hired Lefebvre, which, of course, would have put me on to something bigger and more revealing than a puff personality profile of the new Cubs' manager. I would have gotten a head start into understanding why Himes was a head case—a guy with a great baseball mind, who was so devoid of people skills and so demanding of blind loyalty that he would tear down an organization quicker than he could build a team.

Instead, I made a seamless transition from journalism to sports journalism and laid the road markers for an easy escape route anytime I needed to Feed the Dragon over the next few years.

For all the glaring and humbling failures in that debut piece, there were a few redeeming tidbits. First and foremost, it painted what proved to be an accurate picture of a cocksure, one-dimensional dynamo. It also tipped the astute reader that Lefebvre's perception of reality wasn't always very realistic.

In our meeting, Lefebvre talked about his days in Japan at the end of his career. His first marriage was failing. He was in an alien country. He was out of the major leagues. "I grew up, I really grew up in Japan," Lefebvre said. "I had a lot of chance to learn about myself and about handling situations."

When I put those quotes in the story, I figured Lefebvre probably was sincere. But when he went from there to talk about how his newfound maturity had led him to a Born-Again approach to the media, I knew he had lapsed into self-serving delusion and I wanted it on the record.

"I couldn't read or write Japanese, so I could care less what they wrote about me," Lefebvre said. "I didn't get caught up in that and, right now, even to this day, I don't really read a lot of journalists. Not because I don't respect them. It's just that I know when you're on top of the world they write good things about you and when you're not going well they write bad things about you. I'm not going to get caught up in that."

Right. And the Pope's converting to Islam on Good Friday.

It didn't take long for Lefebvre to forget the enlightenment of the Far East. Within three months, he was so livid at some of the things I'd written—the kinds of things he said he didn't bother to read any more—that he threw a capillary-popping tantrum in the hallway of a Houston hotel at 1 in the morning.

Actually, my relations with Lefebvre began to crumble the first few days of that first spring training when he adopted what came across as a condescending attitude. I'm still not convinced to this day it was intentional. In fact, I'm inclined to believe Lefebvre meant well and simply didn't know better. Whatever. I wasn't alone in cocking an eyebrow in confusion when Lefebvre insisted on turning his daily post-practice interviews into a kindergarten for beat writers. He would have one of the team's two public relations representatives—either Sharon Pannozzo or Chuck Wasserstrom—gather all the reporters together at a set time every afternoon. Then, when he was ready, Lefebvre would march us *en masse,* like a gaggle of infants, across the field, usually in front of the players, who were doing their cool-down exercises, but always in front of dozens of fans, who were simply hanging around. We were made to look like mopes, begging for crumbs, which, I suppose, is precisely what we were. But it was embarrassing to have to be reminded of it so blatantly and publicly. Then, before any of us could ask one of our penetrating spring training questions—*Any injuries today? Anybody catch your eye out there? Where are you eating tonight?*—Lefebvre would seize the initiative and deliver a patronizing sermon on baseball. "We're going to work on our basics," he said, only half-jokingly, the first day. "Okay, now. This is first base." The next day's post-practice session was a repeat, except it was second base. Then third, home, the pitcher's mound, and outfield before Lefebvre ran out of positions and we ran out of dignity.

It was, admittedly, a trivial slight. And, probably unintentional. But it was a great reminder to me that for all the green grass and sunshine, for all the comforting sounds of balls plopping into gloves and spikes digging into dirt, I was still at work. I had to behave like a professional

and I had the right to expect to be treated like one. Even if I wanted—
and was so inclined—I wasn't there to be friends with James Kenneth
Lefebvre or anybody else in the Cubs' organization. *"It's okay to sleep
with elephants. Just don't cover the circus."*

That early reminder made it easy for me to be critical in my coverage, but not nearly as easy as Lefebvre himself made it. Lefebvre was a
born leader, but an atrocious tactician. Several times during the 1992
season he actually ran out of players in games. Once, when he had two
lefthanders warming up, he walked to the mound to make a pitching
change and signaled to the bullpen with his right hand. The umpires
were baffled. Several of us in the press box doubled over in hysterics.
Fortunately, pitching coach Billy Connors, a true-blue Cub, who developed an inspiring relationship with his players, was down in the bullpen
to sort things out. Otherwise, we might still be out there trying to figure
out what pitcher Jimmy LeFun wanted in the game.

Lefebvre's blunderings were great fodder for comical copy. And,
despite his professed reluctance to read what was written about him,
Lefebvre clearly was paying attention. Our relationship grew increasingly strained. It didn't help that Lefebvre kept finding new ways to
outdo even himself—such as his baffling performance in a game against
the Mets on July 1.

My account of the events in the next day's *Tribune* began: *"For
those who were wondering, Cubs' manager Jim Lefebvre was wide
awake and says he knew precisely what he was doing in the bottom of
the ninth inning of Wednesday's 6-4 loss to the Mets."*

I figured it was a public service to let everyone know Lefebvre was
awake because circumstantial evidence indicated otherwise.

The score was tied at 4 in the bottom of the ninth inning when
Lefebvre sent up newly acquired outfield Kal Daniels to pinch hit.
Daniels, only 28 and a career .287 hitter, had been released by the

Dodgers two weeks earlier because he was batting just .231 and had spent most of the season on the disabled list with knee injuries that had bothered him for years. Daniels' knees were so bad the Dodgers were convinced—rightly so, it turned out—that his career was over. They took him off the roster and made him available to anyone foolish enough to take him. Larry Himes was first in a line of one, and—in true Himes fashion—proud of it.

When Daniels reported to the Cubs, all he and Lefebvre did was answer questions about the knees. Lefebvre downplayed the problems, but admitted he wouldn't start Daniels against the Mets. "He hasn't played in a while, I want him to get back into the swing of things," Lefebvre said.

But with the score tied and one out in the bottom of the ninth, Lefebvre sent Daniels up to pinch-hit. That made perfect sense. Daniels had a lifetime .319 average in Wrigley Field, which is pretty good even taking into account all those hits came off Cubs' pitchers. This time Daniels didn't have that advantage, but he still laced a single to left that Mets left fielder Dave Gallagher momentarily bobbled. A hustling runner would have been standing on second representing the winning run. Daniels, with his bad knees, wisely held first.

The obvious move—the only move—at that point was to send Daniels to the bench for a pinch runner. With one out and the top of the order coming up, the only sure way Daniels was going to score the winning run from first was on a homer. A stand-up triple would have been iffy. A pinch runner, on the other hand, might get to second any number of ways and score on a single.

Lefebvre, though, never made a move. Daniels stayed at first. Three balls and two strikes later, Jose Vizcaino's hit would and should have been a game-winning double to right field. Daniels had the advantage of breaking with the pitch because the count was full. Even so, he still hasn't touched homeplate to this day. He lumbered around second base like something out of a 1950s horror movie about nuclear war—a frightened 200-pound mutant king crab with his arms and broken knees flailing desperately at ungodly contorted angles. Daniels somehow managed to round third, in spite of his pudgy little self, and was careening in the general direction of a Cubs' win when his out-of-shape body surrendered with a massive belly flop that left him wallowing in the dirt six feet from the plate and nowhere to hide.

Doug Dascenzo put the cap on the catastrophe by grounding out to second to end the inning and, despite putting another six runners on base in the next three innings, the Cubs never scored again. The Mets came back to win 6-4. And, like Daniels, there was nowhere for Lefebvre to hide either.

In the crowded manager's office after the game, Lefebvre visibly bristled at every question and experimented with every imaginable justification. His first and most-adamant line of defense was to insist he had nobody better available to run. Never mind that if that were true in the bottom of the ninth of a 4-4 game, it reflected pretty poorly on his managing skills. The reality was he had a natural candidate available in infielder Doug Strange. And there was backup catcher Joe Girardi, who, while never known for his speed, had a well-deserved reputation as a smart runner—good enough to let him bat second in the order for the Colorado Rockies in 1995 when they went to the playoffs. The only position player left that Lefebvre could legitimately argue was worse than a banged-up Daniels, was a healthy Hector Villanueva, the ever-expanding third-string catcher who was the unofficial patron saint of Dunkin' Donuts. Villanueva was best left on the bench to catch if the game went deep into extra innings. But even granting Villanueva a continued leave of absence and ignoring Strange and Girardi, Lefebvre still had at least four healthy pitchers who could have strolled home on Vizcaino's double.

When his first line of defense began to wither, Lefebvre's fall-back position was even more tenuous. He said he stuck with Daniels because he remembered the Dodger outfielder had run well against the Cubs earlier in the year. "I think he scored twice in L.A. from first on a double against us, and scored easily," said Lefebvre, either deluding himself or hoping nobody would bother to check. A glance at my scorebook showed that in six games against the Cubs earlier that season, Daniels only scored once. That was at Wrigley Field, not in L.A., and it wasn't on a double. Daniels trotted home on a throwing error by Sammy Sosa. To make things worse for Lefebvre's case, my scorebook reminded me that in one of those earlier games, Daniels had gotten a clutch hit in the bottom of the ninth. Dodger manager Tommy Lasorda promptly lifted Daniels for a pinch runner, who—you guessed it— scored the winning run.

I expected Lefebvre to go ballistic the next day after reading my story and similar wonderfully scathing dispatches by Toni Ginnetti in the *Sun-Times* and Barry Rozner in the *Daily Herald*. But he kept his cool. He clearly wasn't in a mood to invite any of us over for a Fourth of July bar-b-que, but he took his well-deserved pounding with admirable restraint. Unlike earlier in the year.

The Cubs went through a bizarre rollercoaster ride in their first few months under Lefebvre. After a respectable 6-7 start, they went into a 2-9 tailspin at the end of April and early May. At one point during the dive, they were shut out four consecutive games and five times in six tries. They went an almost unimaginable 34 consecutive innings without scoring. That's almost a week's worth of games without a run. Their line scores, as I wrote at the time, had as many zeroes as the national debt. When the Cubs finally did score, though, they reeled off three consecutive wins and looked as if they were headed back in the right direction until Lefebvre stepped in.

Things started innocently enough. The weather was glorious for the May 8 Friday afternoon opener of a weekend series against the Reds. The Cubs, looking as if they were determined to make up for the recent void of runs in one fell swoop, were crushing the ball. They jumped to a 5-0 lead and were in the process of pounding out 19 hits when the bottom fell out. The Reds scored six times in the seventh inning to go ahead, 6-5. And, although the Cubs came back to tie it, Cincinnati won 10-7 in extra innings. It was a crushing defeat at just the wrong time. It kept the Cubs buried in last place with an 11-17 record. What was worse, everybody in the ballpark knew Lefebvre had been the biggest contributor to the loss. If he'd done one more thing wrong in that game there probably would have been fatalities.

In the course of the final six innings of the game, Lefebvre ran out of position players. He used up two relievers to face just three batters in a middle-inning jam then was so short-handed he had to ask his bullpen ace to go three innings—long enough to hurt his arm and get the loss. Lefebvre kept a left-handed PITCHER at the plate to bat with the bases loaded and two outs against Cincinnati's ace lefthander Norm Charlton. And he rounded all that off by publicly embarrassing and alienating former All-Star Dave Smith, the No. 10 leader in career saves at the time. Smith had been struggling all year and Lefebvre had lost all confidence in him. He pointedly refused to look in Smith's direction until the last available pitcher, Chuck McElroy, hurt his arm and had to come out after giving up the winning run. Smith never even got to throw a warm-up pitch before going to the mound with the game already lost.

I thought my lede in the *Tribune* the next morning summed things up pretty accurately:

"It doesn't get any uglier than this.

"If it does, somebody should be prosecuted.

"Or run out of town."

I briefly mentioned the final scored and the fact the Cubs had squandered 19 hits and a 5-0 lead. Then I wrote: *"It took 12 innings, and a remarkable amount of ineptitude, to do it, but they managed. Maybe managed is the wrong word. Because it was a decision by manager Jim Lefebvre that cost them this one."*

The next day was Saturday and I had the weekend free, after writing my Sunday column, to do expenses and catch up on my statistics and homework. I wouldn't see Lefebvre until Monday night in Houston when the Cubs opened a three-game series against the Astros. Boy, would I see him.

I flew from Chicago to Houston early Monday morning. The team had gone down Sunday night after the final game of the Cincinnati series. As usual, I got to the Astrodome about three hours before game time, made the rounds, went up to the press box and started working on the daily notes. Greg Maddux was pitching, which meant the Astros weren't scoring. And the Cubs weren't hitting, which meant we went extra innings. I had to do one story on deadline, get down to the locker room for a few quotes, then come back up to the press box and do a complete writethru for the final editions. I breezed in and out the locker room, got a few perfunctory quotes from Lefebvre and the usual sus-pects and took about an hour writing and transmitting a new story.

It was about 1 A.M. when I got back to the hotel. I was exhausted. I'd left home for O'Hare to get my flight to Houston about 7 A.M. and had been on the run all day. I remember walking down the hall toward my room in the Westin Galleria with my head down and two heavy bags—one filled with computer gear; one with my score book and various record books—slumping from my shoulders. I was thinking about how tired I was when I looked up and heading toward me was Lefebvre, his perpetually tanned face slightly flushed. I was surprised to see him. Usually, the traveling secretary makes sure the manager stays on a floor away from the beat writers—consciously, to avoid chance late-night meetings just as this. "You write a good story tonight?" Lefebvre asked, his voice a bit slow and dripping with sarcasm. "Tried," was all I said and by then we were about to pass in the hall. "Write one as good as you wrote the other day?"

I stopped. The battle was on. Lefebvre, his breath smelling of his usual post-game beer in the clubhouse, and, I assumed, one or two more somewhere else, tried to remain calm. But his voice steadily rose in volume and anger until doors started popping open one by one on either side of the hallway. I was having a tough time keeping a straight face. First, Lefebvre looked laughable with the veins in his neck bulging and his flushed face getting redder by the moment. Then, over his shoulder, I kept seeing one door after another pop open. A bleary-eyed coach or stranger would peep into the hallway, realize what was happening, and quickly retreat behind a thudding door.

If the scene itself weren't funny enough, Lefebvre seemed intent on adding to it with his ridiculous arguments. He told me with a straight face—bright red, but straight—that his wife was so upset about the ar-ticle I'd written she refused to come to Chicago again with the children. She's too embarrassed, Lefebvre screamed. I found this incredulous. I'd met his wife. Ruth Endersby Lefebvre is an impressive woman, who was graduated from San Diego State University with a bachelor of sci-ence degree and worked as a registered nurse at Stanford University Hospital for nine years. The first time we met, she described herself as an "osmotic baseball scholar"—meaning everything she knew about the game she learned through osmosis, simply by absorbing it. I found it impossible to believe this person would be so embarrassed, second-hand, by a critical game story that she would refuse to show her face in Chicago and would refuse to let her children watch their dad work in Wrigley Field. I told Lefebvre what I thought, which only prolonged and inflated his rage.

The next day, Lefebvre had calmed enough to invite me to smoke the peace pipe over an expensive lunch at the hotel's poshest restaurant. I went and listened to him repeat a little more sanely, but just as inanely, his feelings. We talked in circles, as adversaries are wont to do in such situations. And we parted, having accomplished little beyond padding Lefebvre's comfortable expense account.

A few weeks later, after another hiccup in our now-constantly rocky relationship, Lefebvre told me he had gone "to the highest levels of the *Tribune*" in an effort to get me fired.

I never found out if that were true. All I knew was that if he had—and it seemed perfectly within his character—then he'd failed. We had passed each other that winter in the air going in opposite directions—he to his junket in Europe and me to my new job in the States. We never would quite get on the same flight path. But when he was gone two years later, I was still around. And I must admit, it was sweet to be home.

Chapter 4

Larry, Curly, and Moe

When I left the United States, the Three Stooges were on television. When I came home, it seemed almost everyone was complaining Larry, Curly, and Moe were their bosses. I couldn't understand it at first. Then I watched Larry Himes run the Cubs for a few years.

Tim Kurkjian of *Sports Illustrated* once called Himes "one of the least-liked executives in baseball," a phrase headline writers quickly, and probably accurately, abbreviated to: "The Most-Hated Man in Baseball."

Andre Dawson, a deeply religious player, went so far as to compare Himes to the devil in his book, *"Hawk."*

To me, though, Himes was no more and no less than the embodiment of everything that seemed to have gone wrong with Corporate America as the 20th Century drew to a close. He was a blindly ambitious, egotistical boss who rewarded loyalty to him over competence to the company. He sowed chaos like wildflowers and never realized it because of his complete lack of people skills. Like a frightening number of employers in a frightening number of fields, Himes created an atmosphere where dedicated worker bees willing to put in long hours and spawn innovative ideas were treated no better than 9-to-5 clock-watchers who simply went through the motions.

Himes didn't do it all himself. He got a tremendous boost from his bosses at Tribune Co. in stifling initiative and dedication. It came in the form of a plan called the Hay system, which Tribune Co. imposed on the Cubs and many of its subsidiaries in place of a series of successful bonus schemes in the early 1990s. Tribune Co. didn't invent the Hay system. It was popular with a wide range of businesses in the 1980s and '90s. But Tribune Co. embraced it with a vengeance.

Essentially, the Hay system established a structured hierarchy of job classifications and set out what it claimed were scientific and rational methods of evaluating employees in those classifications. Pay scales for each job grade were rigidly defined, which meant there was little incentive to work hard. A dedicated employee who did excellent work, put in longer hours, was professional and punctual would be paid roughly the same as someone in the same job grade who did mediocre work, came in 15 minutes late, left five minutes early, and basically went through the motions. The only way to break out was to move up in job grades, which often was difficult because the Hay system was pyramid-shaped. The higher the pay grades, the fewer employees who would be admitted.

Considering the low pay ceiling and lack of mobility on the administrative end of Major League Baseball, the Hay system was particularly cruel to the Cubs. The very core of the Cubs, the reason the franchise had become so profitable, was the hard-working attitude of people who never watched the clock, who came in when they were sick, and who pulled each other along. Not even the Hay system could kill that loyalty. But it could—and did—take away the financial rewards.

The Hay system did for the Cubs what Communism does wherever it takes root. It encouraged mindless mediocrity and discouraged excellence—all in the name of a better world. One of my many flaws is that I have tendency to go ballistic in airports whenever I'm leaving a Communist country. It's happened to me too many times. I can't help myself. Airports are tedious and nerve-wracking enough without having to deal with all the insanities imposed by socialist societies. My emotional circuitry overloads under the strain. I snapped three or four times during my years in Beijing when yet another security guard asked to see my passport for the 92nd time in the 100 yards from customs to the boarding gate. It happened to me again just recently in Vietnam where, in the space of 25 feet, I had to deal with four different uniformed bureaucrats to purchase an airport departure ticket. One young woman sold me the ticket. Another woman standing two feet away tore the ticket out of a book and handed it to me. A third guard 10 feet away demanded to see the ticket before I could pass through the metal detectors. And a fourth official nearly tackled me to collect the ticket as I headed for the departure lounge. Four people were employed full-time to do an absolutely mindless task that could just as easily been accomplished by adding $8 to the airplane ticket when it was issued in the first place. In case you ever wondered: that's Communism—that and sending tanks to kill your own people in the streets of Beijing.

I would always get in trouble because my reaction to this massive brain death was simply to refuse to admit it existed. I would walk past the guards as if they weren't there. Almost always, I was stopped and given a stern lecture, which I felt compelled to rebut in somewhat loud tones. But once, actually in Beijing of all places, I walked through so confidently and swiftly that I left the country without purchasing a departure ticket or even having my passport stamped. It was a small victory I still treasure.

Larry Himes didn't need Communism, the Hay system, or any other artificial assist to stifle morale. He was a master in his own right.

Himes had revealed his remarkable weaknesses as a manager long before he came to the Cubs. The White Sox made him general manager in 1986 after an impressive career as an evaluator of baseball talent with the California Angels and Baltimore Orioles. Himes knew a good young ballplayer when he saw one. At least, his track record was as good as anyone in that notoriously capricious profession. And he only enhanced his reputation when the White Sox drafted Jack McDowell, Robin Ventura, Frank Thomas, and Alex Fernandez during his tenure as general manager.

Picking those four players alone would seem enough to ensure a long, happy career for any general manager. But there is more to running a major league organization than making good draft picks. And Himes was an unmitigated disaster at almost everything else.

The day he was fired by the White Sox after the 1990 season, there was a collective sigh of relief on the South Side of Chicago. There was a general assumption, too, in the baseball community, that the only future Himes had was in scouting. That is what he did for the next year and that, undoubtedly, is what he would have done for years to come if the powers that be at Tribune Co. hadn't come to his unwelcome rescue.

The man responsible for hiring Himes and setting in motion events that tore one of America's most-beloved sports franchises apart was Stanton R. Cook, a white-haired, blue-blood with a heart just black enough to get him where he wanted to be—atop the corporate world. Cook was the quintessential homegrown Tribune executive. He was graduated from Northwestern University with a bachelor of science degree in mechanical engineering and joined the *Tribune* in 1951 after a brief stint with Shell Oil. Cook rose steadily through the ranks to become president and chief executive officer of Tribune Co. in 1974.

By all accounts, Cook was a capable man. But his abilities didn't always match his position or his perks. The upper echelon of Tribune Co., as much as any giant corporation, is a cozy, private club where members protect members. Admittance is hard won, but virtually irrevocable. In fairness, the same is true all the way down the corporate ladder at Tribune Co. Rarely is anyone fired from the company's newspapers or other media outlets for anything short of gross misconduct or criminal behavior. Dead wood generally piles up until it rots away, which is why *Time* magazine once, accurately, I think, described the *Tribune* as the Baby Huey of newspapers—an enormously overgrown, underachiever that bumbles along benignly without ever truly living up to its size and strength.

The difference in the upper echelon of Tribune Co. is, that not only does the inner circle protect one itself, its members also reward each other by voting huge blocks of company stocks as bonuses and options while imposing the Hay system on the worker bees. It is perfectly legal and even publicized for those who bother to read. To make sure I never forgot who, or what, I was dealing with on the Cubs' beat, I made a habit of cutting out and putting in my baseball files, the seemingly innocuous stock transactions published in agate type on the business pages of the *Tribune*. Just one example is the "Insider Transactions" column of February 13, 1995, the last item of which reads: *"Tribune Co.: Stanton R. Cook, director, disposed of by gift 1,400 shares of common (stock) at an unreported price Dec. 13 (1994) and now directly and indirectly holds 419,394 common."*

Tribune common stock closed December 12, 1994, and December 13, 1994, at $50.50 a share. In other words, Cook gave away $70,700 worth of stock just before the end of the 1994 tax year and still owned or controlled or had options on shares valued at $21,179,397. That was more than the team payrolls of the Florida Marlins, California Angels, Montreal Expos, or Pittsburgh Pirates in 1994. It was more than the $20.5 million Tribune Co. paid to buy the Cubs from the Wrigley family in 1981. By February 13, 1995, the day Cook's December "gift" finally was reported in the paper, the value of Tribune stock had jumped to $55.625. His shares were worth $23.3 million and climbing. Two years later, after a stock split, those shares would be worth $33.5 million.

For that kind of money, Tribune Co. should have gotten a better caretaker for what amounted to the corporate toy. Cook was publisher of the *Chicago Tribune* and CEO of Tribune Co. until August 1, 1990. He was 65 years old at the time and should have retired. In fact, the Tribune hosted a formal retirement party for him at Cantigny Country Club near suburban Wheaton, Illinois, and presented him with a sculpted wooden replica of his office on the 24th floor of Tribune Tower worth thousands of dollars as a going away gift. Trouble was, like a bad dream, Cook wouldn't go away. He stepped down as publisher of the *Tribune*, but stayed on as chairman of Tribune Co. and arranged a new role for himself as chairman of the Cubs.

The Cubs are one of the best-known and most-loved professional sports franchises in North America. But, in the grand scheme of things, the Cubs are hardly the most important subsidiary in Tribune Co. In 1994, the Cubs had operating revenues of $92 million, which sounds impressive. But that was a mere four percent of the $2.1 billion operating revenues for Tribune Co. as a whole.

Where better than Wrigley Field, then, to stuff an old uncle who refuses to fade away? The job of chairman of the Cubs was big-time enough to pacify Cook's not inconsiderable ego. But it was still small enough, in the grand scheme of things, to diminish his already fading influence within Tribune Co.

Like Grenesko, Cook knew little about baseball beyond the knowledge of the passing fan. On several occasions, I heard executives in the Cubs' front office laughingly refer to Cook as "Stan the Fan" or, when he was doing something particularly outrageous and bottom-line, they would dub him "Stan the Man." But Cook's lack of insight into the game did little to stop his star from rising in the world of Major League Baseball. As point man for Tribune Co., Cook was treated as *de facto* owner of the Cubs and awarded the appropriate trappings of power. He was given seats on Major League Baseball's Ownership Committee, the baseball operations committee, the professional base-ball agreement committee, and the schedule, format, and oversight committees. Most importantly, in December 1992, he was named to the all-powerful Executive Committee, which ran baseball in the ab-sence of a commissioner.

For all the prestige and influence of those positions, though, Cook was widely considered the Mister Magoo of the baseball world. On a personal level, he was much like the Cubs themselves—generally be-nign and bumbling. But on a professional level, Cook was the enemy within. Many owners had bitter disagreements with the way Tribune Co. did business and Cook came to be the focal point of their frustra-tions. The Cubs televised all their games on WGN, the cable superstation that could be seen in every major league market. More than a few owners believed WGN cut into their own club's attendance be-cause it was easier for fans to stay home and watch the Cubs on TV than it was to get in the car and go to the local ballpark. Other owners re-sented the fact that Tribune Co. had staggering resources at its disposal if it ever wanted to launch an all-out buying spree for players. That never happened. The Cubs consistently kept their payrolls around the mid- to upper-middle range among major league teams. But when Cook personally intervened March 1, 1992, to sign Ryne Sandberg to what was then the largest contract in history, warning flags and blood pres-sures went up across baseball.

"Stan the Fan" was clearly a happy man the day he stood in the ball-room of the Hilton Hotel in Mesa, Arizona, listening to the announce-ment of Sandberg's signing. He shuffled his feet, folded his arms, and mumbled the patrician equivalents of golly-gee and ah-shucks every time Sandberg thanked him for his role in the negotiations. It was Cook's finest hour. Or so he thought—never dreaming that Sandberg would walk away from the game long before his Goliath contract expired. Or that one of the main reasons Sandberg, "The Franchise," would walk away was because Cook ruined the game for him and scores of others—from the front office to the back parking lot—by hiring Larry Himes as general manager of the Cubs.

The decision to hire Himes in November 1991 caught almost everyone by surprise. Even the senior-most officials in the front office at Wrigley Field were kept in the dark until hours before the announcement. When word finally leaked out, the general reaction was stunned disbelief, mixed—particularly from the White Sox—with more than a few chortles. If any team but the Cubs had announced it was hiring Himes as a GM after his tumultuous run with the Sox, the general reaction of the baseball world would have been denial. But Tribune Co. had worked hard to build an impressive record of ineptitude in its first decade in baseball and anything was possible—even hiring Larry Himes as general manager.

As an organization, of course, the White Sox were ecstatic to see the Cubs slit their own wrists. The fact that a Sox reject was wielding the rusty razor only made it all-the-more wonderful. But one thing I noticed about most Americans—that you don't see in every other culture—is the healthy respect rivals have for one another. We want our competitors to be good. It's no fun beating someone who doesn't work hard or try hard. You see it in almost every field. Lawyers can lose a case and still feel good about themselves because the other side beat them fair and square. In our society, we realize you can't win 'em all. But you sure *better try* to win 'em all.

That attitude thrives in baseball's front offices even more than it does on the field. The players get all the attention. But the real heart of the 30 Major League franchises are the women and men who slave happily and tirelessly behind the scenes. The work ethic of everyone from the people who answer the phones to the scouts in the boonies and the vice presidents who negotiate the contracts is, on the whole, nothing short of staggering. There are sluggards and incompetents, of course. But, generally speaking, baseball's hardest workers are sitting at their desks, not in the dugouts. Everybody admires Ernie Banks and Cal Ripken for the way they loved the game, for the respect they showed it every day and the fun they had playing it. They are legends and they deserve to be legends. But there isn't an organization in baseball that doesn't have 20 Ernie Banks and Cal Ripkens doing everything from loading equipment trucks to running photocopy machines. They have names like Arlene Gill and Nancy Nesnidal; Scott Reifert and Ed McGregor; Hugh Alexander and Willie Thompson. And they all deserve to have their numbers retired.

The public may not know who they are, but everyone in baseball knows who's doing the real work and who's skating. And the greatest reward is mutual respect, which is why, the morning Himes was hired, Ned Colletti, director of baseball operations and one of the hardest workers with the Cubs, got a phone call from a friend high up in the White Sox organization. "Make sure you document everything," the friend warned. "Keep notes. Protect yourself. This guy's trouble." A few minutes later, Colletti got almost identical whispered advice from a senior executive in Tribune Tower, who was equally astounded and frustrated that Cook would hire Himes. "We just entered the long dark tunnel," the Tribune suit said, all-too-prophetically.

If Cook had done his homework, or if he had a few reliable friends in the game, he, too, would have been warned off Himes. But "Stan the Man" insisted on being his own man. He was awed by Himes' résumé, which, in addition to being impressive on its merit, was staggering in its bulk. The closest Himes came to being humble was having an "H" in his name. He once told his executive assistant, Arlene Gill, that if she ever had to sign his name on any documents to make sure the signature was big. A big signature, he had read somewhere, was a sign of power.

Himes' résumé was dozens of pages long, printed in booklet form, and laid out everything from his considerable experience to his philosophies on leadership. Taken at face value, the résumé was so daunting anyone would seem justified jumping at the chance to hire Himes. But what the carefully edited autobiography failed to reveal, what even the most-imposing document could never explain, was how miserable Himes was at dealing with people. Cook never found out because he never bothered to check around. At least, he never asked the right people. His circle of confidants on baseball affairs was embarrassingly small. And he preferred to keep it that way—even if the Cubs had to pay the price.

One of the first things Larry did with the Cubs was to hire Curly and Moe—otherwise known as Syd Thrift and Jim Lefebvre.

Thrift was an eminently likable and highly intelligent man with an impressive baseball pedigree. He founded the Kansas City Royals Baseball Academy, was general manager of the Pirates, served as senior vice president of baseball operations for the Yankees, was a consultant to the Giants, and joined the Baltimore Orioles in 1995 as director of player personnel. He was an ever-smiling, ever up-beat missionary of the "Can-Do" spirit that seemed to be waning everywhere I looked. But he had one major flaw. And, ironically, it probably stemmed from the great success he enjoyed with the Royals' Baseball Academy, which, from 1969-72, tried to make a science out of a game. Thrift was a sucker for any gimmick, gadget, and gizmo that might somehow, some way give his players an edge nobody else had. Syd Thrift was every snake oil salesman's dream come true.

Himes was cut from the same cloth. He loved to spend his bosses' money by the sack full wherever he could. Within days of taking over the Cubs, he was grumbling about the sorry state of the spring training camp in Arizona. Getting new and improved facilities in Arizona became an obsession with him. Stymied at first from implementing the grandiose plans he preferred, Himes passed the first couple years making nit-picking changes. He spent $25,000 one spring to put blue mesh netting on the outfield fences around the minor league camp at Fitch Park. Ostensibly, he did it to give the players more privacy at work. All he accomplished was alienating hundreds of fans, mostly retirees from the Midwest, who showed up and sat for hours on end watching the players walk through practice under the hot desert sun. The fans could still see the workouts from the metal grandstands set up in the middle of Fitch Park, but gone was one of their happiest pleasures—simply driving down Center Street and catching a glimpse of the ballplayers in their bright blue Cubbie workout jerseys standing around on fields of fresh-mown grass.

The Cubs have two training facilities in Mesa, Arizona: the minor league camp at Fitch Park and the major league camp at HoHoKam Park, three blocks north. Himes wanted to merge the two, but couldn't because the land between was owned by several individuals and organizations. One block was an apartment complex that, obviously, was there to stay. But two blocks up from Fitch, and just a block from HoHo, was a large cotton field. Himes wanted to buy it, move the Fitch facilities closer. He also wanted to tear down "Dwight Patterson Field" at HoHoKam Park and replace it with a scaled down replica of Wrigley Field, complete with elaborate new administrative offices both at HoHoKam and Fitch.

Himes' dream collapsed because the landowner refused to sell the cotton field. And the mini-Wrigley Field floundered because the city of Mesa wasn't about to foot the mega-millions it would cost when they already had a perfectly acceptable stadium. The city eventually approved and built a beautiful new 12,500-seat stadium in 1997, but it was a mere shadow of what Himes originally wanted.

For the three years he ran the Cubs, Himes kept pressure on the HoHoKams, the non-profit, public service organization that hosted the Cubs, by threatening to move the training facilities several miles east to an area called Red Mountain, where, coincidentally, he had just built his dream home. That never happened and Himes never got his fantasy camp. But when he finally was replaced as general manager, Himes was given the title of Director/Arizona Operations and Special Assignment Scout. It was a typical Tribune Co. face-saving move and, some say, Cook's final act. Himes could stay on the payroll in a senior management position, thus finishing out the two more years he needed to collect his Tribune pension. He could work from his home in Arizona where he would be out of everybody's hair and wouldn't have to deal with people. And the Cubs could continue to tap his sole legitimate asset—his talent as a scout. Himes, at first, took the new position to mean he finally had power to push through his schemes. And one of the first things he did was give his successor, Andy MacPhail, the blueprints of the spring training facilities he wanted to build. MacPhail needed only a glance to see it was folly. He gave the blueprints back to Himes and told him to try again. Only this time, MacPhail said in effect, be a little more realistic.

That was later, however. While he was running the show, there was no stopping Himes. He and Thrift set about spending Tribune Co. money in a frenzied mission to find a magic formula that would turn the Cubs from lovable losers to wondrous winners. They ordered new weight equipment and bought elaborate machines to test hand-eye coordination. They had players hitting baseballs while standing on bouncing tires. They subjected potential draft picks to psychological tests and leadership quizzes. Himes and Thrift established a complex system of skills goals for every player and called in coaches and staff to measure progress every 20 games—carefully charting if a pitcher dropped off three percent in first-pitch strikes or a hitter was up one percent in runs created.

Once, they even toyed with the idea of hiring a craniologist who claimed he could isolate good hitters by feeling their skulls to see if they had the same bumps and shapes as Lou Gehrig or other greats of the game.

The perfect backdrop to all that craziness was Jim Lefebvre, who should have been wearing a pleated skirt and carrying pompoms instead of a Cubs' uniform with the No. 5 on back. He ran around feverishly for two years with a rah-rah-sis-boom-bah attitude that would have been more fitting at a Friday night high school football game or Cub Scout jamboree than a major league clubhouse.

The more I looked around, the more I realized there was no getting around it: Tribune Co., through its affiliate WGN-TV, had given the world Bozo the Clown. Now it was bringing back the Three Stooges.

"I'll tell Larry this to his face, but what happened with this organization is that they were seeking a magic formula—a quick fix," said Andy MacPhail, who was brought in three years later to clean up the mess. "Don't try to be smarter than everybody else. Don't try to find a magic formula. The answer ain't in a weight machine. It's the game. It's the basics: the bat and the ball and have fun, play hard. Sometimes you just gotta do the fundamentals well. If you do that, if you understand the cyclical nature of the game, your time will come. Also, you've got to have enough confidence and faith in your own ability and understanding of the game. They may all be down on us this year. They may make fun of us this year. Okay, we're horseshit. But we'll get 'em in the end. We'll take our time. We'll do it the right way and celebrate when it works. There's always this feeling—particularly with this club, the Cubs—that you just feel like you gotta do something. 'Dang, I gotta do something to validate my job or what I'm doing or just to show I can.' But sometimes you gotta do nothing. Sometimes you just gotta watch. That's hard to do."

Himes was incapable of watching. Just as he was incapable of delegating authority, trusting his deputies, or building relationships.

The first real glimpse I had of how bizarre Larry Himes could be came the last week of my first spring training with the Cubs in 1992. Rumors had been flying for days that the Cubs and White Sox were working on a big trade. Joe Goddard of the *Chicago Sun-Times* was covering the Sox in Sarasota, Florida, that spring and had been on top of the story with help from Dave Van Dyck, the superb senior baseball writer at the *Sun-Times*. On the Cubs' end of the deal, though, Toni Ginnetti of the *Sun-Times* and I were coming up dry. Himes had the lid on tight and I was too new on the beat to have the sources to pry it loose.

Just the hint that Himes would make his first big trade with his former team was news. But when the deal finally came down, it was a shocker. The Cubs traded George Bell, the former American League MVP who averaged 27 homers and 100 runs batted in the previous eight seasons, for Sammy Sosa, a speedy 23-year-old with a cannon arm and a reputation for unbridled, but reckless potential.

Himes also got left-handed reliever Kenny Patterson in the deal and dumped Bell's $3.1 million salary while picking up two players who, combined, would make only $820,000 that season. It was a brilliant trade for the Cubs. Patterson was basically a throw-in, who lasted one forgettable season with the Cubs. Sosa, however, emerged as one of the superstars of the game, arguably the closest thing to Roberto Clemente in a generation. Meanwhile, Bell batted just .240 for the White Sox over the next two seasons and, mercifully, was out of baseball after throwing a classless, egotistical tantrum during the 1993 playoffs.

Understandably, Himes was on edge for days leading up to the trade It emerged later there were serious doubts he could pull off the deal. Bell had been limping noticeably on a bad ankle all spring—since the previous September, in fact. The day of the trade, he had to leave a spring training game against the Oakland A's and go to a Mesa hospital for X-rays. The X-rays proved negative and Bell was back in the locker room, dressed in his favorite starched, creased, skin-tight blue jeans, and $200 loafers by the time the game ended.

We didn't know then Bell had been traded, but it quickly became obvious. Himes had sent word to the press box late in the game that he had an announcement to make. We should be in his office 15 minutes after the last out, a delay he presumably made as a courtesy to those of us who wanted to speak with players before they left and to those reporters who had to file stories immediately for the wire services or broadcast outlets. The first thing we saw when we walked into the locker room was Bell shaking hands with his teammates. We didn't have to call in Sherlock Holmes to figure out what had happened. Someone, I think Toni Ginnetti of the *Sun-Times,* walked up to Bell and said: "George, have you been traded?" He told us, yes; told us who was coming in his place, and started answering a litany of predictable questions.

Bell was part-way into a rant about how unfair he thought it was to get word he had been traded on such short notice—as he was headed out the door for the day and just as the team was about to break camp to head north—when Himes walked into the clubhouse and realized his big announcement wouldn't be such a shocker anymore.

Himes went nuts. His soft, pink face flamed. He barely managed to keep his voice under a yell as he stepped in and demanded all the reporters gather in his office immediately. Several of us stayed a few minutes to finish with Bell, then walked across together to the administrative offices where Himes was standing behind his desk looking apoplectic. His teeth were clenched. His face was flushed. And every muscle in his fit body seemed taut as piano wire.

As soon as Himes saw the last of us walk in, he lost the self-control he liked to think he had. Himes raised his right arm, opened his palm flat,

Surrounded by the winning Afghan tribesmen after a game of Buzkashi *in which two small armies on horseback wrestle for possession of a 130-pound headless calf. The calf inevitably gets torn to bloody shreds. As weird as* Buzkashi *sounds, it was nothing compared to some of the behavior I witnessed on the baseball beat.*

and slammed it down on his compulsively neat desk top with a crack that would have sent half the veterans of Desert Storm scurrying for cover.

"I *HAAAAATE* to be scooped," Himes screamed.

The room, of course, went dead silent. Everyone was stunned. I half-expected to hear the theme music from "Twilight Zone" slowly fade in.

Doo-doo-doo-doo … Doo-doo-doo-doo … Doo-doo-doo-doo…

I saw a lot of strange behavior in my time as a foreign correspondent. I remember a bizarre, carefully orchestrated news conference at Malacañang Palace during the "People Power" uprising in the Philippines when Chief of Staff Gen. Fabian Ver walked up to President Marcos, leaned over his shoulder and asked him on national television: "Shall I sic the tanks on them, sir?" I once watched one of my bosses,

Leon Daniel of UPI, mock the Soviet system by turning somersaults on the cobblestones of Red Square while goose-stepping soldiers changed the guard in front of Lenin's tomb at 5 in the morning. And I doubt if ever again will I be awed by anything as I was on a brutally bright day in February 1989 when I stood on a dusty field outside an Afghan refugee camp in Peshawar, Pakistan, with Michael E. Malinowski, a Chicago-born U.S. diplomat, and watched scores of bearded tribesmen on howling, sweating horses tear apart a 130-pound headless calf in a magnificent ceremonial game called Buzkashi.

Larry Himes had a way to go to top those memories. But he certainly earned an honorable mention in my personal Wall of Weirdness when he slammed his hand on his desk and yelled to a startled group of reporters that he *HAAAAATE-d* to be scooped on a trade.

I wish I had realized then how telling that incident was. Himes was giving us a glimpse into his tortured, insecure soul. I was simply too dumbfounded by the sheer absurdity of his behavior to absorb anything but the obvious. I should have known then and there that Himes was such a desperate control freak he could never truly trust even his most trustworthy assistants. And I should have seen what it meant for the Cubs.

That first warning sign may have been the most blatant and bizarre, but Himes repeatedly revealed his true self in a dozen ways. And none was more unnerving or damaging to morale than the way he handled player transactions. Forget about trades. Those are relatively rare occurrences in baseball. But every team makes scores of relatively routine moves throughout a season. Things like players going on and off the disabled list, struggling players getting sent down to the minors or prospects being called up. And every time one of those moves is made, more than just the players are involved. Someone has to handle the paperwork. Transportation and hotel rooms have to be arranged. Uniforms need to be changed and issued. Medications need to be ordered or documented. Exercise routines have to be modified. Press releases have to be issued.

A lot of people have to do a lot of hard work to get one major league player in the right place at the right time. Too often, Himes seemed oblivious to it all.

Less than a month after the desk-slamming incident in Arizona, Himes made it clear he wasn't about to be scooped again on a player move. To prove it, he embarrassed his own manager, one of his players, and three or four key members of his organization.

It happened 12 games into the season when Himes decided to send catcher Rick Wilkins back to the minors. Wilkins, who would hit .303 with 30 home runs the next season, had only 10 at-bats at that point. But Himes, a former All-America catcher at the University of Southern California in 1961, had seen enough. Even though the season was just under way, the Cubs already were in fifth place, $5\frac{1}{2}$ games out. Philadelphia was the only team with a worse record in the division and the Phillies had just scored three runs in the top of the 10th inning that afternoon to beat the Cubs.

The routine after major league games is for the clubhouses to be closed to the media briefly, usually less than 15 minutes, so players, coaches, and managers can have a few moments to themselves. During the waiting period that day, Himes cornered Wilkins and gave him the unhappy news he was being sent down. That was fair enough. But Himes didn't bother to tell anyone else right away. He didn't tell the traveling secretary, who had to make arrangements to get Wilkins to Iowa and his replacement, Derrick May, to Chicago. He didn't tell equipment manager Yosh Kawano, who had to issue uniforms. He didn't tell trainer John Fierro. And he didn't tell his people in the media relations department, who had to put out a press release and answer questions.

But most surprising of all, Himes didn't even bother to tell manager Jim Lefebvre.

A gaggle of reporters was gathered around Lefebvre's desk in the crowded manager's office asking about the questionable tactics and woeful pitching that had turned a 3-2 lead after eight innings into a 7-5 loss after 10. I was standing in my usual spot in the back of the room waiting for the crowd to clear when I saw Himes stroll in. It was unusual for the general manager to come into the manager's office while reporters were still there after a game, but it wasn't unprecedented. And I didn't think much of it until I noticed Himes appeared somewhat agitated. He was shifting his weight from foot to foot and trying to peer around the heads of reporters to get Lefebvre's attention. Finally, when the questions were beginning to turn from the specifics of that day's game to broader issues about the team, Himes raised his hand and his voice: "Jimmy, I need to speak to you right away," he said in his best authoritarian voice, which was pretty authoritarian.

Lefebvre was obviously surprised and a little embarrassed. But he recovered quickly and politely asked the reporters to leave for a few minutes. The door closed behind us and as we walked down the blue carpeted steps to the main clubhouse, several of us noticed Wilkins throwing his equipment into a bag at his feet. He was sitting at his locker with his head down, clearly upset. When we approached him, Wilkins told us he was being sent down and spoke plainly about how unfair it seemed to him after just 10 at bats.

A few minutes later, we were allowed back into the manager's office where Lefebvre announced, somewhat sheepishly, that Rick Wilkins had just been sent down to the minors. *Oh, really*, we said, without actually having to utter the words.

The Wilkins episode was repeated over and over with different players. Never so clumsily that Lefebvre had to be embarrassed again. But other members of the organization were put in awkward positions and given unnecessary work repeatedly because Himes cut them out of the loop. Two separate traveling secretaries—Peter Durso and Jimmy Bank—had to deal with the frustrations of being told after the fact about moves involving players they were responsible for transporting. Equipment manager Yosh Kawano, a veteran of more than half a century with the Cubs, looked up more than once during the Himes regime to find some kid he never heard of telling him he was supposed to get a uniform. Himes even hid many player moves from his personal assistant, Arlene Gill, and his vice president for baseball operations, Ned Colletti—the two people responsible for the complicated and, potentially, costly paperwork required of even the most mundane transactions.

I mentioned earlier I came to think of Himes as one of the Three Stooges. And I did. But there were times, too, particularly in the dark mutinous days of his final year with the Cubs, that Himes reminded me a lot of Lieutenant Commander Queeg. All he needed was the steel balls.

Much has been written and blubbered—and has yet to be written and blubbered—about how Himes let Greg Maddux walk away at the end of the 1992 season after winning the first of what turned out to be an unprecedented, and still almost-unfathomable, *four consecutive* Cy Young Awards. It will go down as one of the magnificent blunders in history by a sports franchise that made blundering an art form. But those of us who were there when it happened know how it came to pass. And most of us understood the comic clash of egos and lunacy it took to bring it about. It wasn't nearly as black and white as revisionist history has painted it.

Himes, justifiably, has taken a lot of bashing over Maddux. But usually for the wrong reasons. The revisionists make it sound as if only Himes had dangled a little more of mighty Tribune Co.'s endless dollars in front of Maddux, all would have been right with the world. Maddux would have stayed. He surely would have kept winning—as he did when he moved to Atlanta—and the Cubs would have been World Champs again for the first time since Teddy Roosevelt was in the White House.

The cold, hard truth is that, in the end, money wasn't the issue. If Maddux had taken the contract Himes and his then-top assistant, Ned Colletti, offered in July and November of 1992, he would have made more than he did by going to Atlanta. The difference in *guaranteed* salary between what the Cubs offered and Maddux accepted from the Braves was just $500,000 over five years. Throw in potential bonus money and Maddux took a cut to go to Atlanta. If he had stayed in Chicago and done what he did for the Braves—pitch more than 1,050 innings, finish among the top five for the Cy Young three times, be named to the All-Star team, and win his usual Gold Gloves—Maddux would have collected more than $1 million in bonuses from Cubs. The five-year deal Colletti carefully put together would have been worth close to $29.5 million. Instead, Maddux signed for $28 million in Atlanta.

Popular myth has it that Maddux was unappreciated by the Cubs. His pride was hurt by that. He exercised his God-given right to seek employment elsewhere and then lived the fantasy of every American worker by sticking it to his former bosses when he took another team to the World Series. That simplistic fairy tale is one reason Maddux could turn his back on Chicago and still remain a hero to Cub fans. Well, that and the fact that Chicago fans always appreciate great performers.

The reality of the Maddux saga, though, is a little less storybook; a little more muddled. Maddux simply didn't want to stay in Chicago. Or, more accurately, he didn't want to stay in Chicago badly enough to stop his agent, Scott Boras, from making it impossible.

Boras is one of the most successful of a generally loathsome breed— the sports agents of the 1990s. His goal in life is pure and simple: to get the most money possible for his clients—and, thus, himself. Few people are better at it than Boras. And Boras was at his best during the Maddux negotiations—thanks, in large measure, to Larry Himes.

Himes had many failings as a general manager, but few would fault his ability to evaluate talent. He was well aware he had one of the greatest pitchers in the game in Maddux. But he was always prepared, from the moment negotiations began, to lose Maddux, if the stakes got too high. And Boras was there to make sure the stakes got too high.

As usual, in baseball, what happened at the end of the Maddux negotiations was the result of months, even years, of miscalculations by both sides. Cook made a colossal blunder in December 1991, a year before Maddux left, when he first refused, then belatedly approved a five-year, $25 million deal that Maddux and Boras were willing to accept with some revision. Cook was thinking ahead to the Sandberg negotiations the next spring and figured Maddux could wait. It was Cook's first major decision as chairman of the Cubs and deserves to go down alongside the Brock-for-Broglio trade as one of the great bonehead baseball moves of all time. Instead of wrapping up Maddux the year before he won his first Cy Young and having him for four more years, Cook set the stage for the pitcher of a generation to walk out the door.

Boras was incensed and probably a little embarrassed when that package fell through and was determined to make the Cubs pay dearly for their mistake. He never was able to come close to dealing rationally with the team again. From that moment on, he seemed more interested in a vendetta than a deal. That isn't to say a deal was impossible. Boras may be a lot of things, but he isn't a fool. He would have recommended that Maddux sign with the Cubs in spite of his feelings—but only if he was convinced the price was high enough to make them feel like fools for their past sins.

The price of contrition Boras settled on was $32.5 million for five years. That's the figure he set out in July 1992, when Himes, Colletti, and Tribune Co.'s chief contract negotiator, Dennis Homerin, met with him in San Diego at the All-Star break. The Cubs countered with $27.5 million plus another $1.5 million in possible incentives—a deal that would have made Maddux the highest-paid pitcher in history at the time. Maddux never sat in on those meetings. He relied on Boras to relay what was happening. When Maddux heard how far apart the two sides were, he was incensed.

The first day after the All-Star break, the Cubs were in Pittsburgh to play the Pirates. I had worked the All-Star Game in San Diego with Jerome Holtzman and just had time to shower and change clothes to get to Three Rivers Stadium the usual three hours before game time. I was hoping for a quick, boring game so I could get home to the hotel, grab some sleep, and get back into the rhythm of the day-to-day routine for the second-half of the season. It wasn't going to happen. The moment I walked through the visitors' dugout and onto the spongy artificial turf of Three Rivers, I was accosted by the team's public relations representative who had been waiting anxiously for me to arrive. Maddux wanted to see all three beat writers as soon as possible. He had something he wanted to say.

Such summons are rare. We all knew two things immediately: it wasn't good news and it was going to be a long night. We were right. Jim Lefebvre turned his office in the visiting manager's office over to us for a private mini-news conference and Maddux opened things by calmly coming straight to the point: "I am going to go ahead and go through free agency," he said, meaning he was through negotiating with the Cubs on a long-term deal. "Things didn't work out. I've given them two opportunities to sign me ... That's it. I'm going to put my name in the hat and see what happens." One of the first follow-up questions, of course, was whether Maddux would give the Cubs a chance to compete with other teams once he did, indeed, declare free agency. "I don't know the answer to that," he said, shaking his head and pursing his lips in the girlish pout he flourishes so often on the mound. "I don't know. I don't know. I really felt I should have been signed last year."

Maddux never came out and actually said it, but he made it clear he thought his career with the Cubs was over. I certainly was convinced then and there that nothing the Cubs could do would bring Maddux back—nothing. My story in the next day's paper began simply: "Say goodbye to Greg Maddux."

Boras never came close to getting the $32.5 million he sought, except, perhaps, from the Yankees. But Maddux didn't want to pitch for the Yankees. In the end, it came down to the Braves and the Cubs. What it really came down to was a chance to go to the World Series. And, in the end, Maddux made the right choice. But only because Boras and Himes left him no other.

In his heart of hearts, Maddux wanted to stay in Chicago. Hours before he signed with Atlanta, he called his best friend, pitcher Mike Morgan, and asked Morgan if he could somehow talk to somebody to find a way around all the egos and bitterness. Morgan tried. But it was too late. Boras was adamant to the end. He insisted Maddux never would sign with anyone for less than $30 million. Three hours after he told the Cubs that, Maddux signed with Atlanta for $28 million. On the other side of the table, Himes never left a door open for Maddux to walk through. He was convinced, like I was in July, that nothing could be done to bring Maddux back. What he didn't realize, in these negotiations and others through the years, was that he was a big part of the reason it was impossible. Contract talks are usually bitter. With millions of dollars on the line, both sides, by definition, must play hard ball. But what Himes never realized was that it's possible to play hard ball and still show the other side respect. Twice during the Maddux negotiations, Himes put offers on the table and demanded an answer one way or the other within hours. Once he gave Maddux two days to make a decision. The next time, he set a one-day deadline. The Braves, on the other hand, came to Maddux and said: "Look, here's our offer. Think it over. Take as much time as you need. Obviously, we'd like an answer as soon as possible. But whatever you do, get back to us before you make any other moves. We want you to pitch in Atlanta and we're willing to work with you to make it happen."

Himes was incapable of that kind of civility. He was in a war and the enemy was always faceless. He told me once his favorite movie actor was Steven Segal. He saw himself as the stereotypical Segal character—a noble, loner struggling against all odds to save the world without ever getting the appreciation he truly deserved.

The Maddux war unofficially ended on Friday night, November 20, 1992. Obviously, whether Maddux would stay or go was the hottest sports story in Chicago at the time. The three beat writers—Barry Rozner, Joe Goddard, and myself—were working like crazy to stay on top of events and all hoping it would end soon so we finally could start our winter break. I was making the endless routine phone calls about 6 P.M., expecting, and getting, nothing, when, out of the blue, someone in the organization suggested I give Himes a call. I had spoken with him earlier in the day and learned nothing. I told this to the person on the phone. "I'd give him another call if I were you," the voice said.

When I got through to Himes, he was a different man. Suddenly, he was answering direct questions with direct answers. Something had changed. Himes wanted to use me. By the time I hung up, I had a lead story for the next day's paper that said Maddux had rejected the last offer the Cubs were willing to make and Himes was beginning to actively pursue other pitchers with the money he had set aside for Maddux. I think it was the only time Himes really helped me with a story. And, of course, the reason he did was to put one final bit of pressure on Maddux and Boras and to begin laying the groundwork for his argument to the fans that he had no choice but to let Maddux go.

The story made a big splash, of course, and Himes called a rare Saturday news conference at Wrigley Field the next morning to deal with the scores of radio stations and newspapers who were trying to follow it up. I was feeling unhealthily smug when I showed up in the crowded room and felt even better when Joe Goddard of the *Sun-Times* came over to congratulate me on breaking the story. Goddard is a friend and secure enough, after more than two decades covering baseball, to accept the inevitable, if rare, beat by the competition. The two of us were standing in the back of the room chatting when Himes entered and beckoned everyone to sit around a huge rectangular conference table. Himes started his news conference by thanking everyone and saying right off the top that the story Joe Goddard had in the paper today was accurate. Goddard and I looked at one other—each unsure who was more baffled. Then we just smiled, shrugged, and starting taking notes. It was vintage Himes. A Joe was a Joe was a Joe. Most people meant nothing to him. We were just bit players in his one-man action film.

    The Maddux watch seemed to last forever and, frankly, I was glad it was finally ending. I would be sorry—personally and professionally—to see Maddux go. But, at least, the waiting was nearly over. I only felt that way twice before in my career and both times the endings were just as unhappy. Once was in May 1980, when Josip Broz Tito, the strongman of Yugoslavia, finally died after lingering so excruciatingly long that every journalist in the known world literally ran out of things to write. The other was in the fall of 1988 when Emperor Hirohito died in Japan. Unlike Tito, the emperor only lingered on his death bed for about three weeks. But that was more than enough time to exhaust even the most intimate and unnecessary details of the story.

    Normally, I didn't cover Japan, but the *Tribune* bureau was unstaffed for a while and the emperor's death was big news. I was based in Manila at the time and hadn't been home more than a couple days in the past six weeks. I had rushed off to Pakistan to cover the suspicious death of President Mohammad Zia ul-Haq in a plane crash. No sooner did I get home than I was off to the remote island of Mindanao, 1,000 miles south of Manila, to cover the start of the trial of a mountain tribesman accused of murdering a 70-year-old missionary from Chicago I had befriended and written about 14 months earlier. Before the trial was even under way, I was on a plane to Bangkok to cover the anti-government uprisings and military crackdown in Burma.

    I was elated when the office called and asked me to go to Tokyo to babysit the emperor's death watch. It promised to be a respite from the break-neck pace of the past month. I could set up in a posh hotel in downtown Tokyo and write a nice leisurely story a day with an occasional feature or analysis to fill out the Sunday paper. And when I learned one of my closest friends, Rick Hornik of *Time* magazine, was being sent to cover the story, I secretly wished I could stick around a month or more. Like many wishes I've had in my life, I quickly came to regret that one. The emperor's death watch was one of the weirdest, most excruciating events I ever covered. Our one source of news every day was a medical briefing that provided the most-intimate biological details of a dying man. The Japanese papers would take the gory specifics and splatter them all over their front pages in colorful charts showing how many cubic centimeters of blood the emperor had passed with his bowel movements, how many times he had vomited, and precisely how much urine he had passed since the last bulletin—all without carefully and pointedly ever mentioning the emperor had cancer. It seemed mildly amusing at first and immensely illustrative of the cultural differences between the Japanese and most other societies in which I had lived and worked. But after a couple days, it simply became too much. I started longing for a good military uprising, an assassination, flood, or an earthquake—anything to get me out of Tokyo. After Emperor Hirohito, even the Maddux marathon was a pleasure.

Himes did just what he threatened to me on the phone and reiterated at his Wrigley Field news conference. He went out and spent the $29 million he set aside for Maddux to get three pitchers and a couple of throw-ins to take his place. Over the next three years, Jose Guzman, Dan Plesac, and Randy Myers combined to go 22-28 with 113 saves and throw $499\frac{1}{3}$ innings. Maddux alone went 55-18, threw $678\frac{2}{3}$ innings and won three more Cy Young Awards.

By any standard, that was a bad swap. But Himes had to lie and betray decent people to get even that good a deal. Guzman was easy enough. He was out of the majors in 1989, 1990, and part of 1991 with an injured arm. He bounced back to have an impressive 16-11 season with the Rangers in 1992, but, even at that, Guzman had to be astounded when Himes offered a four-year, $14.3-million contract. Actually, it was Guzman's agent who was astounded. Barry Meister was ready to sign a deal with the Cubs for $12.5 million. But Himes, misread the signals and rushed in after his underlings already thought they had a deal to up the ante another $1.8 million. Guzman couldn't grab a pen quick enough. Of course, that was before he blew his arm out again and could still pick up a pen.

Myers and Plesac, though, were different stories. Both lefty reliev-ers were eager to cash in on part of the Maddux money. But Plesac only came to the Cubs because Himes duped him.

A native of Gary, Indiana, Plesac was an All-America basketball player at Crown Point [Indiana] High School before attending North Carolina State University, where he won All-America honors in base-ball. He was 6-foot-5 and Apple Pie as they come. Always smiling. Al-ways a friendly wave and hello for everyone he met. He was everything Himes wasn't, including honest.

Plesac was a No. 1 draft pick of the Milwaukee Brewers in 1983 and was in the big leagues by 1986, saving 14 games his rookie season. He made the American League All-Star team the next three years and had 133 saves by late in the 1991 season when he developed arm trouble and the Brewers felt he lost his touch for closing. They began experi-menting with him as a starter. Plesac made 10 starts in 1991 and another four in 1992, but felt more comfortable working out of the pen and ex-ercised his right to become a free agent at the end of the season. He wanted nothing more than to sign with a club that would give him a shot at being a closer again.

Himes was willing to give Plesac that chance. He was impressed with the lanky lefthander and went after him as soon as he made up his mind the Maddux deal was dead. Himes met with Plesac's agent, Tom Selakovich of St. Charles, Illinois, at the winter meetings in Louisville, Kentucky, to work out a deal. Unbeknownst to them, though, at the same time, Himes had Randy Myers and his agent, David Fishoff, in an-other room at the same hotel.

Myers was coming off a 38-save season as the closer for the San Diego Padres. He had been the closer, before that, for the 1990 World

Series champion Cincinnati Reds. And before that, for the New York
Mets. If Plesac had known the Cubs were courting Myers, he would
have tried to sign with another team. He was smart enough to know that
in a race between two lefthanders for the closer's job, he probably
would finish second to Myers. But Himes never let him know it. For
several hours, Himes and his deputies shuttled back and forth from one
room to the other trying to sign both lefties. Neither pitcher knew the
other was in the running. Himes closed both deals within minutes of
each other, then told Selakovich that the chance to sign Myers had come
as a surprise. He hadn't known Myers was available when he signed
Plesac. He was sorry. He never would have done that to Plesac. In other
words, he flat out lied.

At the same time the Maddux, Plesac, Myers fiascoes were playing
out, Himes was orchestrating a travesty of equal—arguably, greater—
dimension. He was telling Andre Dawson to take a hike.

Dawson was 38 years old, at the end of the 1992 season, with
chronically bad knees that had been operated on seven times. He had an
unremarkable .274 batting average over the last two seasons and clearly
was in the waning days of his career—if not finished. Himes thought he
was finished. Dawson said he could play two more years.

Andre Dawson probably was the classiest gentleman I met in my
time in baseball. He is, to borrow a favorite phrase of Cubs president
Andy MacPhail, "the kind of guy you'd want your sister to marry." He
is more than that. He is the kind of man you want your son to grow up to
be. No one, not even Dawson's supporters, can fault Himes from a baseball point of view for letting Dawson go. But even at his advanced age
and in his near-crippled condition, just having Dawson around made the
Cubs a better team—made any team better. He was a leader of men. And
the Cubs, more than most teams, sorely needed leaders in those days.

Once in spring training, shortstop Shawon Dunston—never canon-
ized for his durability—was asked by a reporter how many games he
thought he could play that season? Dunston was typically frank. He said
he hoped to play 130, maybe, 140 games. Dawson, sitting nearby, heard

the answer and immediately launched into Dunston. The season hadn't even begun, Dawson berated Dunston, and you're already writing off 20 or 30 games. What's the matter with you, Shawon?

Any other player who confronted Dunston like that was liable to be met instantly with a blur of flailing arms and flying obscenities. But not Dawson. Dunston took the reprimand from Dawson like a docile pup. That's because Dawson was a father figure to Dunston, who idolized his own father. There wasn't a player in the Cubs' clubhouse in 1992 who didn't look to Dawson as the epitome of everything good and decent in a man and a ballplayer. Himes telling him to take a hike was the equivalent of tearing the heart out of the club—especially coupled with the loss of Maddux.

Technically, Himes didn't tell Dawson to take a hike. He made a token effort to sign him. But the offer of a $300,000 pay cut at a time when salaries were skyrocketing for even the most paltry players was so humiliating that Himes had to know Dawson would refuse. What's more, Himes typically made his first offer his last. Take it or leave it. And never mind what you've done before in your career.

Himes had a strong argument that all he was doing was trying to put the best team on the field. But, as George Steinbrenner has proven time and again, the best team isn't always made up of the best or highest-paid players. Almost everyone, except Himes, who was around the Cubs that year believed the team would have been far better keeping Dawson in right field—and in the clubhouse.

I say that knowing full well Dawson was a disappointment the next two seasons with the Boston Red Sox. He played just 20 games in the outfield and batted a meager .260 as a designated hitter. For that, he was paid $9 million. But Dawson hit 29 homers and drove in 115 runs in 753 at-bats. And, far more importantly, he was, as always, an inspiration to his new teammates and coaches—making them better and bettering the team in the process. Nine million dollars is a staggering amount of money by any standard. But given the bizarre realities of baseball in the '90s, Dawson was worth somewhere around that—both as a player and a presence. During those same two years, 1993-94, Teddy Higuera earned $6.75 for winning two games and losing eight with the Milwaukee Brewers. John Smiley picked up $8.5 million for a 14-19 record with the Reds. And Doc Gooden and Darryl Strawberry combined made nearly $19 million for spending more time in rehab centers than they did on ballfields. Those four players—Strawberry and the three struggling pitchers—appeared in a total of 164 games and earned more than $34 million in 1993-94. Dawson, nearly crippled by the pain in two knees that would have to be replaced by artificial joints at the end of his career, appeared in 196 games. And he never once embarrassed himself or the game—on or off the field.

One bitter and recurring complaint against baseball in the 1990s is the perception that players have lost all sense of loyalty. Those who bemoan this sorry state constantly point to the fact that players rarely stay with one team their entire careers. That is nothing new. The same thing was happening 40 and 50 years ago. The difference, of course, was that back then players left because owners traded them. They didn't have a say in the matter. Now, they do. Thanks to the courageous efforts of people like Curt Flood, many veteran players have the fundamental right to shop their talents on the free market—just like the rest of us. They have to wait a few years, but they are paid well in the interim. And they have agreed, through their union, to the rules of the game. Players still get traded without having a say in the matter, but they also eventually have the right to walk away and the owners can't do a thing about it except pay them more.

Loyalty is a two-way street. Often as not, the blame for a failed relationship rests as much with ownership or management as it does with a player.

"Loyalty isn't exactly the right word," says Andy MacPhail. "There is clearly a benefit to continuity, but I had to come to terms with the fact that if a player couldn't contribute, I always felt it was my responsibility—if I could—to make a change. Bing. Bang. I did it. As a result, understanding that, I never begrudged a player for leaving. If he could improve his situation, his family's situation, why should I begrudge that? I don't."

In the case of Dawson and the Cubs, the circumstances were a little less cut and dry. All Andre Dawson wanted at the end of the 1992 season was a two-year contract that would carry him to the age of 40 and allow him to finish his career with the Cubs. He said so privately. He said so publicly. Admittedly, Dawson and his agent, Dick Moss, were asking a hefty price. They went to the winter meetings in Louisville, Kentucky, believing Dawson's fair market value should be around $11 million or $12 million for two years. They never came close to getting that. But that didn't really matter. What Dawson really wanted was to be afforded the respect he had earned. He never felt Himes showed him—or any player—the proper respect. Dawson said time and again that Himes never even acknowledged him with so much as a "hello" the first 10 months Himes was with the Cubs. That hurt and puzzled Dawson. But it was easy for many of the rest of us to understand. Himes was intimidated by Dawson and by anyone else who was respected and admired by their peers.

The White Sox flirted with signing Dawson, which would have been a great public relations coup in addition to filling the need for a designated hitter that Bo Jackson eventually played to Cinderella perfection the next season. But the White Sox weren't willing to come anywhere close to the $9 million the Boston Red Sox eventually gave Dawson. That was an impressive bundle for a player his age and in his physical condition. Few teams could justify spending that much for Dawson—not when it turned out $10 million would buy Jimmy Key's 35-10 record over the next two years or $5.5 million would bring Dave Winfield home to Minnesota.

Winfield is a relevant example. The Twins, consistently operating with one of the three or four lowest payrolls in the American League, parted with $5.5 million before the 1993 season to get Winfield at age 41 and bring him back to his native Minnesota. Skeptics dismissed the move as a thinly veiled marketing ploy. But the reality was that in two seasons—one of them shortened by a strike—Winfield had 31 homers, drove in 119 runs, and picked up his 3,000th major league hit with the Twins.

Andy MacPhail was general manager of the Twins at the time. He emphatically rejects the suggestion that he brought Winfield home either out of an idyllic sense of loyalty to the game or as a crass marketing ploy. "We went out and got him because he had 28 home runs and 100 RBIs and we didn't have any power on our club," MacPhail said years later. "He was a helluva ballplayer. He just had the winning hit in the sixth game of the World Championships (for Toronto). All the other things were important and plusses—the Minnesota ties, the leadership, where he had been. But principally, and most importantly, we were adding a player.

"The human element cannot be overlooked. You play this game over a six-month period. You play 162 games. Talent alone is not the only barometer as to who is going to be playing where. But talent is a big part of it. You can't overlook it. It's part of the equation. But playing a guy solely for leadership or bringing a guy in solely for marketing is, I think, a big mistake because people want tangible results. Leadership is great, but if a player doesn't produce or contribute, how can you market him."

And judged by those standards, MacPhail says bringing Winfield home to Minnesota was a disappointment. "To be honest with you—and nothing against the guy because he is terrific—but, if I would have known then what I know now, we would have gone in a different direction. Nothing personal, but for the kind of money we spent, we could have gotten more bang for the buck. For example, another part of the equation was his 3,000th hit. We factored that in, I'm not denying it. We drew 14,000, 17,000, and 19,000 when he was going for it. The [published] attendance, I think, will be different, because—and this will show you where the game has gone—the ultimate attendance might show up at 40,000 or 30,000, but what happened is they sold tickets to speculators who bought about 10,000 tickets with the idea of selling them for more than they were paying and it didn't work out."

MacPhail says if he had been with the Cubs at the time, he would have made the same choice Himes did on Dawson. "To me, I understand people being disappointed at Andre not being retained. But he just couldn't do it. He just couldn't play. You start talking about giving him a two-year contract at that point in his career and you're talking about the occult to me. The team might have been better if Dawson had been there because of his leadership, but how do you know? How do you measure it? I remember seeing Andre at the time and he demonstrated he couldn't run. He belonged in the American League. You can't ignore those factors."

What would have changed, if MacPhail had been in charge of the Cubs at the time, though, was the way that Dawson was treated earlier in his career. The Cubs only signed him when he groveled and gave them a blank contract and told them to fill in the numbers. Then he went out and led the National League with 49 homers, 137 runs batted in, and was named Most Valuable Player for a last-place team. His reward was being forced to go to arbitration that winter. "I've had guys do things that I thought were conciliatory and didn't push it to the max when they had the leverage," said MacPhail. "In those cases, I'd always try to go the extra yard for my guy. We had the same thing in Minnesota. Randy Bush always signed his contracts. No bullshit. Easy. He probably played a year longer than he would otherwise."

Himes wasn't responsible for the early contract squabbles with Dawson. But the kind of thinking MacPhail mentioned, the notion that loyal employees sometimes deserve to be rewarded, was alien to Himes. In the first 27 months Himes was on the job, more than 120 people in the organization were fired, forced out, or left in frustration. Included in that turnover were players, scouts, coaches, vice presidents, assistant trainers, traveling secretaries—even dietitians and video operators. Many of those talented people went on to make other organizations better. Two of the most notable were Dick Balderson, who was forced out as vice president of scouting, and Ned Colletti, who was unceremoniously fired as vice president of baseball administration. Colletti went on to become assistant general manager of the Giants. Balderson joined the Colorado Rockies and helped take them from an expansion team to the playoffs in three years.

Both Colletti and Balderson enjoyed tremendous respect in the often-petty baseball community. Colletti, in particular, was able to walk the fine line between two volatile worlds—the front office and the players. He was the best thing Himes had going for him. Colletti put a human face on a robotic regime. And he did it while still being a hard-nosed executive. He was involved in four major arbitration cases with the Cubs, winning three and losing one. Arbitration is one of the most-bitter experiences any player can go through. The very definition of the process requires the team to denigrate its own players, to accentuate their shortcomings, and downplay their assets—all with the goal of saving money. Colletti was able to do that and still remain friends with the players he beat. He won arbitration cases against Leon Durham, Andre Dawson, and Mark Grace. Yet all three of those players still call him friend. The one arbitration case he lost was against Shawon Dunston, who followed Colletti to San Francisco for one season before returning to the Cubs.

If Colletti was good and popular, then why would Himes fire him? The answer was simple: because Colletti was good and popular. Himes felt threatened by the Collettis of the world. He was so egotistical and insecure that he only felt comfortable around underlings who knew how to kowtow to the boss. What's more, by December 1993, Himes had reason in his eyes to perceive Colletti as a real threat. The Pitch & Hit Club, which hosts a popular baseball dinner for Chicago's die-hard fans every January, had just voted to give Colletti an award as Chicago Baseball Executive of the Year. Himes found out about the award through Scott Nelson, a Himes disciple. Within days, Colletti, a solid and dedicated baseball executive, was out of a job.

The wholesale turnover under Himes wasn't particularly an anomaly. In the first 14 years under Tribune Co., from 1981 to 1995, the Cubs had five general managers and 13 field managers. Chaos was a constant. Job security was as obsolete as the inflatable chest protector. Himes, though, brought the madness to new lows. His me-against-the-world attitude alienated talented lieutenants, frightened off loyal foot soldiers, and created a climate of poison for almost everyone with the Cubs.

In 1994, the Cubs had a respectable team with a starting lineup that included: Sammy Sosa, Ryne Sandberg, Shawon Dunston, Mark Grace, and Steve Buechele. The pitching rotation was decent and Randy Myers was the closer in the bullpen after having just set a National League record with 53 saves the year before. In spite of all that, the Cubs got off to a 12-24 start and my bosses at the *Tribune* gave me free rein to write a front-page analysis on why I thought the team was so inexplicably disappointing.

"The answer is poison," I wrote. "There is a poisonous atmosphere in the Cubs' clubhouse. A core of key, veteran players is so disenchanted with the regime of general manager Larry Himes that there is almost a collective will to fail. The thinking seems to be that if the Cubs look bad enough, surely the team's owners, Tribune Co., will get rid of Himes, who is in the final year of his contract. Whether the ill-feelings toward Himes are justified or not, they are palpable."

Needless to say, Himes was furious. The next afternoon, the Cubs were playing the Giants at Wrigley Field and I was standing around watching batting practice when Himes walked up to me calmly and asked to speak with me. I said, of course, and Himes said, no, not here, let's go somewhere private. He led me through the dugout, into the clubhouse and behind the closed doors of the trainer's room, which is off-limits to the media. For several minutes, Himes was placid and reasoned. He wanted to know how I could write something like that—what made me feel there was a poison in the clubhouse? I explained that I had noticed it for more than a year. It was something I picked up being around the team day in and day out. That was one of the reasons newspapers spend so much money to have reporters work and travel with their clubs all season long. But I assured Himes the story was based on more than mere intangibles. I had spoken with several key players in recent days off the record about my feelings. They said I was absolutely right and spent considerable time elaborating their sentiments. Himes demanded to know what players. I refused to tell him. He then volunteered his own list of suspects, which, was frighteningly off target. Frustrated and acutely aware how damaging the story could be in the final year of his contract, Himes vented his anger by screaming for several unproductive minutes before finally sending me on my way. It was a waste of time. But, at least I got to see the dark bowels of the forbidden trainer's room. This one looked like every doctor's examining room I've ever been in.

A story like the "Poison Clubhouse" is difficult for a beat writer because it stirs such deep emotions, isn't shored on tangible facts, and, once it's in print, you can't count on your sources rallying 'round to say: "Yep. That's right. He nailed that one." All you can do is ride out the storm, knowing you did your homework and believing you said something that needed to be said. But, every now and then, somebody you respect finds a back-handed way of tipping their hat to you. I felt manager Tom Trebelhorn did just that when some of my colleagues, forced to do a follow-up, asked him for his comment on the story. Trebelhorn chose his words carefully, admitting the article had ruined his morning, but subtly indicating there might be more than a grain of truth to it. "Within this ballclub, we'll address these things and try to find an antidote to this poison," he said with—what I took to be, anyway—a wry smile.

Himes created the poisonous atmosphere, but he wasn't alone. Syd Thrift and Jim Lefebvre were talented men, who had flourished in different environments. Under Himes, though, they simply compounded the chaos. They both had their supporters—Lefebvre, in particular, among the players *after* he was fired. But I wasn't alone in thinking of the big three of the Cubs those days as stooges. Peter Durso, the irascible, outspoken traveling secretary who fled the Cubs for the Colorado Rockies after one miserable year under the Larry, Curly, Moe Show, summed up the frustrations of many with a quote he used often:

"The chances one organization would hire three clowns like Larry Himes, Syd Thrift and Jim Lefebvre all at once are about the same as Willie, Mickey and the Duke running into one another at midnight on New Year's Eve on a street corner in Nome, Alaska."

Chapter 5

Welcome Back to Reality, Pal

If the opportunity ever presents itself, I'd highly recommend swapping a foreign correspondent's trench coat for a seat in the Wrigley Field press box. For one thing, your odds of being shot are drastically reduced, although not entirely eliminated. For another, you can eat the food, you can drink the water, and you get a lot more fan mail.

Just tagging along in the wake of a major league ballclub is a wondrous ride, starting with the office accommodations. I had a lot of great offices, in a lot of marvelous places. But none rivaled the splendor of a seat behind homeplate at Wrigley Field.

In Beirut, I worked out of the legendary Commodore Hotel for several long stretches each year from 1979-83 and for four months during the Israeli invasion of Lebanon in 1982. The Commodore was nothing special to look at, just a careful pile of cinder blocks nestled against a cracked and derelict swimming pool in a neighborhood turned to rubble. But the Commodore featured some awesome amenities, including a sturdy basement that doubled as a bomb shelter and five Telex machines and a half dozen international phone lines that kept working through months of Israeli shelling—thanks, of course, to the conscious efforts and surgical precision of the Israeli Defense Forces. A package deal at the Commodore included the dubious privilege of semi-regular entertainment from an easy going half-Egyptian, half-Lebanese organist named Joe, who serenaded us with ear-splitting Arabic caterwauling that was so painful we almost welcomed the next bombardment. Joe would work himself into a frenzy as the night wore on, each song growing progressively louder and more nerve-shattering until it seemed musician and instrument had reached the limits of physical endowment.

Just then, Curtis Wilkie of the *Boston Globe* would encourage both to staggering new heights. A graduate of Ole Miss with a mumbled Mississippi drawl that made him sound drunk long before he was, Wilkie would rise slowly from his bar stool and bellow above the din: *"Crrraaannnkkkkk iittttt upppp, Joooo-uh!"* Old Joe would beam across the room at Wilkie, nod his head, and happily crank up the volume.

The Commodore also had an impressive support staff that included gun-toting guards to protect its journalist guests, fearless taxi drivers who would go anywhere even when you wished they wouldn't, and an ancient, smelly parrot who lived in a brass cage next to the empty swimming pool. The parrot could curse like a sailor in five languages. But his real claim to fame was being able to re-create the high-pitched whine of an incoming artillery round with such fearful realism that rookie reporters invariably dove for cover in ashen panic while grizzled veterans howled and called for one more round of scotch to celebrate yet another hilarious rite of passage.

My office during the Philippine Revolution was a teak-paneled

With Reuters photographer Pat Benic, my lifelong World Series companion, on the roof of the Manila Hotel watching 100,000 Filipinos demonstrate against soon-to-be-ousted dictator Ferdinand Marcos.

room in the grand old Manila Hotel with a terrace that overlooked the pool, the gardens, and magnificent Manila Bay. If you strained your eyes and stretched your imagination, you could just glimpse the fortress island of Corregidor on the horizon. The sunsets I watched from that hotel room still come to me in my dreams. They were more than color and light. They were treasures from the sea and sky—so beautiful that more than once I thought I would cry. Then again, maybe those were just the heightened emotions of the time. A favorite hobby among a small brigade of Filipinos in the years leading up to the revolution was hotel arson. The *Tribune* office where I watched most of those fiery sunsets and wrote about the fall of Ferdinand Marcos was fully equipped with an oxygen mask, a fire-resistant poncho, and a nylon rope ladder for emergency escapes. It was hard to say whether the Manila Hotel was more or less likely to be firebombed because it was a favorite hangout of the first family. Every Wednesday night, First Lady Imelda Marcos would show up in a new pair of shoes and trod down a red carpet that was laid out specially for her through the lobby and up to her favorite table at the glass-roofed Roma Restaurant. Her son, Ferdinand Marcos, Jr., known to everyone as "Bongbong," preferred to spend his nights in the Tap Room, a dark, smoky tavern almost directly beneath my room/office on the third floor of the hotel's old wing. I chuckled at the irony when, five nights before his father fled to exile aboard a U.S. helicopter, "Bongbong" walked onto the small stage in the Tap Room and asked the band if he could sing a song. Filipinos love to sing in times of trouble. And, of course, nobody was going to deny "Bongbong" an opportunity. But I couldn't believe the song he chose. It was *"Yesterday"* by the Beatles. *"Suddenly, I'm not half the man I used to be; There's a shadow hanging over me. Oh, I believe, in yesterday."* The lyrics were just too perfect for the son of a soon-to-be-ousted dictator. I spit out my drink and rushed upstairs to that lovely office to write the scene down before I forgot it. It fit perfectly in the Sunday wrap-up a week after Marcos fled.

In Warsaw, my office was a separate two-bedroom house in the backyard of the three-storey Stalinist spa we called home. The main house had an elaborate satellite TV system, a wonderful white pine sauna, and a maze of horrendously ugly, but immensely practical, folding metal grates on every door and window to protect us from the soaring crime rate that was the unwelcome cost of economic reform in newly democratic Poland. The main house was so big we turned the entire lower ground floor into a formal dining room and wine cellar. In the back yard, a pear tree rained lush fruit every fall. My two translators had their own office in one bedroom of the guest house. Mine was in the other. And the whole little self-contained cosmos was 10 minutes in opposite directions from the government offices where I did most of my interviews and the brooding forest where I walked Havoc, the fat yellow Labrador who followed me around the world.

Wondrous as all those offices were—and will forever be in my memory—none even remotely compared to Wrigley Field. Some people work and plan years to see the ivy-covered walls just once, then spend the rest of their days reliving the moment as if it were a son's 18th birthday or a daughter's college graduation. I got to go to Wrigley Field 70 times a year. And I cherished every game. I knew when I took the job I wouldn't be a baseball writer for life. I understood I was living something special and I determined to savor it.

Baseball writers are no different from any other mopes. They grumble about having to come to work. They moan when a game goes extra innings or gets delayed three hours by rain. They belittle each other and most everybody they come in contact with. After I got my rookie season under my belt, I dutifully joined the chorus of grousers. It was expected. But, truth be told, I never really had my heart in it, especially when the Cubs were home. I could be in the worst mood. I could be exhausted, sick, mad at my wife, furious with my bosses, frazzled by the traffic, or simply zoned out. But it all seemed to wash away when I walked up the ramp behind the third-base stands at Wrigley Field heading for the press box.

Wrigley is the only big-league ballpark in America without a press box elevator. Tribune Co. wisely refused to put one in because the only way to do it structurally would have ruined the famous facade. So to get to the press box, you have to walk up the same series of long ramps that fans use to reach the upper deck. The first part of that walk nudges through the bowels of the ballpark, in front of the concession stands, and past the rest rooms. But there is a stretch where the ramp turns back down the third-base line just above field level and you get your first glimpse of Wrigley's magic.

I usually got to the ballpark three hours before games. The stands, of course, were empty, but a few players would be on the field already. I loved the sight of those long rows of billiard-green seats giving way to soft emerald grass sprinkled with players in pristine white pants. Add to that the comforting sound of bat on ball, the familiar smell of popcorn and stale beer, the bright glare of a picture-perfect sunny day or the raw bite of a bitter Hawk wind. It was enough to make Warsaw seem a lifetime away.

The splendor of Wrigley Field was only part of what made that office so terrific, though. Just as wonderful were the characters who populate the place when the gates are still shut and the next game is hours away. Hall-of-Famers like Harry Caray, Jack Brickhouse, and Jerome Holtzman. Thoughtful, witty veteran writers like Bill Gleason, Dave Van Dyck, and Gene Seymour. Scouts like Hugh Alexander. And baseball legends like Yosh Kawano, who, for more than half a century, doubled as clubhouse manager and heart and soul of the Cubs. Getting to know them—getting to call them friends and have them call me friend—was one of the highlights of coming home. Think about it. Which would you rather be doing: Sitting in a mud shack outside the Golden Temple in Amritsar, India, in 110-degree heat interviewing a teenage Sikh fanatic about the men he's killed, and wants to kill, with the AK-47 assault rifle cradled in his arms? Or lazing in the dugout at Wrigley Field two hours before a Cubs' game swapping baseball stories with Harry Caray, Jerome Holtzman, and whichever National League manager happened to be passing through town? It took me 14 years and several trips around the world, but I finally got it right. I wouldn't have traded a single day I spent overseas. But I'm sure glad I did it all before I got an office in Wrigley Field. Otherwise, I might never have gone out into the real world.

One reason Wrigley Field is so wonderful is because it isn't the real world. It's a magic place where people go to escape the real world for a few hours. When you are stopped at a red light in downtown Warsaw on a gray, snowy day with the sun already setting at 3:30 in the afternoon and a drunken pedestrian teeters, then passes out across the hood of your car, you know there's nothing you can do except try to muddle through. When you're sitting in the bleachers at Wrigley on a sun-splashed summer afternoon and the drunken college kid next to you falls across your lap diving for a home run ball that lands 100 feet away, you know there's no place else you'd rather be.

Warsaw is the real world. Wrigley is closer to Wonderland. At the very least, it's the rabbit hole Alice fell into. Wrigley Field is a cozy little Never-Never Land somewhere between the real world and the weird biosphere of baseball where Mad Hatters and March Hares strut unnoticed and Tweedledee and Tweedledum could be co-captains on most teams.

Sometimes it takes an outsider to point out just how truly weird the world of baseball can be. British novelist P.G. Wodehouse did a masterful job in his classic short story "The Pitcher and the Plutocrat," about a spoiled rich kid who becomes a baseball player when his father squanders the family fortune. The story was written decades ago, but two of the themes he lays out—brain death and a skewed sense of reality—are as valid in the modern world of baseball as they were in the era of the dead ball. Early in the story, the aristocratic father is pacing his library worrying about how to break the news to his son that the family is broke. Wodehouse describes the old man as "wrapped in thought."

"This was unusual," Wodehouse writes, *"for he was not given to thinking. To be absolutely frank, the old man had just about enough brain to make a jay-bird fly crooked, and no more."*

When the father finally breaks the news, he tells the son his allowance is cut off. The son must find work.

"Work. Well, of course, mind you, fellows do work," the son says. *"I met a man at the club only yesterday who knew a fellow who had met a man whose cousin worked."*

Much to the father's horror, the son becomes a professional baseball player. He takes an assumed name to spare his family indignity and pitches the New York Giants to the National League pennant.

I thought of that story often during my years on the baseball beat. Not that I ran across many players who were so rich and coddled from birth that they never knew the meaning of a day's work. Such members of that species as exist in baseball are generally confined to the front offices or the owners' boxes. But I did run across an abundance of characters on every level of the game who had just about enough brain to make a jay-bird fly crooked, and no more. And I could easily imagine many of the biggest stars I came to know living out the rest of their lives in such comfortable isolation that they might never again befriend a woman or man who worked for a living—save, perhaps, as a fellow athlete or athlete-turned-broadcaster.

Every player who makes it to the major leagues for more than a cup of coffee has an understandably difficult time keeping things in perspective. Most come from lower- to middle-income families. Most have only a basic education. All are making phenomenal amounts of money. Combine a 25-year-old with a high-school education, the pampered upbringing of a star athlete and a slick agent. Toss in more money a year than most people make in a lifetime. And it's obvious how easy it would be to lose touch with the real world. It's more than easy; it's practically inevitable.

Big-league ballplayers live in a cloistered world where they never carry a bag, never have to book a flight, never even have to take a cab if they don't want. They pay for their own meals at home—if a fan, sponsor, or agent doesn't grab the check. But they need never pay on the road, unless they're unduly determined or ravenous. The daily meal allowance in 1996 was $60.50. By 1997, it was up to $67. In either case, more than enough to feed any human being in any city in the world, except, perhaps, Tokyo. And most major-leaguers rarely have to buy more than one meal a day on the road. There is always a cornucopia of fresh fruit, sandwiches, hot entrées, soup, and desserts in the clubhouse before and after games and on airplanes on travel days. And while players do, in fact, pay for some of that food by tipping clubhouse attendants—often quite generously—they still can easily pocket several hundred dollars in meal money every road trip.

Players foot the bills for their own housing and transportation at home, but they're on the road more than half the baseball year at club expense. At checkout, on travel days—otherwise known as "getaway" days—players go to the front desk of the team hotel and pay only their "incidentals." In plain English that means mini-bar expenses, telephone calls, room service, laundry and in-house movies—pornographic or otherwise.

Many executives, even journalists and baseball writers, enjoy similar corporate perks. But the degree is incomparably different, both fiscally and psychologically. From the time players show up at a ballpark on getaway day until they return home, all their needs are handled by the club. Their luggage is picked up for them at the airport, put aboard waiting trucks, and whisked to the team hotel while the athletes themselves climb into separate luxury buses or, in some cases, privately hired limousines. Former American League MVP George Bell was one of those players who preferred a private limo to the team bus. He would even show up at spring training—invariably several days late—in a stretch white limousine roughly the size of a luxury cruise ship and with many of the same amenities.

When players arrive at the team hotel, they need never bother with such drudgery as checking in. Their keys are usually waiting in white envelopes on a table in the lobby or in a private side room. Often, two or three members of the hotel sales staff are on hand to help any befuddled athletes who have trouble finding their own names. Usually available, too, are complimentary soft drinks, juices, and, if the team allows, beer—just in case the athletes are parched from the long bus ride or are worried about getting thirsty on the arduous trek from the lobby to their rooms. Once safely inside those rooms, players rarely have to wait more than a few minutes for their bags to be delivered.

The architect of all this pampered treatment is a person known as the "traveling secretary." Each team has one and they are among the

hardest working, most underpaid, under-appreciated, and neurotic creatures in game. They do everything from making travel arrangements for
the team and management to doling out complimentary tickets for players, their friends, relatives, and groupies. Traveling secretaries coordinate limousines, golf outings, concert tickets, and dinner reservations.
They write the checks to pay the visiting team's share of gate receipts
and hand out cash by the heap for meal money during spring training
and road trips. They make sure players being brought in or shipped out
get where they're supposed to be on time. They are part mother, father,
priest, rabbi, fixer, and finagler. Their jobs force them to be everything
to everyone. But far too often they're treated like nothing by too many.

I can count on the thumbs of five catchers' mitts how many times I
saw players walk up to a traveling secretary and express appreciation for
the lavish perks and considerations they received. All but one or two
times, it was a rookie or a journeyman player—guys like infielder Gary
Scott when he was with the Cubs or catcher Bill Schroeder when he was
with the Brewers. Almost everyone who stuck around more than a few
months came to take the pampered lifestyle as their due. Not just the
things like having their bags carried or spikes cleaned, but things like
hotel and plane reservations that could take the traveling secretary
weeks to arrange.

Obviously, traveling secretaries get paid to do those things. But not
a staggering lot. In 1996, salaries for traveling secretaries started as low
as $22,500—less than one-fourth the minimum for even the most-mar-
ginal major league player. That figure was exceptionally low, an aberration spawned by the spend-thrift ways of Marge Schott, who was both
the Scrooge and scourge of baseball. Most clubs paid their traveling
secretaries a little better. The average was between $40,000 and
$55,000, which might seem respectable, even enviable, to many fans
who have to survive in the real world. But it was piddling by corporate
standards and abysmally small in proportion to the effort and production
most traveling secretaries contributed to both the bottom line and general morale of the team. Consider this: the average annual salary of a
traveling secretary works out to about what Jack McDowell earned for
pitching two innings in 1995. And traveling secretaries don't get four
days off between starts.

There was the *RARE* traveling secretary who compensated for the disappointing income by cashing in on the considerable influence and access that comes with the job. One particularly resourceful character used to pick up an extra $400 a month by scalping some of the complimentary tickets every club provides players.

A chore many traveling secretaries dread every day is dealing with the "comp list"—the sheet that hangs in every clubhouse before every game so players, coaches, and managers can sign up for free tickets. There is always a limit on the number of tickets that can be requested. And the limit varies from park to park and day to day. Invariably, of course, there are players who need more tickets than they're allowed in certain cities and players who don't need any. So a lot of horse trading goes on in the locker room. The particular traveling secretary I mentioned used the inevitable cracks in the system to ensure a regular supply of tickets to a certain fan—in return for a flat $400 monthly retainer.

Those kinds of shady—if colorful—transactions have become increasingly scarce. These days, players are far more likely than traveling secretaries to abuse their perks, leaving complimentary tickets for a golf pro, say, in return for free green fees at some of the poshest courses in the country.

Another routine chore of traveling secretaries is to provide a detailed itinerary before each road trip. The carefully printed sheets contain phone numbers and addresses of every hotel where the team will be staying, contact numbers for all visiting ballparks, the precise times for every game or workout, and the estimated departure times for each flight. Short of pinning a note on every player's shirt, you'd think that would pretty much cover all contingencies. But at some point every couple of trips—at least with the Cubs—there would be a confrontation over the itinerary. I would cringe when I'd hear players walk up to the traveling secretary and demand—quietly at first, then, eventually, angrily—to know exactly what time the flight to such-and-such a city was going to land. They either had relatives or girlfriends to meet. They had plans to make. And they needed to know what time the flight would land.

Bear in mind, these are grown men; men whose entire young lives had been built around the game of baseball and who had gotten so good at it they were being paid staggering amounts of money to play every day. But somewhere along the way they got lost—so lost they forgot the fundamentals. One of the great beauties of baseball is it isn't governed by a clock. In the legendary words of Yogi Berra: "It ain't over 'til it's over." So, if no one knows how long a game is going to last, how is a traveling secretary going to know when a post-game flight is going to take off—let alone land in another city? It seems pretty simple. It can't be done. But, I swear, I saw the scene repeated time and again. I'd watch players get angry and curse a traveling secretary because they couldn't let their friends or family know exactly when the team plane would be landing. Even more painful and frightening was to see someone like veteran pitcher Anthony Young fuming about *the same thing* two or three times in one season. It boggled the mind. But it definitely helped me understand how Anthony Young set a major league record losing 27 consecutive games in 1992-93. Every time I looked at him after that I had this mental image of a jay-bird flying crooked.

Foreign correspondents don't have traveling secretaries, but they do have fixers. A fixer is usually a native of the country where a journalist is living or working, who, like a traveling secretary, makes everything possible for little pay and only token appreciation. I had some terrific fixers—and some unbelievable bozos—in my years overseas.

In Czechoslovakia, back when it was Czechoslovakia, my fixer was Arnold Keilberth, a gentle, gray-haired man who loved to read Hemingway and gave me the Czech-language copy of *Winnie The Pooh* I still have in my private library. Keilberth came to my rescue once when I was pulled off a train and arrested just inside the Czech border because a journalist I was traveling with from Vienna to Prague was so incredibly naïve that he brought photocopies of all his background files with him. The journalist worked for the *Detroit Free Press* and was making his first trip behind the Iron Curtain. He had been told not to bring the files—in

After years of bumbling around behind the Iron Curtain, it was magical to be in Berlin for the fall of The Wall.

fact, I was the one who told him—but he ignored the advice. The first Czech guard who looked at my friend's carry-on bags found hundreds of pages of suspicious photocopied documents that he couldn't read and promptly ordered the train to make an unscheduled stop at a remote village where we were hauled off to the local police station. My friend and I spent the night in separate closet-sized rooms sitting in straight-back wooden chairs. Neither room had windows and both were lit by a single, bare light bulb. I spent nine excruciating hours looking into the nervous eyes of a far-too-young, pink-cheeked policeman, who kept his gun drawn and resting in his lap to discourage any James Bond bravery. One phone call to Arnold Keilberth early the next morning enabled me to go free and my toddler-guard to holster his pistol.

Like all great fixers, Keilberth was more than a bail-bondsman, translator, and travel agent. He was a great newshound, too. Later on that same trip, when I finally reached Prague, Keilberth gave me the tip—no, he gave me all the details and contacts—that made it possible for UPI to scoop everyone with the news Soviet leader Leonid Brezhnev was on his way to Czechoslovakia to deliver an important speech. That speech turned out to be a politically explosive reaffirmation of the

Brezhnev Doctrine, which vowed armed Soviet intervention to prevent any changes in the Communist governments of the Warsaw Pact at a time when the Solidarity movement was pressing reforms in Poland.

Keilberth was just one of many terrific fixers I had over the years. Without question, the best was Kasia Znaniecka-Vogt in Poland. She was brilliant, beautiful, well-connected, and amazingly attuned to the strange world of Western journalism. She recognized the weaknesses in each of the endless parade of *Chicago Tribune* correspondents inflicted upon her and found ways to correct or hide those flaws. Her story ideas and suggestions were better than anything that came from the *Trib* foreign desk. And her sources were legendary. On top of all that, Kasia had the impressive knack all truly great fixers have of being able to do the impossible—even when it came to trivial personal requests. Shortly before we left Warsaw to come home, my wife decided to host a masquerade party for her favorite holiday, Halloween. She asked Kasia if she knew where we could find some costumes. Unflustered as always, Kasia said she would check around. Two days later, Kasia took us to an unmarked brick building that occupied much of an entire square block in downtown Warsaw. Two smiling potato-shaped ladies met us at the door and kissed Kasia on both cheeks. They led us up a flight of stairs and unlocked a metal door that opened onto an enormous room—the length of the city block—that was packed with row after row of deliriously colorful costumes, masks, capes, hats, boas, and shoes. We were in the costume department of the Polish Opera House and we spent the next two hours running around giggling and playing dress-up like a bunch of pre-schoolers until we finally chose appropriately gaudy costumes for each of us and a spare one for Kasia's husband, Steve.

Besides Keilberth and Kasia, I was blessed with a string of superb fixer friends led by Aleli Nucuum-Jones in Manila, Erica Hall in Vienna, Chris Drake in Cyprus, Rachel Silver in Jerusalem, Anwar Iqbal in Islamabad, and Chieko Kuriki in Japan. But there were some laughable losers along the way, too. The first translator/fixer the Chinese government assigned me when I got to Beijing in 1984 was hopelessly incompetent. I knew right away he was going to be trouble. The first thing he did, even before we met, was to ask me in a long-distance phone call to buy a television set and a VCR and bring them in for two

Chinese friends. Mr. Jiang's English was only marginally better than my Putonghua, which was non-existent. And his initiative was worse. At my request, he once arranged a meeting with the Diplomatic Housing Services to discuss some annoying, and long-since-forgotten, problem with our apartment-office in the Jianguomenwai foreigners' complex. Mr. Jiang had been working in the apartment for two years, showing up dutifully five days a week, 12 months a year. When we sat down for the meeting, Mr. Jiang translated the usual opening pleasantries, then the government official I was meeting asked a question. Mr. Jiang turned to me and said: "He wants to know where you live." I furrowed my brow and looked at Mr. Jiang like he was crazy.

"What do you mean, he wants to know where I live?"

"That's what he says: he wants to know where you live."

"Mr. Jiang. You know where I live. You go there every day."

Mr. Jiang seemed truly puzzled. He was lost in thought for a few scary moments, then snapped his head up alertly and said: "Oh, yes. That's right." Only then did he pass along the answer any right-thinking translator would have provided immediately.

That same week, I knew it was time to replace Mr. Jiang after I asked him to book an airline ticket for me to Hong Kong. He obviously was confused, so I repeated that I needed to book an airline ticket to Hong Kong. He said O.K. About an hour later, Mr. Jiang came into my office and said: "I've booked the phone call to your son in the States. It will be ready tonight at 7 o'clock."

"Thank you, Mr. Jiang. Good-bye, Mr. Jiang"

Baseball's traveling secretaries, like journalism's fixers, still wield powerful influence. But not nearly as much as they did as recently as the early 1970s. Until then, traveling secretaries basically ran major league teams on the road. They were as powerful as many managers—more powerful than most. Their influence eventually waned with the advent of a powerful players' union and the ever-stricter fiscal and ethical standards that swept across Corporate America in the '80s and '90s. Major

League Baseball, and the traveling secretaries themselves, tightened those standards even more in 1992 when a former traveling secretary of the New York Mets was implicated in an embarrassing situation involving the sale of a bit of baseball history. The item in question was the baseball that went through Bill Buckner's legs in the sixth game of the 1986 World Series, allowing the Mets to come back from seeming certain defeat against the Boston Red Sox—the only team in baseball with a history even remotely as heartbreaking as the Cubs.

Outfielder Mookie Wilson of the Mets hit the anemic dribbler that Buckner misplayed. And when Ray Knight scored on the play to end the game, umpire Ed Montague retrieved the ball. Montague gave it to Arthur Richman, then traveling secretary of the Mets, in case Wilson wanted it for a keepsake. Wilson wasn't interested and, instead, autographed the ball and gave it back to Richman, who kept it in a closet in his Greenwich Village apartment for six years. Then, in 1992, after he had moved to the New York Yankees as a senior vice president, Richman sold the ball to a Manhattan memorabilia store that auctioned it off for $93,500 to actor Charlie Sheen, who starred in the movies *Major League* and *Major League II*. Among those Sheen outbid was ESPN anchor, Keith Olbermann, who offered a paltry $47,000.

Richman promised to donate the proceeds of the sale, after taxes and commissions, to sports-related charities. But the mere perception of impropriety was enough to taint every traveling secretary in baseball, which was a shame. The bad apples are few and far between. And they usually get plucked from the barrel pretty quickly. The Red Sox once hired a former Boston cop, who served a year in federal prison for extortion, to be their traveling secretary. He was relieved of his duties as soon as his record became public.

The strike-ruined spring of 1995 was a nightmare for traveling secretaries. Late one night that spring I wandered into the Cubs' training complex in Mesa, Arizona, to find Jimmy Bank, the team's traveling secretary, alone in the cramped administrative offices up to his elbows in post-it notes, memos, and crinkled fax paper. He had a Faith Hill CD blaring on his boombox and we quickly degenerated into a lecherous discussion of how much more pleasurable country and western music had become since the lovely Ms. Hill arrived on the scene. The discussion was disappointingly brief, however. Jimmy had little time for fantasy. He was swamped trying to juggle literally hundreds of plane reservations and hotel bookings for the regular players who might or might not be coming to camp, the minor leaguers who might or might not be playing in their stead, and the so-called "replacement" players who were keeping baseball alive temporarily, but who would be sent packing as soon as the strike ended.

A native of Alabama with a drawl as long and slow as Frank Castillo's best swing at the plate, Jimmy looked like warmed-over oatmeal. His skin was pasty. His eyes were baggy. And his usual quick laugh was out in the bullpen for the night. These were extraordinary times—with the strike and everything. And Jimmy wasn't alone. There were 27 other traveling secretaries going through the same nightmare just as anonymously. But, watching Jimmy work, I wondered if even one of the scores of pampered young men appreciated the effort that went into something as simple as a hotel room or an airplane reservation. I knew the answer, but I had to ask. When I did, Jimmy wrinkled his brow and looked at me as if I'd just told him his beloved University of Alabama was giving up football. His only reply was to summon the laugh he'd banished to the bullpen. The cackle was loud enough to drown Faith Hill.

The fact that many players dismissed traveling secretaries and other hard-working club officials with an-almost master-servant condescension was all the more galling considering how astoundingly helpless some players could be. Pitcher Willie Banks was a classic example. Just before the Cubs got rid of him in the middle of the 1995 season, Banks learned his girlfriend was about to deliver their baby. The team was in Cincinnati and Banks wanted to fly out for the birth. He received permission from manager Jim Riggleman to leave the club, but was still around hours later when I bumped into him and another player on the elevator at the team hotel. It was the second time in half an hour I'd seen Banks and his buddy on the elevator. They seemed lost. I learned later that Banks was frantically searching for the traveling secretary because he didn't know how to book a flight on his own. Neither did his friend. They were in a panic until another teammate came to the rescue.

That incident only reinforced Willie's reputation. He was an incredibly talented pitcher—so talented, in fact, that he was picked ahead of future Cy Young winner Jack McDowell in the June 1987 draft. But Banks never came close to realizing his potential. The rap against him was that he lacked the mental discipline to be a great pitcher. He would throw wonderfully for four or five innings, then fall apart. The more I watched him, the more I came to believe his critics were right: he simply couldn't stay focused. He would be tossing a no-hitter one inning, then taking a loss and a shower the next. Fortunately, win or lose, he didn't have to make plane reservations very often.

When Banks was pitching well and things were going his way, he was hilariously funny. One day during the strike-delayed spring training of 1995, Banks showed up in camp for a few minutes and had a couple of us in stitches. Then, as he was wont to do at times, he turned suddenly serious. "When my career in baseball is over, I'm going to be a standup comedian," Banks said.

The way he pitched for the Cubs, I figured he was just getting a head start.

One thing about Willie Banks: even when his career was unraveling, even when he was trying to wrestle with the almost-unbearable pressure of seeing his dream life in the big leagues going down the drain, Banks still found time to be a gentleman. He was quick to ask favors of the traveling secretary, but just as quick to say please and thanks. That was true of too few veterans. One notable exception, in addition to Banks, was Shawon Dunston. He once stopped Jimmy Bank on the charter plane after a particularly harrowing adventure. The Cubs had flown from Chicago to upstate New York for a frenzied one-day trip to play in the Hall-of-Fame game at Cooperstown and left right after the last out for Pittsburgh to resume their normal schedule the next night. Everything imaginable had gone wrong that day: problems with the equipment trucks, the bus company, the airlines, everything. Bank had juggled it all so professionally that most players never even noticed. But one had. Bank was walking down the aisle of the charter plane just before takeoff when Dunston stuck his hand out and offered it to the traveling secretary. "Man, I wouldn't have your job for all the money in the world," Dunston said, shaking his head and closing his eyes. "You're doing a helluva job."

Bank and I talked about that painfully rare incident more than a year later. "The infrequent show of appreciation is well remembered," he said. "A simple thank you goes a long, long way."

Players aren't the only ones who lose touch with the real world and simple social graces. Traveling secretaries are at the beck and call of management, too. And the lack of appreciation from the front office can be even more galling. I know a traveling secretary who was with an American League club that had one of those typical shakeups after a particularly bad season. The traveling secretary survived the purge and was beginning to feel reasonably secure in his job again when one of the new bosses called him in about a month later. After the usual pleasantries, the new boss looked the traveling secretary in the eye and said simply: "We need to know what you do in your job in case you die."

It's a wonder the traveling secretary didn't die of a stroke right then and there.

"A lot of traveling secretaries feel alone," Jimmy Bank admitted reluctantly over dinner one night. "We're in a weird position between management and the players. We don't really belong to either world, yet we're ruled by both."

Ed Lynch learned to live in two baseball worlds—and the real world for a time in between.

Lynch was the fortunate soul chosen to succeeded Larry Himes as general manager of the Cubs on October 10, 1994. Fortunate because it was a no-lose situation. Anybody who stepped in would be better than Himes. And anybody who stepped in would work under Andy MacPhail, the third-generation baseball executive, who had been brought in as president and chief executive officer of the Cubs when Himes was sent packing to well-heeled exile in Arizona.

That isn't meant to take anything away from Lynch. Nor is the fact that, by his own admission, Lynch had a lot to learn when he took the job. He was just 38 years old and the highest position he had held in a major league front office was as "special assistant" to Joe McIlvaine, executive vice president of the New York Mets. And Lynch only held that job for one year. Before that, he was with McIlvaine in San Diego as director of minor league operations for the Padres. Like me, when I took my job with the Cubs, Lynch had to accept the reality there probably were dozens of candidates more qualified than him for his position. But Lynch was the one who got it. And he didn't get it because Tribune Co., MacPhail, or the Cubs were running a work-release program for wayward baseball executives. He got it because MacPhail thought Lynch had the right pedigree for the position. And because MacPhail had the rare luxury of being able to afford to wait until Lynch grew into the job, which he did. But there were a few growing pains along the way.

I was one of those growing pains. So was the strike that began when Lynch was still with the Mets and ended during his first spring as general manager of the Cubs. The day the strike ended, we were in Arlington, Texas. The Cubs' replacement players—a group of young men I both liked and respected—had just lost 6-5 in 12 innings to a team representing the Texas Rangers. It was the only time the replacement players took the field in a major league ballpark and they put on a wonderful show. Phil Stephenson, a former Cub, crushed a 415-foot home run in the new Ballpark at Arlington and Sean Ryan, whose uncle played for the Philadelphia Athletics and whose brother was a top prospect in the Cubs' organization, went 2-for-3 with a double. But the star of the day was Joey Terilli, a personable, pint-sized 26-year-old ex-minor leaguer, whose hometown was Dallas, just up the road. Terilli left 73 comp tickets for family and friends, then delighted them all by slapping a bases-loaded double in the sixth inning.

We learned during the game that the nearly eight-month strike was finally over and that all but a few of the players who kept baseball alive through one of its darkest, greediest periods, would be summarily sent home. The players, though, weren't formally told until they went back to the team hotel. They knew, of course, what was happening. Luis "Mambo" DeLeon, who was scheduled to pitch Opening Day in Cincinnati on Monday, had already gotten a call from his wife in Puerto Rico telling him she heard on television the strike was over and the replacements were being sent home. DeLeon told his wife it couldn't be true because the Cubs hadn't given the players the news, but he knew he was only deluding himself. At age 36, he wanted desperately to recapture the glory days of a decade earlier when he was briefly a pitching sensation with the San Diego Padres. He had pushed his aging and injury-wracked body all spring, knowing the striking major league players and many fans would taint his dream even if it came true. Then, just hours before the months of hard work and emotional strain were about to pay off, the Cubs called a meeting. All replacement players were to report to Lynch's dark-paneled suite in the Arlington Hilton. The moment DeLeon heard about the meeting, he accepted the harsh reality with his characteristic good humor. He walked into Lynch's suite carrying a fishing pole and a smile.

Lynch was in an awkward position himself that late afternoon. As a former major leaguer, he understood far better than any of us the gambit of emotions from animosity to ambivalence that the striking players felt toward the replacements. But he knew, too, what the replacements had done for the game. He saw both sides of the emotionally charged situation, but he was focused on one thing: getting the so-called "real" players into camp so he could finally start feeling like a "real" general manager.

The Cubs treated the replacement players kindly and professionally, if a bit brusquely. Other teams, notably the St. Louis Cardinals, San Francisco Giants, and Texas Rangers, handled the strike settlement with considerably more class—rewarding their temporary players financially and emotionally. The Cardinals generously made sure every player got

$30,000 in bonuses they would have received if they had started the season. The Rangers volunteered $5,000 bonuses. And the Giants went out of their way to make the fill-in players feel like the heroes they were. General Manager Bob Quinn gave each one of his temporary players an official Giants' game jersey and broke down in tears as he thanked them, from his heart, for helping save the game.

Lynch couldn't be expected to feel the same way. Quinn was a fourth-generation baseball executive. Lynch was a rookie general manager chomping at the bit to get to work and start impressing people. Most of us would be just as self-focused in his situation. He was like a kid about to explode waiting for the first day of college or the start of a new job. The excitement was twitched across his face when he agreed to sit down for a few minutes with the three beat writers around a table in the closed lobby bar of the hotel. The replacement players were filing by, boarding the team bus for the last time, taking group pictures and slapping each other on the back. We needed a few quotes and some insights into where Lynch thought things would go from here. The striking players were due to report for a new, abbreviated spring training in several days. How long did Lynch think it would take the pitchers to get ready? How many pitchers would he carry on the roster when the season started? Was he worried about injuries after such a long walkout? What would be his first priority: signing Mark Grace or trading for a center fielder?

We reeled off the obvious questions, then started winding down the interview. Lynch was in a jolly mood. I mentioned he probably had a few sleepless nights ahead of him now that he genuinely was climbing into the general manager's saddle at long last.

"A few sleepless days, too," he said, slapping his right thigh and chuckling. "There goes those noon naps."

It was a nice quote—perfect for the moment. In just a few words, Lynch captured the essence of the long, difficult task ahead of him and tempered it with just a hint of self-deprecation. To me, it was the kind of quote that could only come from a confident, determined leader, willing to poke a little fun at himself. So I used it in the next day's story.

I, frankly, hadn't given the quote a second thought until Lynch stopped me in the reception area of the minor league offices at Fitch Park in Mesa, Arizona, where the returning players were scheduled to report.

Lynch asked if he could see me in his office for a second and I said, sure. I was a bit surprised when he closed the door behind me. The atmosphere at Fitch Park is usually pretty casual. I was thoroughly flabbergasted when seconds after the door shut, Lynch erupted into a rage. He told me he never thought I would use that quote in the paper. I told him: Ed, you were sitting right there when I wrote down the quote in my notebook. He said: Yeah, but he never thought I'd put it in the paper. Lynch yelled at me for several long minutes, his voice so loud a friend told me later every word could be heard in the reception area and down the hall to the manager's office. I couldn't believe what was happening. But I was more amused than angry. And every time Lynch paused to catch his breath, I simply rolled my eyes and chuckled in disbelief. That, of course, did nothing to calm him down. "Don't roll your eyes at me like I'm a three-year-old," Lynch screamed, the veins in his neck bulging.

Ed Lynch is a big man—a big, big man. He was listed at 6-foot-6 and 230 pounds when he pitched for the Mets and Cubs from 1980-87. He hasn't gotten any smaller. So when it appeared my body language might provoke this giant into newer, more dangerous depths of despair, I decided I needed to be a little more articulate about my feelings. I told Lynch I was rolling my eyes because he was behaving like a three-year-old—not a particularly diplomatic entreat on my part, but an honest one.

"Come on, Ed," I said. "Do you honestly believe anyone who read that story thinks the new general manager of the Cubs is taking naps all day during spring training?" The quote, I insisted, was used in a positive way to underscore how hard he had been working already and how willing he was to work even harder in the days ahead.

I was calculating whether I could beat Lynch to the door if he lunged across the desk when desperation drove me to one final argument: "Ed," I said, "if you read that same quote about Dave Dombrowsky or Walt Jocketty, would you honestly think for one second that those guys were sleeping their days away?"

Linking Lynch with two other rising stars in the general manager ranks sent him to a neutral corner. Lynch is a bright man. Once he controlled his Irish temper, he realized two important things: 1) that the quote could very well be viewed positively, as it was intended; and 2) that screaming at a beat report over such a trivial incident was neither smart nor productive. He apologized profusely and, I believe, genuinely. We never had another blow up. And, with MacPhail's quiet behind-the-scenes guidance and much hard work on his own, Lynch steadily evolved into a secure and talented general manager.

Lynch was born in Brooklyn and spent most of his major league career with the Mets, though he did go 9-14 with four saves in 81 appearances with the Cubs in 1986-87. He became the first former Cub since "Jolly Cholly" Grimm to return to the club as GM. He also is one of the few general managers in the history of baseball with a Juris Doctor degree.

Earning his law degree from the University of Miami was the first step on the road back to baseball for Lynch, who knew a good thing when he lived it. The real world is a fine place, but why stay there if you can swaddle in the bassinet of baseball and get paid handsomely for it?

"I remember my first day in law school," Lynch once told me. "Believe it or not, after my first class, I'm out in the hallway signing autographs. Here's a bunch of first-year law students, who are pretty much 10 years younger than me. I was 32, they were all 22. And I'm standing there signing autographs. I'm feeling great. Then the next week or so, I'm in class getting berated by this professor. To him, I'm just a lowly first-year law student. I almost wanted to say to the guy: 'Hey, don't you know I was on "Game of the Week" a couple years ago?' Then I realize this guy probably doesn't give a shit. It was a rude awakening, a very cold slap in the face."

Almost every player gets that cold slap in the face. Unfortunately, it usually comes *after* they've left the game. While they're playing, the perks and adulation bestowed on them—and the incredible pressure they are under to perform at peak levels—make it almost impossible for athletes to fathom life in the real world.

"A guy who works for IBM for 20 years, he might get feedback from his boss once every six months," Lynch says. "He might get some negative feedback from his co-workers once every other year. But baseball is all condensed where every day it's a high and a low. A pitcher, you win or you lose. You save the game or it's a blown save. People cheer you or they boo you. Everything is condensed so tightly. The emotions run so high and low, so high and low, it's very difficult to keep your compass set on reality."

In a lot of ways, that is just as true for foreign correspondents. The emotional swings are certainly as dramatic, if not more so. The big difference, of course, is that foreign correspondents are out in the real world, dealing with real people. They are constantly exposed to the best and worst on the planet, from abject poverty and senseless cruelty to the most awe-striking art and accomplishments. The pressure to perform at peak levels, day in and day out, is nearly as great as for professional athletes. And the perks can sometimes be just as daunting as anything anyone in baseball ever experiences.

At one point in my career with the *Tribune*, my wife and I were living in Manila and Beijing at the same time. It sounds weird to have two full-time homes in two worlds 1,800 miles apart. But it actually was quite logical and practical. The *Tribune* wanted, and needed, a bureau in China, yet the hottest story in Asia at the time was in the Philippines. The Marcos regime was crumbling. Corazon Aquino, the widow of a man martyred by Marcos, was about to become president. And the future of the two largest U.S. military bases outside the United States was in the balance. I was spending months at a time in the Philippines, staying in the lovely old Manila Hotel, which had been Douglas MacArthur's headquarters during World War II. I was running up huge bills there and paying rent in Beijing as well. My bosses in Chicago figured they would save money renting a place in the Philippines instead of putting me up in a hotel. It all made perfect sense, but it certainly wasn't normal. One week, I'd wake up in colonial splendor in a 4,000-square-foot house with a pool and a coconut palm in the front yard next door to the Egyptian ambassador's residence. A week later, I'd be sitting in a dingy, two-bedroom apartment in a pre-dilapidated concrete high-rise building in Beijing where the winter air reeked of coal dust and an ill-tempered, gun-slinging Chinese guard in a sack-fitting uniform watched my every movement when he wasn't busy with what seemed to be the national pastime—spitting on the sidewalk.

Some time during that aberrant stage of our lives, we suddenly stopped and stunned ourselves with the realization that a dozen people in two countries were working for us, most of them full time. The paper paid for most of them. We hired some. But we had a driver, a cook, and Mr. Jiang working for us in Beijing—all of them government spies. The cook, Xiao Li, allegedly spoke no English, but at least once a month we'd catch her hunched over the Telex machine reading incoming messages from Chicago. In Manila, we had two live-in maids, a driver, a pool boy, and a gardener. I had a secretary in my office and she had an assistant, who helped with clipping newspapers and maintaining my files. I was also president of the Foreign Correspondents' Association of the Philippines one year. In that capacity, I inherited a full-time office manager and two assistants.

Try keeping your compass set on reality in those circumstances. I knew I'd lost track of True North one time when I flew into Hong Kong on a layover between Manila and Beijing. I won't say I was upset, but I have to admit I noticed, and felt a little disappointed, when the Regent Hotel dispatched a gold Rolls Royce to pick me up at the airport. The Hong Kong Regent is routinely rated atop, or near the top, every list of great hotels of the world. Its service, even by Asia's exceptional standards, is phenomenal. And sending a gold Rolls Royce to meet guests at the airport was a classy touch. But I was expecting the gun-barrel gray Daimler. The Roller was for VIP guests. Since I'd spent six weeks at the Regent when I first came out to Asia in 1984, I was officially listed on the hotel books as a VVIP—a *very, very* important person. I usually got the Daimler. Once there was even a pitcher of margaritas and a Jimmy Buffett tape waiting on the walnut bar of the car when I got in. A gold Rolls Royce positively paled in comparison.

Fortunately for me, or unfortunately, I suppose, I spent more time in ramshackle hotels than the Regent and more time in beat up Daihatsu taxis than sleek Daimlers. I'd no sooner lose perspective than I'd be dispatched to cover some slice of human misery destined to reorient my compass. Hong Kong was just a momentary flicker of the needle. I certainly didn't find a Daimler, or even a paltry Rolls, waiting when I came home from Warsaw to start working at Wrigley.

Unlike reporters, big-league ballplayers rarely have to deal with regular reality checks. The first time many of them restore contact with the normal world is when their time in the majors is finally up.

"You know, in my last year, I made in the neighborhood of $600,000 throwing a horsehide sphere with accuracy," Ed Lynch told me one day in the general manager's office at HoHoKam Park. "Then I get out and I'm interviewing for jobs and I realize that people bust their butts for $40,000 a year and are so proud of the fact that they are making that much money and supporting their family. It really woke me up and gave me an appreciation of just how good I had it. Now the second time around (as a GM) I'm reaping a lot of benefits of this industry. The fact that I can come to spring training for six weeks; the fact that I can go to Wrigley Field and call it my office, the fact that, maybe, I can get a table in a restaurant that somebody else can't get—I really have a great appreciation of that and, certainly, I try not to abuse it, maybe, as much as I did as a player.

"But, you know, it's all relative. When you're in the minor leagues, you get all excited if somebody says: 'Hey, did ya hear? We're gonna have pizza after the game tonight.' Then, six years later, you find yourself on a chartered flight complaining: 'How could they serve this wine with a steak?' And you don't even understand that it's happening to yourself because we're all human."

Human, yes. But real people? Not a lot of players fall easily into that category. At least not while they're still wearing spikes.

"I remember when I finished my playing career—11 years, eight in the big leagues—my wife and I went to the movies," Lynch said with an embarrassed chuckle. "There was a long line to get in and I looked at her and I said: 'Jeez, I can't believe I have to wait on this line to get in this movie.' She just looked at me and said: 'Welcome back to reality, pal.'"

Chapter 6

We Don't Need Another Ego

When I was packing to leave Warsaw for the baseball assignment, I took time out to have dinner with Charles T. Powers, a good friend who was the *Los Angeles Times* correspondent in Eastern Europe then and became a novelist before his unexpected death in late 1996. Chuck was a great cook, a malicious Sunday afternoon badminton player and an ardent baseball fan. One of his icons in the sprawling split-level chateau he called home in Warsaw was a ball Stan Musial autographed for him when Musial came to Poland a few years ago to donate some baseball equipment to a youth league. Powers was excited, and a bit puzzled, about my new assignment. He wanted to know everything: How did I think I'd like it? Would I regret giving up living overseas? Could I handle cranking out all the daily copy? But somewhere between the *ossobuco* and his homemade chocolate chip cookies, Chuck hit on a question I'd been asking myself: How are you going to deal with all those spoiled jocks?

From my first day on the beat until the morning I quit and started packing to go back overseas, I never was able to come to grips with the star status accorded even the most woeful baseball players—let alone the giants of the game. More importantly, I never was able to come to grips with, or explain to readers, how easily most players themselves embraced the adulation as merely their richly deserved due.

I had stood in the Great Hall of the People with Deng Xiaoping and walked through the gold-leafed palace of Philippine strongman Ferdinand Marcos. I sat down with Yasser Arafat, Lech Walesa, King Hussein of Jordan, and the leaders and opposition figures of a half dozen other countries from Bulgaria to Bangladesh. They all had massive egos. They all had enormous self-confidence and charisma. But none was more cocksure, more narcissistic or egomaniacal, than most 25-year-old banjo-hitting baseball players I came across.

Part of it is the enormous pressure the players are under to succeed and the realization that few people on the planet can do what they do. Part of it is the distorted lives they lead from the moment they're singled out as star athletes as early as grade school. But those are merely mitigations. The amusing reality is many players are afflicted with massive egos out of all proportion to their contributions to the game, let alone life. And few realize it.

Dallas Green, who built the 1984 Cubs team that went to the postseason for the first time in 39 years, once looked around the clubhouse when he was managing the New York Yankees and noticed some of his players hiding from the media after a game. Locker room hide-and-seek is common practice in major league baseball. Players who make bonehead plays that cost a game or pitchers who give up the back-breaking hit often retreat to the trainer's room, showers, eating area, or other confines of the clubhouse that are off-limits to the media. They will hide there as long as it takes until most reporters have given up or rushed away to meet deadlines. "Isn't it something?" Green was quoted in *The Sporting News*. "The egos are such that they can accept the accolades, but they'd beat you over the head for writing what they did wrong."

Baseball players hardly have a monopoly on egotistical imbalance. Demagogues and dictators everywhere lust for praise and rarely brook even the tamest criticism. I can personally attest that is true from demagogues as seemingly different as the editor of the *Chicago Tribune* and the president of Iraq.

A lucky break enabled me to become the first Western correspondent into Iraq during the Iran-Iraq War in September 1980. I was working in London at the time for United Press International. London was UPI's headquarters for Europe, the Middle East, and Africa. So when Iraq launched its invasion of Iran, we were in charge of covering the story. We had correspondents in the Middle East, but they worked mostly out of places like Jerusalem and Cairo. We relied on part-time writers and tipsters, known as stringers, to supply coverage out of places like Iraq, where it was either difficult to get full-time correspondents accredited or where, under normal circumstances, there rarely was enough day-to-day news to warrant full-time coverage.

The boss in London at the time was an accomplished and intelligent gentleman named Alex Frere, whose kindness and quick thinking helped save my life once and catapulted my career another time. Frere came to the rescue of my panic-stricken wife and arranged a battery of doctors to care for me when I lapsed into unconsciousness with bacterial meningitis just before Christmas 1979. Nine months later, long after I'd made a full recovery, Frere became my professional salvation when he pulled me off the London newsdesk and sent me to the Iran-Iraq war. Neither country had any resident Western correspondents at the time, so the logical place to head was Kuwait, which bordered Iraq on the south and was closest to the fighting in Iran's southwest Khuzestan Province. Frere gave me a few minutes to turn my desk duties over to a close friend, David Cowell, then called me into his glass-walled office in the middle of UPI's typically shabby, chaotic, and warm-spirited newsroom just off Fleet Street. He handed me 100 pounds sterling, which, at the time, was worth about $250—a king's ransom for usually frugal UPI. Frere also gave me a stack of signed letters on UPI stationery attesting I was a duly accredited correspondent and told me to go find the war.

I was so excited I was beside myself. I called my wife, who was working for ITT as a press officer just two blocks away on the Strand and told her the great news. Or, at least, what I thought was great news. It was raining when she walked up the street to meet so we could share the cab I was taking home to pack. It was always raining in London. So I didn't notice at first she was crying. Then, as the black cab pulled away into the Fleet Street traffic, my wife started sobbing uncontrollably. I couldn't understand it. To me, going off to a war was the greatest thing in the world. The thought that it might be dangerous, let alone fatal, never entered my mind. All I could see was my name in lights. Well, maybe not lights, but certainly in bold type above page-one stories all across the world. I was going to be Ernie Pyle, Walter Cronkite, and Edward R.

Murrow rolled into one. I couldn't have made the comparison then, but I know now my ego was soaring somewhere off in the rarefied heights usually reserved for .280 hitters and above.

I pried myself from my weeping wife, got to Heathrow Airport just in time to bumble aboard a conveniently delayed flight to Kuwait, and realized as the wheels left the ground that I didn't have the vaguest clue what I was doing. Fortunately, Alex Frere had told me the first thing I needed was a visa to Iraq. Unfortunately, when I landed, it was late on a Friday, the Moslem holy day. The Iraqi embassy was closed. But I was far too excited to sit around a hotel room, so I took a cab to the embassy anyway, just to learn where it was. When we pulled up, I asked the driver to wait while I checked the main gate. It was dark already, but lights were blazing in the embassy and just as I reached the gate a group of men inside burst into noisy celebration. The sounds of clapping, singing, and high-pitched wails of giddy ecstasy rolled out the embassy building onto the street. I put my face to the wrought-iron gate and peered in to see a half dozen men dancing around the eerie glow of a tiny television perched on a chair near the open front door of the embassy. The Iraqi Evening News was on and Baghdad's answer to Dan Rather had just announced Saddam Hussein's troops were marching into Khorramshahr, a port city in southwest Iran.

The report turned out to be ridiculously premature. Saddam's glorious troops were stalled in the dark brown sand outside Khorramshahr and would be for another two weeks. But nobody in the Iraqi embassy knew that. All they knew was what Baghdad Dan was telling them and he was telling their army was unstoppable.

I, of course, had no idea what was happening—my command of the Iraqi language being roughly the same as, if not a little worse than, most New Orleans natives. But it was clear the lads inside were in a jolly mood. It couldn't hurt to try to talk to them. I stuck my arm through the iron bars of the gate and managed to attract the attention of a guard who had abandoned his post to join the celebrations. I hurriedly told him I was an American journalist and I needed to get a visa. When would the embassy be open? When should I come back?

"Come in, my friend. Come in," said an excited young man in a rumpled gray suit behind the guard. "There is great news. Our soldiers are victorious. You say you are an American journalist? You must go to Iraq and tell the world about this great news. Come in. Come in. I will see that you get a visa."

I think of that night at the Iraqi embassy every time I see the *Wizard of Oz* when the guard to the gates of the Emerald City refuses at first to let Dorothy and her friends in and then relents after the Scarecrow points out Dorothy is wearing the ruby slippers given her by the Good Witch of the North. "Oh, so she is," the guard squeaks. "Well, bust my buttons. Why didn't you say that in the first place? That's a horse of a different color. Come on in."

Iraq wasn't exactly going to be Oz. In fact, if I'd had any idea all my wishes were going to come true that night, I'd have clicked my heels and wished for a lot more than an Iraqi visa. Who knows? Maybe I could have gotten the Cubs the pennant.

Blind luck and great timing got me the visa a hundred other correspondents coveted. And blind luck and great timing stayed with me for a couple weeks. I managed to keep ahead of most of the competition and was the first to report from inside Khorramshahr after the city fell that Iraqi troops had looted the port. That didn't seem particularly surprising. As I mentioned in my dispatches: the victors have always enjoyed the spoils of war. But it was funny—and it did make an interesting story—watching Iraqi soldiers haul off vacuum cleaners, bedroom furniture, and all sorts of useless sundry from the metal cargo containers stacked around the sacked port. Then, obviously weary from weeks of digging trenches in the desert, many of those same soldiers simply moved in and transformed the barren containers into battlefield condos.

Since I was based in London, and since I had been ahead on the story, the British press tended to use my copy prominently. Even when the papers published stories without a byline under the heading: "from our wire services," they often included several paragraphs quoting UPI corespondent Joseph A. Reaves on the scene. And when I had the story about looting, the British tabloids went wild. They splashed it all over their front pages. The *London Evening Standard,* the paper most commuters bought to read on the Underground on their way home, ran a two-column banner front-page headline that read: "Key Iran Port Falls." Beneath that, under the smaller headline: "Waterfront looting," was a box of copy, which began: "UPI reporter Joseph Reaves said Iraqi troops wasted no time in looting house-sized metal containers stacked up along the waterfront."

The story ran in the evening papers of Monday, October 6. By Tuesday evening, I was racing for the Iraqi border to keep from going to prison.

An Iraqi Information Ministry official showed up the next afternoon in the tiny lobby of the Hamdan Hotel in Basra, where I'd been living the past 16 days, and angrily demanded to see my passport. I was surprised by his attitude because the same information officer had been fawning over me for two weeks. I was too frazzled to make an immediate connection between the looting story of the day before and the sudden hostility. And I was too dimwitted to find some excuse that would have bought me time before handing over my passport. Instead, I dutifully reached into my shirt pocket and produced the precious blue document that has been my talisman in a thousand places over the years. The information officer took the passport from me, flipped quickly through the pages, and found the one with my miraculous Iraqi visa. He bent the spine of the passport angrily, laid it open on a glass coffee table, and produced from his pocket a rubber stamp that came down with a thud on the middle of Page 15. There, across my Iraqi visa, stamped in Arabic and English, was the word: *"Cancelled."*

My former friend, who only two days earlier was telling me how wonderful my writing and reporting had been, informed me I should confine myself to the hotel. He had an errand to run, but would be back shortly and wished to see me again.

As soon as the information officer left, a concerned group of wiser and far more-experienced colleagues told me to pack what I could and get out of the country immediately. They already had heard I was to be arrested and sent to Baghdad. The looting story had enraged Saddam Hussein himself. And Saddam, it seemed, would have fit right in with Dallas Green's New York Yankees. He was good at accepting accolades, but tended to whack a few heads when things went wrong.

The next few hours were scary. I left the Hamdan Hotel in a taxi followed by a pair of four-wheel drive security vehicles. Acting on the advice of an incredibly wise colleague, I had the taxi take me directly to the local office of the Information Ministry. I got out, sent the taxi on its way, and walked in the front door. The goons who followed me must have thought, as my colleague hoped, that I was turning myself in to the ministry. They relaxed long enough for me to slip out another door, walk rapidly around the corner, and meet my waiting taxi driver, who pocketed a $150 tip for speeding me 35 miles down a dusty two-lane highway to the border village of Safwan without getting caught. The driver had to leave me there and I walked up to the border checkpoint wondering what to say about my canceled visa, or "cancelled" as it was spelled in testimony to the still-lingering British influence in the Middle East. I finally explained that UPI had sent in a replacement to cover the war and the Information Ministry only allowed one reporter from each organization at a time. Feeble as that sounded to me, the border guard bought it. I guess he probably figured it was a lot smarter letting journalists out of the country than allowing them in.

There was, at the time, about a 100-yard stretch of no-man's land between the Iraqi border post and the checkpoint on the Kuwaiti side. The walk between the two was one of the longest I ever took. The sound of my shoes on the asphalt seemed louder than the artillery I'd been hearing the last few weeks. I kept expecting to see two jeeps full of security goons come barreling down the road. It never happened, though, and two hours later I was soaking in a hot bubble bath eating a room-service cheeseburger in one of Kuwait's luxury hotels.

UPI didn't pay very well, but the company gave its people some terrific opportunities. And the bosses were always grateful. When I called Alex Frere from Kuwait City that night, he insisted I take some time off and enjoy myself. That sounded just fine and I knew where I wanted to go. I flew to London, met my wife and we got on a plane for Houston, where she had worked as a reporter for the *Houston Chronicle* until we married the year before. Less than 72 hours after I left Iraq, Lynne and I were sitting in the orange seats of the Astrodome watching Joe Morgan hit the 11th-inning triple off Tug McGraw that made Dave

Smith and the Astros winners in Game 3 of the National League playoffs. I had grown up listening to Gene Elston and Lowell Pass broadcast the Astros on WNOE Radio in New Orleans. Next to the Cubs, the 'Stros were my team.

In true Cub-like fashion, the Astros blew a 2-1 lead to lose in five games to the Phillies. But it was a phenomenal series. Four of the five games went extra innings. The lead changed hands three times in the final game. Pete Rose batted .400 and made a series-saving catch of a high pop foul that bounced off catcher Bob Boone's mitt and nearly landed in the first-base dugout. Even indoors on plastic grass it was one of the best baseball showdowns anybody would ever want to see. And I have Saddam Hussein to thank for getting me there.

Nobody on the 1993 White Sox ever threatened to put me in a Baghdad prison, at least not to my face. But I know a few guys who would have liked the idea.

That was a great team—a championship team—built by, and around, a wonderful core of people. But it was spoiled by a small, nasty knot of players whose egos could have given Saddam Hussein a run for his money.

I only covered the White Sox that one season. The *Tribune* believed its baseball writers should switch teams every year—the theory being the move would expand the writer's contacts throughout baseball, which it did. However, I thought the benefits were outweighed dispro-portionately by a loss of continuity. A writer who stays with a team four consecutive years is going to have a better collective memory, more sources, and be treated by the front office and players far differently than someone who shows up every other year—or even three out of four. But I didn't have a say in the matter. The only reason I accepted the baseball beat to begin with was because it meant covering the Cubs. I was a lifelong Cubs fan and a lifelong National League fan. I'm one of those stubborn codgers who still loathes the designated hitter rule. The arguments in favor of it all make sense. More offense. Prolonging the careers of players the fans want to see. I just think it diminishes the game. So what if the pitcher strikes out a lot? Think how exciting it is when a pitcher gets a hit. Or, even better, how great it is when a pitcher lays down a perfect bunt in a crucial situation. It's wonderful to watch the wheels turn in the dugouts when a manager has to agonize over whether to keep a pitcher in the game or pinch-hit. That's baseball. And it's beautiful. Don't get me wrong. I don't think the American League is an abomination. It's like the old saying about sex. Even bad baseball is great. Still, given the choice, I'd go to a game between two National League expansion teams before I'd go to the AL playoffs.

The year I came home from Warsaw, Alan Solomon was supposed to cover the Cubs. He had covered them in 1990 and, under the standard operating procedures, moved over to the White Sox in '91. Solomon was a big Cubs fan, too, and he was looking forward to moving back to the North Side of town in 1992. But Dick Ciccone, the managing editor who offered me the baseball job, knew the only way he could lure me back to Chicago from Warsaw was to cover the Cubs. I wouldn't have jumped for the White Sox. Ciccone told me not to worry: he would work things out with Solomon. But Ciccone made me swear I'd go quietly to the Sox in 1993. I agreed, half thinking that if I didn't enjoy the baseball beat, I could always quit after one year and go to the University of Tennessee as originally planned. Or, perhaps something unexpected might intervene to keep me in the National League—as happened between the 1994-95 seasons when the Cubs had such a massive shakeup that the *Trib* figured it would be better served sticking with the reporter who had covered the changes and already established a relationship with the new regime.

Neither miracle escape evolved after the 1992 season. I fell in love with the baseball beat, my wife got a great job and we decided to settle in for a while. Quitting was out of the question. And neither the Cubs nor the White Sox went through any dramatic changes during the winter. So the routine handover rules were in effect. I hinted at the possibility of getting my promise rescinded and staying with the Cubs. But the appeal fell on distinctly deaf ears.

If you look closely, you can probably still see the black heel marks up Addison Street, along Lakeshore Drive, and down 35th Street where

I was dragged from Wrigley Field to New Comiskey Park before the '93 season.

I didn't want to, and, frankly, it hurts to admit it, but I had a great time with the White Sox. I'd still rather watch a last-place Cubs' team than the World Champion Sox, but that '93 season was a joy.

General Manager Ron Schueler was terrific to work with. He was professional, personable, honest, and as forthcoming as his job allowed. In other words, he was everything Larry Himes wasn't.

Manager Gene Lamont was, and is, a prince among men. I learned more about baseball in one all-too-brief season with him and his bench coach Joe Nossek than I had in my entire life as a playground infielder, full-time fan, and rookie writer. Lamont took the time every single day of the season to explain what was happening, why it was happening, what it meant, and when and where it would change. He trusted the writers. He worked with us. And he made all of us who followed the team that season better. I don't think I ever covered a story any time or anywhere in my career when I felt more secure about what I was writing. That was good for me, good for the fans, and good for the White Sox. The credit goes to Gene Lamont.

The White Sox media relations staff under Doug Abel was excellent, particularly Abel's administrative assistant Mary Dosek and Abel's three top aides: Scott Reifert, Dana Noel, and Barb Kozuh. They were impressive professionals and incredibly pleasant souls, which becomes awfully important during the marathon course of a baseball season.

What surprised me most about the White Sox, though, was the team itself. From the moment I walked into the clubhouse, I knew those Sox players were winners. A lot of it had to do with the incredible array of talent: Frank Thomas, Jack McDowell, Alex Fernandez, Roberto Hernandez, Tim Raines, Robin Ventura, Ozzie Guillen. But there have been teams with far greater talent that never became winners. That White Sox team had the rare quiet air of confidence that could make a lot of bad years melt away and turn one season into magic. Unfortunately, that White Sox team also had a few brooding souls whose egos were boundless enough to make the magic black.

The White Sox cruised to the American League West title in 1993 and clinched it in storybook fashion in front of 42,116 fans waving white socks when Bo Jackson lofted a high, arcing rainbow of a three-run homer that just cleared the left-field fence at New Comiskey to beat the Seattle Mariners, 4-2. It was a Cinderella climax to a scullion season. Jackson, a former All-Pro running back with the Los Angeles Raiders who was in danger of being crippled for life from a football injury, had also homered in his very first at-bat that April, just one year after having a plastic hip implant.

The *Tribune* pulled my story of that game out to the front of the newspaper and quickly made a bundle selling souvenir T-shirts and poster replicas of the page, which carried the uninspiring banner headline: "Bo's blast is a clincher." The newspaper had done the same thing with my "Holy Cow! Cubs win!" story in 1984 story and Andy Bagnato's account of the NL East title game in 1989. Needless to say, neither Bagnato nor I ever collected an extra nickel off Mother Tribune's marketing. Still, just seeing those shirts and posters was a booster rocket for the ego and I felt nearly as good as the White Sox players for a week. That is until George Bell stepped up to turn the Lovefest in a Loser's Ball.

Bell had hit 25 homers and driven in 112 runs the year before, in his first season with the White Sox. But he struggled through 1993 and eventually lost his job as designated hitter to a platoon of Bo Jackson and Danny Pasqua. When the playoffs came, Bell assumed he would be the DH. And it wasn't an outrageous assumption. Despite his stutters that season, Bell had been a productive hitter throughout his career. He had even been Most Valuable Player in the American League in 1987 when he hit 47 homers and drove in a league-high 134 runs for the Blue Jays.

The fact that the Sox were meeting Toronto, the team he'd played for his first nine seasons in the majors, undoubtedly exaggerated the embarrassment Bell felt about being benched. He stewed in relative silence watching Pasqua go hitless as DH during the first two playoff losses in Chicago. But when the Sox traveled to Toronto for Game 3 and Lamont announced Bo Jackson was stepping in to DH, Bell was incapable of containing his considerable ego any longer. He found a devious way to strike back. Bell met with a friendly writer from a Toronto tabloid who had written his biography after Bell won the MVP award. In the midst of their interview, Bell unleashed a classless, childish, and calculated diatribe against Lamont.

"I don't respect Gene Lamont as a manager or as a man," Bell said in what, of course, was a sensational story in the middle of the playoffs. "What he's doing to me is cruel. He's not showing me any respect."

The cruel and disrespectful thing Lamont was doing was sitting a player who had become an albatross. True, Bell still had a solid lifetime batting average of .282. But he hit only .217 in 1993—56 points less than pitcher Shawn Boskie hit for the Cubs. Bell had finished the season, and his career, as it happily turned out, in an 0-for-26 slump. What's more, Bell batted .065 against Toronto that season. His lifetime average against his former team was a paltry .129. And he was a combined 16-for-91 (.176) against Toronto's four starting pitchers in the playoffs: Juan Guzman, Dave Stewart, Pat Hentgen, and Todd Stottlemyre.

Lamont had every reason in the world to keep Bell on the bench. But Bell was so blinded by his ego, and so spoiled by a career filled with success, that he was incapable of comprehending the big picture. Bell's tirade wasn't a matter, as some apologists have suggested, of a player with a keen sense of competitiveness wanting desperately to be in the biggest games of the season. It was a matter of George Bell's incredible sense of self overshadowing any concept of team.

Lamont, of course, was acutely embarrassed by the brouhaha. And, when I saw him the day the story came out, he was visibly angry. But he kept his cool—and his class. He refused to rip Bell in public, either to his own beat writers or to the long parade of reporters covering the playoffs. Lamont refused to get down in the gutter with Bell and, in doing so, did a world of good for the image of the White Sox organization and the city of Chicago.

It wasn't reported at the time, because Lamont didn't want it written. But the morning the story came out, Lamont called Bell into the visiting manager's office in the SkyDome. The conversation quickly degenerated into confrontation. Lamont, a former catcher with the Detroit Tigers, threatened to stuff Bell's head in the toilet and was about to carry out the threat when two of his coaches intervened. Lamont didn't want the near-fight reported because, he said, his first priority was getting his team focused back on the playoffs. He wanted to put the Bell incident behind them as quickly as possible. That was understandable and the right thing to do. But it was unfortunate because the story would have been good for Lamont. The public and many in the media, particularly the radio sports talk shows, had the mistaken impression that Lamont lacked fire, that he was too Caspar Milquetoast to manage a big-league ballclub. That perception was one reason Lamont went from being Manager of the Year at the end of the 1993 season to being fired just 144 games later at the start of the strike-shortened 1995 season. But the perception was simply wrong. Lamont may have looked low key. He may have walked away from more than one argument with an umpire that, perhaps, another manager would have fostered to fire up a team. But Lamont was tough as they come. And the Bell debacle wasn't the only time he showed it behind closed doors.

Earlier that same season, Lamont had quietly, yet firmly, stifled ugly snit fits by two other pampered egotists: catcher Carlton Fisk and second-baseman Steve Sax. Both were washed up as players. And both refused to see it. Fisk and Sax had enjoyed such success, fame, and adulation over the years that neither could keep his compass set on reality. Lamont coddled both their egos—Fisk's for half a season and Sax's all year—for the good of the team.

Carlton Fisk was, and is, an idol to many fans—and players, too. He was in the major leagues 24 years and came into his final season needing just 25 more appearances to break Bob Boone's record for games caught. The fact that Fisk was 45 years old and couldn't catch anymore was irrelevant. He dropped the first two pop fouls hit behind the plate in spring training. Pitches plopped in and out of his mitt almost as often as they landed. Runners stole at will when he was in the game—22 steals in 25 games without one runner being caught. And all the while, the White Sox had one of the best defensive catchers in the game in 29-year-old Ron Karkovice.

None of that embarrassing failure and ineptitude mattered to Fisk. He was determined to get the record and the White Sox, to their credit, felt they owed him the opportunity. That was great. But Lamont drew the thankless task of making it happen. Few gave him credit when it was all over, but Lamont overcame some amazing obstacles to lead the White Sox to the division championship that year. Every other team in baseball had 25 players on its roster. Lamont went much of the season with only 21. Fisk was more a liability than an asset. Steve Sax was dead wood with a lead glove. So was George Bell. And as wonderful and storybook as it was having Bo Jackson and his plastic hip in the big leagues, Lamont would have had a far easier job winning with another full-time defensive two-hipped outfielder on his roster and a solid No. 2 catcher for half the year.

Fisk had spent his entire adult life in baseball. In his final years, he loved to pontificate about how the younger generation of players didn't appreciate the game the way he did; how things had changed for the worse; how he was only hanging on because he loved the game. Fisk went on *ad nauseum* in an unbelievably narcissistic interview in *USA Today* during his final spring training about how he felt a duty to protect the game's traditions; about how he and his generation were the keepers of the flame that is baseball. "The flame is in the process of being extinguished only because [the younger players] play for different reasons than was intended ... None of the players that carry the flame use the dollar sign as motivation." This was the same Carlton Fisk who cashed in his own reputation so he could linger years beyond his time; the same Carlton Fisk who measured his own self-worth in dollars; who constantly bickered with the White Sox over money—and with the Red Sox before that. It was the same Fisk who banded with two other Boston players in a joint bargaining ploy that became so bitter and personal Red Sox owner Tom Yakey decreed on his death bed they all be traded.

That same Carlton Fisk who appointed himself keeper of the flame spent his final days with the White Sox sniping behind his manager's back, grumbling like the simpering, spoiled soul he had become after two decades in the self-indulgent world of baseball. He had two lockers in the far corner of the Comiskey clubhouse and usually could be found there with his nose pressed against the wall like a school kid being punished and his back turned like a shield to the cruel baseball world he thought was treating him so unjustly in the end. Fans who only saw the admirable, hard-working Fisk on the field could never imagine the petty, pouting person he could be in the clubhouse. But most people who got even a glimpse of the inner sanctum of the game knew.

Nationally syndicated sports show host Chet Coppock gave the fans a pretty accurate summation of Fisk's final days when he said in typically blunt fashion: "In case you're unaware, on his good days, Carlton's about as happy-go-lucky as a guy doing 6 to 10 [years] at Pontiac [State Prison]. He can be a pain in the neck. He's self-centered. His first and last concern has always been Carlton Fisk."

Dave Van Dyck of the *Chicago Sun-Times* covered Fisk for 13 seasons and knew him in Boston before that. When the White Sox finally released Fisk, Van Dyck wrote a brilliantly balanced column under the headline: "Let's Remember Fisk in the Happier Times." Van Dyck rattled off Fisk's staggering statistics and included some laudatory insights from former Red Sox manager Don Zimmer, who compared Fisk to the great catchers of all time. Van Dyck personally castigated the White Sox for provoking Fisk in his final years and contrasted that to the Texas Rangers, who promoted Nolan Ryan, the only other player from the 1960s besides Fisk still active that late in the 1990s. Then Van Dyck ended his column with some well-chosen words that cut both ways: "Someday, they'll write a baseball epithet for Fisk. It will read: 'He played hardball the hard way, even when he hardly played ball.'"

Fisk definitely played hardball with Lamont. And for no good reason. It wasn't Lamont's fault Fisk was over the hill. In fact, Lamont did his best to protect Fisk from himself. But Fisk was so busy keeping the flame he never saw the light.

One day early in the 1993 season, I went to Lamont to get his reaction to another particularly churlish remark Fisk had made. Something about Lamont being a pup of a manager who failed to take advantage of the vast wealth of baseball wisdom Fisk had at his command. Lamont politely declined to respond. "Listen, Joey, I can't say anything," he told me. "The guy's a hero, a legend. I can't get into a pissing match with him in print. I'll never win. And it won't do anybody any good."

Lamont never denigrated Fisk publicly. And he did a masterful, almost impossible, job of juggling the lineup so Fisk got enough playing time to set the record without ruining the team's chances of winning the division. Once Fisk got the record, the Sox wisely released him and he started the mandatory five-year waiting period in retirement before being eligible for the Hall of Fame. Ron Schueler tried for an entire weekend to move Fisk to another team. But nobody else needed a Sunday beer-league catcher—not even one who was headed for the Hall of Fame.

The White Sox did the honorable thing for him and the fans and threw a Carlton Fisk Night at Comiskey where his teammates presented him with a Harley Davidson motorcycle. I didn't know whether to cry or cheer when he rode off into the sunset. Like a million other fans, I loved the Carlton Fisk who waved that home run fair in the 12th inning of Game 6 of the 1975 World Series at Fenway. It was hard for me to accept our love was misplaced. We confused the goodness and happiness of the moment with the man himself. The moment was rapture. The game is wondrous. Carlton Fisk merely had the great, good fortune to be part of it. And the sad, familiar fate to accept it as his due.

How does that old song go?

"We don't need another hero ..."

Or is that ego?

Steve Sax was 12 years younger than Fisk, but just as washed up. And just as blinded by his ego. Sax was a five-time All-Star with the Dodgers and Yankees who had come to the White Sox a year earlier in a trade that put Schueler's reputation on the line. Schueler gave up cash and three touted pitching prospects for Sax, who responded by hitting .236 and committing 20 errors in his first season in Chicago.

Sax still had three years to run on a four-year contract that guaranteed him $12.4 million. That, and the fact the boss's reputation was on the line, would have convinced many a more-timid manager to take the easy way out and live with Sax in the lineup. Not Lamont. He told Schueler he didn't think Sax could play, then called Sax in the last week of spring training and told him the same thing man to man. Lamont made a public display of announcing that Craig Grebeck would be the everyday second baseman. Grebeck was a utility infielder who hadn't played a single game at second base the previous season. Giving him the job over a five-time All-Star took a lot of guts.

Several days later, in Las Vegas on the final weekend of spring training, Grebeck hurt his hand. Lamont had the perfect alibi to take the pressure off himself, give the job back to Sax, and save face for everybody. Instead, Lamont stuck to his convictions and dug deeper down the depth chart to give the second-base job to Joey Cora, who had been around the big leagues five seasons and played just 308 games.

Lamont went out of his way to salvage as much from Sax as he could. With three years still left on a massive contract, the White Sox didn't have much chance of trading Sax—particularly if his own manager didn't think Sax should be in the lineup. Sax never started another game at second base for the Sox. But Lamont did use him as a designated hitter, pinch runner, or pinch hitter in 21 games. And, despite his better instincts, Lamont got Sax into 32 games as an outfielder.

Sax had only played one game in the outfield in the major leagues before 1993. That was six seasons earlier with the Dodgers. It didn't take long to realize why he only played one game and why he wasn't going to prolong his career much by moving to the outfield now.

The White Sox were in Milwaukee in early May, 27 games into the season, when Lamont gave Sax a rare start in left field. Sax had started two other games in left already and gotten into another game late as a defensive replacement in the outfield. Those earlier appearances had been uneventful. This one wasn't. My story in the next day's paper began: *"Steve Sax has played just five games in the outfield in the majors, but already he's on his way to becoming a legend. Not the way Willie Mays was a legend. Far from it. Sax in the outfield resembles Stan and Ollie more than he does Willie. But that's why he may be a legend some day."*

Sax saved the game that day with a tumbling catch on what should have been a fairly easy play in the bottom of the eighth inning. The score was tied at 1 with two outs, but the Brewers had the potential winning run on third base when Bill Doran hit a rocket to left field. Sax broke hard to his right and back a few steps before discovering the ball was headed off in the direction from which he just came. He made a quick button hook, flailed his arms like a construction worker about to fall off a steel beam and somehow found himself close enough to the ball to make a tumbling catch. I wrote in the paper that the somersault knocked the ball free and would have cost the Sox the game "except that Sax is such a superb outfielder he was able to make the ball land on his thigh, trap it between his legs and lift if free with his bare hand before it hit the ground. Just another routine play by a legend in the making."

A Sax quote followed: "I was just fortunate I had a long glove," he said as he laughed all the way to the dugout and was mobbed by those among his teammates who weren't doubled over holding their sides.

In truth, what Sax said was a little different from the quote I used in the paper. What he really said, as he undressed at his locker, was: "It's a good thing I have a long dick, or I never would have caught that ball."

A few minutes later, in the manager's office, Joe Goddard of the *Sun-Times* asked Lamont if he heard how Sax said he trapped the ball. When Goddard told him, Lamont shook his head, rolled his eyes, and said with an embarrassed chuckle: "If that's how he did it, I never would have caught it."

Those two lines said a lot about both men. Lamont was a quiet leader, so supremely self-confident he was willing to joke about even the most-sensitive of all male subjects at his own expense. While Sax, on the other hand, was simply another filthy, crude, sexually obsessed man in a world populated by filthy, crude, sexually obsessed men. In baseball, when two friends talk to each other, a preferred form of address is: "Hey, bitch." And that's among friends. Just imagine where the conversation goes if two players dislike each other.

One of my most vivid memories of Steve Sax was sitting across the aisle from him on the team bus on the way back from Yankee Stadium one night and listening to a half hour of the most sexually graphic rant I ever heard in my life. I'm no angel. I can hold my own with most people in crude conversations, but Sax had even me looking for a place to hide. Not as desperately, though, as he had me and others scrambling for hiding places in the clubhouse sometimes. Sax used to love to come out of the shower naked, grab himself so his right hand looked like it had grown an extra finger and yell to a reporter or some other unsuspecting outsider: "Hey, baby. How'd you like some of this?"

Even if you went outside baseball and threw in half the legendary lecherous foreign correspondents I knew, Sax still would have been in a league of his own. But, like many professional baseball players, he was a paradox. This same foul-mouthed, egomaniac was the picture of fatherly kindness whenever the team was on the West Coast. Sax could always be seen playing catch with his son and daughter on the field before games at the Oakland Coliseum—and clearly enjoying it. I could never quite reconcile Steve Sex and Steve Sax in my mind. But some-how it made sense when I heard, after he retired, he was considering running for the California legislature. I thought he'd probably hit on the perfect career move.

Three months after the Milwaukee tumbling exhibition, Sax put on another freestyle gymnastics seminar—this time in the outfield at Comiskey Park. Instead of saving the game with his pratfalls this time, though, Sax almost lost it. And instead of being a lazy, laid-back game against Milwaukee in May, this time it was in crucial showdown in the heat of the pennant race against Sax's old team, the New York Yankees.

Sax tumbled heels over head on a routine flyball by Bernie Will-iams in the sixth inning that gave the Yankees a 3-2 lead. Frank Thomas tried to pick up Sax by launching a frightening a 431-foot home run to tie the game in the eighth inning and adding a ho-hum 410-foot shot in the 10th inning. But even those heroics weren't enough to save the game as the Yankees scored three times in the top of the 10th to win, 6-5.

Fairly deep down in my story the next day, seven paragraphs after it jumped off page one to an inside page, I mentioned Sax's latest somer-sault show. I described it as another of "his now-patented plays" des-tined to make the blooper highlight films.

"Sax looked as if he were filming one of those beer commercials—you know, the ones where they combine two outrageous sports into one—say sumo wrestling and high diving," I wrote. "In Sax's case, though, he went the commercials one better. He combined freestyle swimming with floor tumbling and a vague approximation of baseball and turned a fly ball by Matt Nokes into a run-scoring double."

The next paragraph read: "It wasn't all Sax's fault. He was playing right field for only the fourth time in his major-league career. And the right field he was playing looked like a scale model of Lake Michigan [after two rain delays]."

Sax wasn't impressed with my assuaging sentiments. The next afternoon, he waited until I was sitting on the bench in the White Sox dugout before the game. I had to walk through the clubhouse to get to the field and I had seen Sax inside, though I didn't give a thought to the story in the morning paper. The game had ended at 1:28 A.M. It was just one of 162 regular season games, 35 spring training games, and six playoff games for the Sox that season. And, of course, it wasn't the first time that season I'd written about Sax stumbling around a baseball field. So I was surprised when Sax stormed into the dugout and started yelling: "Where is Joey Reaves?" I was right in front of Sax, sitting with several reporters, including Cheryl Raye, who worked for the White Sox flagship radio station at the time, WMAQ. Cheryl later would expand on a tip by *Chicago Sun-Times* columnist Mike Sneed and break the story that Michael Jordan was holding secret workouts to sign a baseball contract with the White Sox.

Sax came up to the group of us and said: "Which one of you is Joey Reaves?" which, of course, was ludicrous. He was trying to embarrass me by implying to the other reporters that I was so inconsequential he didn't even know who I was, despite the fact I'd interviewed him when he lost the second-base job, ridden buses with him, talked with him after dozens of games, and been around him every day for seven months. When I didn't bother to answer his ridiculous question, Sax came over and started yelling in my face. "What do you think you're doing writing something like that? You don't know what the f— you're talking about. Let's see you go out there and try to catch that f—ing ball. I don't see you out there, you sorry piece of s—. Let's see you catch the mother f—ing ball in the middle of a mother f—ing swamp." He bellowed for minutes, attracting the attention of everyone on the field, which obviously was his intent. He repeated himself time and again and worked himself into an ever-greater frenzy as I sat on the top rung of the dugout bench with my back against the cool concrete wall. My colleagues shuffled their feet and tried to look off in another direction in a kindly effort to spare me further embarrassment, while Ozzie Guillen caught my attention from the batting cage and gave a dismissive wave with his right hand as if to say: "Forget it. It's just Saxie."

The only thing I could do was sit there and accept it all in silence. It was obvious to me that Sax was venting a year's worth of frustration. What I'd written had little or nothing to do with what was happening in that dugout. Sax had simply suffered yet another frustrating and mortifying experience after years of professional excellence and he couldn't take it anymore. He had finally reached his breaking point. He needed to lash out at someone or something and I was in the wrong place at the right time.

If Sax had let it go and that and walked away, I would have kept silent. But he insisted on pressing the personal attack. He tried to round up his wild, unfocused rantings with a final well-honed barb: "You need to learn how to do your job."

As much as I understood Sax's frustration, my own ego wouldn't let me suffer an insult like that in front of my peers from a player I didn't feel worthy of my respect on any level. I weighed my thoughts for a second, then, to my surprise, said in a calm, reasoned voice: "Steve, I know how to do my job and I'm good at it. If you were half as good at your job as I am at mine, I wouldn't have to write those things about you."

When Sax finally wandered off muttering the vilest obscenities about me and my dead mother, Cheryl Raye looked at me and said: "I don't know how you did that. I would have been so embarrassed." I merely tilted my head, pursed my lips, and arched my shoulders in a macho display of supreme indifference. But the truth was: I don't know how I did it. I was so embarrassed.

The biggest embarrassment of that season, though, was the way Jack McDowell pitched in the playoffs. McDowell won the Cy Young Award as the best pitcher in the American League that season, going 22-10. But when the bell rang for his first playoffs, McDowell was out to lunch. The Toronto Blue Jays hammered him in both his post-season starts. He gave up 10 runs in just nine innings and lost the two most important games of the championship series—the opener in Chicago and the fifth game in Toronto after the Sox had rallied from an 0-2 deficit to tie things at two games apiece.

McDowell was different from most players. He didn't just want to hit the media over the head when they wrote bad things about him. He wanted to hit them over the head when they gave him accolades, too. McDowell was born to do two things: pitch in the major leagues and brood through life. His nickname was Black Jack and he lived up to it—win or lose. Or so it seemed. And it seemed particularly true after he took a powder in the playoffs.

But I always had the feeling McDowell's brooding was rooted in something other than pure ego. I'd watch him and think: there's more here than meets the eye. That wasn't a feeling I had often on the baseball beat. Most of the time, when I got to know a player, I would think just the opposite. I'd be reminded of a United States ambassador I knew, who once summed up his impressions of the Philippines by saying: "There's less here than meets the eye."

The closest I came to getting a glimpse of McDowell was during an hour-long taped conversation we had on a spectacularly sunny afternoon at Comiskey Park in the dog days of August a few weeks before the White Sox clinched the division title. We had the obligatory daily journalism discussions about where he thought his contract negotiations would lead next winter, whether he wanted to stay in Chicago the rest of his career, could the Sox stay together long enough to establish a dynasty? But we also talked at length about Jack McDowell himself—about how he came to be Black Jack; how he seemed so morose in what should have been one of the happiest summers of his life.

"One of the reasons I wasn't having a whole lot of fun earlier in the year is I felt like I was under the magnifying glass a lot," McDowell said. "I felt I wasn't being given the benefit of the doubt very much. I don't care how many games I'm going to win. There's always something more you could do. I could have thrown 35 no-hitters. That's something I learned hard earlier this year: the higher I achieve, the more pressure there is to achieve. The more people are going to expect. "

That was disappointing. I had been out of the country a long time, but I knew one thing hadn't changed: the more you succeed in America, the more people demand from you. That is one of the things that helped make this country great. Success isn't easy. But it isn't supposed to be easy. And if you are capable of success, then you're probably capable of greater success. You would think someone as smart as Jack McDowell would have understood that long before he won 20 games in the majors.

The more we talked, the more it became apparent Black Jack was the product of years of frustration—some of it with the fans; much of with the White Sox front office, and most of it with the media.

"I think a lot of me of me has to do with media representations of the players and the game and individuals and expectations," McDowell confided. "I see how directly all that translates to people. People on the street read something in the paper and all of a sudden that's the label they have on a situation for the rest of time. That can be a little frustrating because there's nothing you can really do about that."

McDowell was absolutely right. The media often create unrealistic and inaccurate perceptions. People forget that reporters have bad days, too, just like everybody else. But one bad day, one factual mistake, or careless interpretation by a writer or broadcaster, can translate into years of misperception about a player. And there's nothing the player can really do about it.

Still, McDowell's "Black Jack" image was hardly the product of misperception or media bungling. It was real and cultivated. McDowell thought more and worried more about the game, and his place in it, than most players. And he didn't always like where his thoughts led him.

"You've got a whole generation of kids growing up now who care about what kinds of cars we drive, how much money we make—more so than what kind of glove I'm using, or what kind of spikes I'm using or how I wear my stirrups. Those were the kinds of things I was interested in when I was a kid looking at big league players," he said that afternoon as he gazed out over the green grass of Comiskey.

"But you know the weird thing about it. A lot of people use the money thing. They say, 'Well, if you weren't making that kind of money, you wouldn't be the way you are.' I kind of think the money thing is just thrown into the equation too much. It's kind of like a catch-all for all the problems. You know: 'Players make too much money, that's why the game's in trouble. Players make so much money, that's why they should be perfect.' But everyone thought players should be perfect before we were making all this money. In baseball of old, you were supposed to be perfect. You were the hero. You were the great guy. You could do no wrong. It's the whole thing of the kid saying: 'Say it ain't so, Joe.' The kid was asking: 'How could this happen? Some guy we respected and thought should be perfect and now we find out he wasn't.' That's always been there. It was there before all the money. And it's still there."

By the time that enjoyable conversation was winding down, I realized McDowell was like so many highly successful people in America. He was two people. And he often had trouble deciding which one.

"Yeah, definitely, I think there's definitely two personalities," he admitted. "I became more aware of that when I started dating my wife. I'd come up to her after the game and she would say: 'Are you the baseball person now or are you not?' She was kind of half joking, but kind of not joking. She'd say: 'Are you still intense? Can we talk about other things yet?'"

Eventually, McDowell would. Wonder if George Bell ever did?

Chapter 7

War Paths, Base Paths, and Crossed Paths

There's nothing quite like driving into a war zone together in a silver Mercedes to cement a relationship. Maybe Mark Grace and I should have tried it.

My son and I did. Kelly was in college in the States in 1991, but had come to Warsaw to spend the summer. My wife, Lynne, was back in Texas on a brief trip near the end of June when the *Tribune* foreign desk called and told me to get to Yugoslavia. The neighboring republics of Slovenia and Croatia in the north had declared independence and the Yugoslav federal army was threatening to retaliate. Dozens of people already had been killed and scores wounded in scattered fighting that threatened to degenerate into all-out civil war. The preamble to Bosnia had begun.

"Kelly, get your passport. We're going to cover a war," I said, jokingly. I could have left Kelly behind in Warsaw until Lynne returned, but I didn't really think there was any serious danger. I'd been going in and out of Yugoslavia for more than a decade. I knew the blood-thirsty history of the Balkans and understood Yugoslavia was a strained hybrid that was destined to unravel—probably bloodily. But I doubted the worst was at hand yet and figured it wouldn't hurt Kelly to get an up-close look at the real world. It certainly would put a whole new perspective on life at Michigan State and finally give me a chance to show my questioning son how I made a living.

The first time I had second thoughts was when the four combat helicopters suddenly appeared in attack formation from behind a band of low hills on the horizon. We had just crossed into Yugoslavia for the second time in two and a half frantic days of traveling. Thursday morning we flew from Warsaw to Vienna and picked up the only rental car available without a reservation at Schwechat Airport—a giant, four-door silver Mercedes-Benz with an electric sun roof. As soon as we got the car, we headed for the Yugoslav border, 160 miles south-southwest. We felt victorious slipping across into Slovenia at a place called Sentilj, just north of Maribor, but the elation was fleeting. We were quickly turned back by a pair of no-nonsense soldiers.

Our goal was to reach Ljubljana, the picturesque capital of Slovenia, which the federal air force was threatening to bomb if the republic refused to back down on its independence proclamation. But the radio was reporting all border crossings from Austria into Slovenia were sealed and our experience at Sentilj seemed to confirm the reports. It was getting dark, so we turned around and headed back up the autobahn to Graz, Austria, where we got a hotel room for the night and I checked in with the foreign desk in Chicago. I dictated a brief story on what I'd seen at the border and told the foreign editor I planned to try an end run the next day. I'd drive across the southeastern tip of Austria into Hungary and then south to the Croatian border. We would try to cross into Yugoslavia that way and worry about making our way through Croatia to Slovenia once we were inside. Friday was lost trying to execute that plan. We were stuck in a two-mile-long line of cars at the Austro-Hungarian border for four hours. Then, after driving south in the fading afternoon light, our first attempt to pass through the Croatian border was rebuffed. We ended up backtracking yet again and spending another night in a typically severe Stalinesque hotel in Szombathely, Hungary.

At dawn Saturday, we were back on the road, headed for yet another border crossing. This time, we finally succeeded. We left the town of Letenye, Hungary, and crossed into Croatian territory 67 miles northeast of the capital Zagreb. But just inside the border, we spotted another roadblock. I was determined not to be turned back again, so I cut off the main highway to bypass the checkpoint. The main highway, E-71, was only two narrow lanes at that point. The back road we turned onto was nothing more than a dirt path barely wide enough for the Mercedes. But it was smooth enough and we were making good time traveling through some spectacular scenery. Then Kelly spotted the green and brown camouflaged helicopters off to our right at about two o'clock.

"Dad, look! What's that?"

"Holy, shit," I said, thinking they couldn't be after us, but frantically trying to figure out what to do. The road was lined with deep ditches. There was no way to turn off and nowhere to go if we could. We were in the middle of gently rolling green countryside. The nearest cover was behind the low bank of hills on the near horizon. But that's exactly where the helicopters were coming from.

"Roll down all the windows, now! And get down on the floor!" I shouted to Kelly, who complied a lot quicker than most teenagers normally do to parental instructions.

Don't ask me why I told him to roll down the windows. I remember thinking something about how dangerous all the shattered glass would be if the windows were shot out. As if that were going to be our biggest problem. The Soviet-built helicopters bearing down on us were carrying 12.7-mm machine guns and 57-mm rockets. Not even a Mercedes could survive that kind of fire power. I did, however, take the precaution of closing the electric sun roof. It was metal and gave the illusion we had that much more protection. But in my rush to close the sun roof, I forgot about the shortwave radio we'd been using to tune into newscasts about the situation in Yugoslavia from the BBC, the British Broadcasting Corporation, which every English-speaking foreign correspondent in the world relies upon to stay in touch with reality when they're in the field. I zipped the sun roof shut so fast that I snapped off the antenna and sent the pocket-sized shortwave radio flying in a blur just past my right temple and nearly out the open driver-side window.

About the time Kelly was hitting the floor and I was dodging the kamikaze radio, the four helicopters roared past some 50 yards behind us. The rapid *thup-thup-thup-thup* of the engines and rotors alone was enough to scare us to death. If I had been anything less than absolutely terrified, I surely would have jerked the steering wheel. We'd have run off the road into a ditch and probably ended up in a hospital. But I was so frightened, I simply couldn't move. My right foot remained mashed on the accelerator and my arms were rigid with fear, both elbows locked and steering straight ahead. We must have been doing 120 miles an hour or close enough to it because the helicopters disappeared in an instant. The only casualties we suffered in the air strike were a broken radio antenna and a lovely Mercedes filled with dirt because some idiot had rolled down all the windows.

Kelly and I were giddy with laughter for an hour. Adrenaline is a cheap high. He kept riding me mercilessly about my idiotically macho command to: "Roll down the windows, now!" And I kept joking about how quickly he hit the floor. But the next time we heard a newscast, we both suddenly felt a lot less like giggling. The helicopters that passed over us had strafed the border checkpoint we'd just crossed. We never found out, officially, if anyone was killed. All the radio reports said was there had been several casualties and the border was closed again.

The rest of that day was more of the same—moments of bizarre, heart-thumping scares followed by giddy laughter and relief. Most of the lows were prompted by absurd mistakes on my part. We managed to slip around that first roadblock, bypass Zagreb, and link up with Highway 1, which should have taken us straight into Ljubljana. But federal troops had sealed off long stretches of the highway. We were constantly detouring onto tiny back roads hardly bigger than some hiking trails in the United States that were still being used by horses and hay wagons here in Yugoslavia.

Once, we were zipping down empty Highway 1 when we saw an army checkpoint. I slowed to a crawl, prepared to stop, but the two soldiers on the side of the road weren't bothering to get up. They kept chatting amiably with each other, ignoring us. I figured—wrongly it turned out—they weren't interested, so I started picking up speed again. I was just about to mash the accelerator to get back to cruising speed when I glanced in the rear-view mirror and saw both soldiers running onto the highway behind us, looking extremely agitated. I slammed on the brakes just as one of the two was beginning to raise his rifle to the firing position. They weren't real pleased with me when I slowly backed up to the checkpoint, my left hand raised high outside the window, and tried to explain my innocence. My blue American passport and trusty laminated press card finally calmed them down and they eventually let us go after checking the car thoroughly. Their job was to stop all vehicles to make sure no one was smuggling weapons into Ljubljana. And they had orders to shoot any blockade runners. I shudder to think how messy things might have been if I hadn't made one last check of my rear-view mirror. Glass would have been everywhere. You know you can't roll down the rear window of a Mercedes.

The last few miles into Ljubljana were the worst. We had to get off the highway and creep up and down a narrow, muddy, potted trail in our battle-tested Mercedes. It took us two and a half hours to go six miles at one point. But we finally rolled into Ljubljana around dusk and made our way to the Holiday Inn on Miklosiceva Street, which I knew, in advance, from my colleagues, was the main press hotel. There's always a main media hotel in any hot spot. It invariably has a telephone or two that works, a great bar, hot water, tiresome food, and takes credit cards. In short, it's the safest and sanest place to be.

As soon as we got into our room, I laid down the law to Kelly. The day's harrowing experiences had convinced me my broad-minded decision to usher my son into the real world had been, well ... pretty stupid. I was determined not to compound my folly.

"This is where you live until we get out of here," I said in my sternest, authoritarian voice. "You can go anywhere in the hotel, but under no circumstances are you to leave this hotel unless you're with me. I mean it, under no circumstances. You understand?"

Kelly assured me he understood. He had brought along several thick books and said he was content to read and sleep away the next few days. In fact, he got off to a quick start, alternately reading and sleeping the next few hours while I set up my computer, made a few phones calls, talked with several colleagues, and started cranking out a story for Sunday's *Chicago Tribune.* I was zoned out in a writing coma and Kelly was half-dozing on the twin bed across the room when the first big blast hit.

Kahhh-booooooooom!

I looked up to see Kelly, literally, elevating two feet above the bed with his legs flailing in the air going nowhere like a cartoon character. He eventually fell back to the mattress, tumbled onto the floor, leap-frogged the other twin bed in a single bound and was huddled in a corner next to the wall before the last "ooom" of the *Kahhh-booooooooom!* melted into the night.

Ah, the agility of youth.

"Jeeeee-zuhsss Christ, what was that?!" he screamed.

The whole scene was so hilarious, I couldn't even get up to find out what happened. We were both clearly all right. The hotel was fine. The only indication of trouble beyond the huge blast was the tinkling of broken glass falling to the street outside. I must have laughed for a minute with Kelly staring at me like I was a madman before I recovered enough to go to the window and investigate. It was nothing. A Yugolsav Air Force jet had swept in low and broken the sound barrier just above the Baroque spires of the old town center. The sonic boom broke a few windows and scared the daylights out of almost everyone without causing any real damage. It was a brilliant psychological ploy, a frightening reminder to all on the ground that next time the jets could be carrying bombs. I'd seen, heard, and felt the Israeli Air Force do the same thing in Beirut many times. And the first time you heard it, you thought surely the entire world must have blown up.

That sonic boom was like an exclamation point on the end of a memorable father-son outing. We heard sporadic gunfire in the distance later that evening while I was filing my story to Chicago. And the wails of ambulances cut through the darkness all night. But the sonic boom—and Kelly's understandable panicked reaction to it—was the real highlight.

The next day, I was up at dawn and scrambling for news. I repeated my admonition to Kelly to stay put in the hotel and told him I would be back when I could. That turned out to be about 14 hours later, around 8 P.M., when I stumbled into the lobby of the Holiday Inn with a notebook full of quotes and impressions. I still had to fashion it all into a story and was headed for the elevator to check on Kelly when I spotted him out of the corner of my eye sitting at the small half-moon-shaped lobby bar with Jim Clancy of CNN. Clancy was an old friend I'd worked with in Beirut. We were posted to Rome at the same time and Clancy and Kelly had a running competition going to see who could eat the most steamed dumplings at a little Chinese restaurant we liked in Trastevere. I was delighted to see Kelly had found him and that Clancy was kind enough to take time off his own hectic schedule to sit down and talk. They both had their backs to me and I was walking over

to thank Clancy and renew our friendship when I heard Kelly say
something, in an unfamiliar bass voice, about helicopter gunships. I
stopped where I was and listened for a few seconds until it was
Clancy's turn to speak. "Yeah, I remember when I was in Beirut with
your old man ..."

I couldn't believe what I was hearing. One day out in the real world
and here was my teenage son swapping war stories at the bar with the
CNN guy. Kelly was leaning forward, most of his weight resting on a
left elbow that was cocked jauntily next to a can of Coke. His right fist
rested nonchalantly on his thigh in a pose of macho confidence I found
incredible considering the image I still had of the gravity-defying dive
he'd made over the twin beds and into a neutral corner of our room only
hours before. I wanted to sneak up behind him and go: "*Kahhh-
boooooooom!*" just to see how high he'd jump. But I couldn't bring
myself to ruin the moment. Clancy seemed to be enjoying himself as
much as Kelly.

A week later, we were still in Ljubljana. Clancy and Kelly had run
out of war stories to tell. And Kelly had run out of books to read. He
was bugging me to take him to the only English-language movie playing in town: *Silence of the Lambs.* I didn't think a horror movie was the
perfect way to unwind under the circumstances and Kelly took the let-
down like a trooper. But it was clear he was starting to chafe under
house arrest and needed to break loose. Lynne was back in Warsaw by
then and it looked as if the story in Yugoslavia would drag on for a
while. So I prevailed on a friend with Voice of America who was leaving to drive Kelly back to Vienna. Most of the border checkpoints were
open again and it was much easier to get out than when we'd gotten in.
I felt pretty safe sending Kelly out with my VOA friend until I saw the
friend drive. He backed into a concrete post in the underground parking
garage as he was leaving. I wondered if the guy would have enough
sense to roll down the windows if he came across any helicopters on the
way out.

Slovenia was an exhilarating experience for Kelly and me. But it wasn't the brightest thing I ever did as a foreign correspondent. It was a mistake that, thankfully, worked out. But it just as easily could have turned into disaster.

That was one big difference on the baseball beat. I could make a lot of mistakes and none of them would turn into disaster. But they could cause a lot of problems. I remember Jack McDowell brooding in our talk in the Comiskey Park dugout about the failings of the media. He was right. Players can't do a thing about misperceptions or unrealistic expectations created by the media. And that is unfair. On the other hand, there is often little the media can do about it, either. Mistakes happen. It's easy to forget that reporters and writers have bad days, too. They can't afford too many or, like the players, they, too, will find themselves out of the big leagues—covering high school lacrosse or working the overnight radio desk in Fargo, North Dakota.

Two of the biggest mistakes I made on the baseball beat involved two of the biggest names I covered on the Cubs: Mark Grace and Ryne Sandberg. One was a mistake in judgment. One was a mistake in fact. I regretted them both, but only one distorted reality.

Halfway through my first season with the Cubs in 1992, I was amazed, as were many fans, at how the team seemed to lack focus. There really wasn't a team leader. The Cubs had Andre Dawson and Ryne Sandberg, unquestionably two of the greatest players in modern history. But Dawson and Sandberg were quiet men. Dawson believed in leading by example. Sandberg never asked to be a leader and didn't want to be one. I talked to Shawon Dunston once a few years later about the season and those two men and about the perceived lack of leadership—about how Dawson could get away with leading by example, but how everyone seemed to think Sandberg should have taken a more active role. Dunston idolized Dawson and played next to Sandberg longer than anyone. "Oh, yeah. Oh, yeah. No question," said Dunston. "But Ryno didn't have it in him. That's not his way."

The player everyone hoped, and expected, would step up as team leader was Mark Grace. By 1992, Grace was in his fifth year in the big leagues. He was emerging as a star in his own right. And he finally had enough seniority in the big leagues, and on the Cubs, to stand up as a leader without belittling anyone else.

Just after the All-Star break that season, I wrote a Sunday column that laid all that out in more detail and mentioned how it seemed Grace finally was stepping forward. I pointed to an incident just a week earlier when manager Jim Lefebvre was upset by a comment I'd made in the mid-season "report card" *Tribune* writers were asked to produce on their teams each year. I had generously given Lefebvre a C-grade on the report card. The team was, after all, 40-47 and eight and a half games out. Only two teams in the league had worse records and the Cubs' clubhouse wasn't exactly the merriest little go-round on the block. On Lefebvre's report card for the newspaper, I'd written: "An A for effort. Works as hard as any manager in the league and takes it harder than anyone when his team loses. But has a tendency to over-manage. Angered his pitching staff repeatedly early in the season by lifting starters who still felt strong ... his rah-rah style grates on some players. And he has an authority problem because most everyone in the clubhouse believes general manager Larry Himes calls the shots. May not have inherited the best team in the majors, but appears to have done little to make it better."

Lefebvre never said anything to me about the report card, but I found out later he'd gone to Grace to ask if the criticisms were true. Were the pitchers upset with him? Did his rah-rah style grate on the team? Was there an authority problem?

I used the fact that Lefebvre had sought out Grace as evidence of my belief Grace was emerging as a long-needed clubhouse leader. The column went on at length in glowing terms about Grace until three para-graphs from the end when I added a mild qualifier I thought was needed to stop things from looking like a press release written by Mark Grace's mother or agent. "Grace is hardly the Father Confessor of the Cubs. And, like everyone, he has his own detractors [including a coach who says he is 'nothing but a phony']. But Grace's friends far outnumber his enemies. He knows how his teammates feel and he is secure enough to tell a manager if he has a clubhouse problem or not. And Grace can do it without coming off as some kind of stool pigeon." I said it took a leader to do that and added it didn't hurt that the clubhouse leader also happened to be leading the team in hitting.

That anonymous parenthetical quote from the coach was the biggest mistake I made on the baseball beat. Not because what he said was wrong. On the contrary, Grace's reaction to the column led to a lot of rethinking and convinced me the coach was absolutely correct. But I violated some pretty basic guidelines of journalism when I used that quote and I'm still stunned and ashamed I did it. Where was my brain? Where were all my years of training? All I can say is, I had a bad day—a bad, bad day. One of those 0-for-4, with four strikeouts and a pair of errors kind of days. Oh, yeah, I missed a couple of signs, too.

The quote from the coach was accurate, both in words and substance. But I had no right to use it. First of all, it was anonymous. And an anonymous quote like that, in that situation, casts suspicion on five other coaches who may or may not have agreed with the sentiment. Secondly, I got the quote only because I was invited to a late-night dinner at a bar in New York with a half-dozen coaches, scouts, and team officials. It was a strictly social post-game gathering three weeks earlier at the original Runyon's, a great tavern walking distance from the team hotel. We were all off-duty. We were speaking freely as colleagues. What was said there should have stayed there or I shouldn't have agreed to be there in the first place.

Where was my brain?

I needed my brain a week later in Houston. I always seemed to be in trouble with somebody in Texas. The last trip into Houston was when Lefebvre cornered me in the hallway and started screaming about the story on running out of players and bungling a game against the Reds in May. This time Lefebvre and Mark Grace were waiting to corner me.

The team had been traveling for 10 days. And it seemed longer because the road trip started in Pittsburgh, the day after the All-Star break, with the surprise announcement from Greg Maddux that he was breaking off contract talks with the Cubs. From there, the team traveled to Cincinnati for three games and then on to Houston for an off-day before a weekend series in the Astrodome.

Because we were gone, few players had seen the Chicago papers in a while. Odd copies filtered into the visiting clubhouses on the road whenever someone from Chicago dropped in. And the traveling media relations representative always had photocopies of any stories about the team that were faxed daily from Chicago. But, for the most part, when the team was out of town, players forgot about what was being written back home. Unless someone brought something to their attention. Apparently, someone brought my Sunday column to Mark Grace's attention. He finally read it in Houston a week later. And when he did, he accepted all the laudatory words as his proper due, then fixated on 11 words near the bottom of the column: "*... including a coach who says he is 'nothing but a phony.'*"

Grace went ballistic. Lefebvre was even more incensed. Their righteous indignation fed off each other and within minutes a clubhouse filled with road-weary players and coaches was in turmoil.

I was upstairs in the press box blissfully unaware of the latest Texas tornado I had spawned. I had my head down banging away on the keyboard when I got a tip that trouble was brewing down below. "You better be careful," my guardian angel warned. "I don't know what you wrote, but they're waiting for you in the clubhouse. And they're mad."

I took a deep breath, walked into the locker room and went straight to Lefebvre's office. He was livid. He demanded to know which coach had said that about Grace. He said he had asked them all and they had all denied saying it. He accused me of making it up and threatened to keep me in a closed room with the entire staff until either I admitted I had fabricated the quote or one of the coaches confessed.

When I finally got the chance to speak, I assured Lefebvre the quote was accurate. And I told him it was perfectly understandable that all the coaches denied it. After I'd written the story, I'd realized what an incredible blunder I had made. I went to the coach and apologized. I told him if the issue ever came up, he could deny having said it with a clean conscious because as far as I was concerned, he never had. Those words were spoken in a social setting—not a professional situation—and I had no right to repeat them. So they were never said. I told Lefebvre there was no way in the world I would allow myself or the coaches to be put in a closed room and belittled by him. I admitted I had made a huge mistake for which I was sorry and that I was going to tell Mark Grace the same thing.

I did. I found Grace sitting on a stool in front of his locker stewing. He refused, at first, to talk with me. When he finally relented, I repeated all the things I'd just said to Lefebvre. Then I added: "Look, Mark, I'm really sorry. I made a terrible mistake. I wish I could take it back, but I can't. But I honestly believe you're making too much of this. It is just one line in a column that was incredibly flattering. I've written nothing but positive things about you since I came on the beat. At least this way it doesn't look like I'm fawning all over you. That's good for both of us."

Grace didn't see the logic of my argument. His point was that he considered all the coaches his friends and couldn't believe any one of them felt that way about him. He was hurt personally. He could live with a writer taking a shot at him, but his ego couldn't bear the thought that someone who really knew the game—someone inside the baseball fraternity—actually considered him a phony.

Baseball writers are required to be out of locker rooms 45 minutes before game time. The only time I ever saw the rule bent was that day as Grace and I sat stool-to-stool in the clubhouse going round and round over the same arguments. We were still jawing at each other when the national anthem was played. Finally, seconds before the first pitch, Yosh Kawano, the clubhouse manager, came and got Grace. We parted without reaching common ground. And we never found it.

For the next three and a half years, Grace was always professional in his dealings with me. He wasn't above sniping behind my back to my colleagues or other players. But he always talked to me civilly and answered every question when I needed him. And I believe I was just as professional in dealing with him. For my part, though, it was easy. Mark Grace was one of the best baseball players I covered. He was a Gold Glove defensive player, a .300 lifetime batter, and, in my opinion, the greatest clutch hitter in the National League in the 1990s. I frankly don't know if the statistics will back that up. There are so many different stats that can be interpreted so many ways. But I do know if I were managing, the last guy I would want to see come to the plate against my team with the game on the line would be Mark Grace. He wouldn't always beat you, but he almost always made something happen—and it was usually bad for the opposition.

Even if I had wanted to tear Mark Grace down as a player, it would have been tough. He was too good. And he was just as good at deflecting criticism of his few flaws. Grace is a woefully slow runner. Once when pitcher Jaime Navarro got thrown out at home, his excuse was: "I must have been carrying Mark Grace's piano on my back." Grace also has far too little power for a first baseman. But he makes up for his home run shortage by stroking more doubles than most players. Admittedly, some of those doubles should have been triples. But Grace is smart enough to know he looks better pulling into second standing up than he does sliding in and getting thrown out at third.

In 1995, Grace led the National League in doubles with 51 and became the first NL hitter since Pete Rose in 1978 to have more than 50 doubles in a season. Late in the year, as he was closing in on the magic number, I noticed several times that Grace held second when even he clearly could have made it to third. I was prepared to write a nasty note in my column about it but wanted to be fair and give Grace a chance to comment before I ripped him in print. I told him straight out what I thought. He smiled, put his foot up on the stool in front of his locker, and said: "Yep. You're right, Joe. I stretched a lot of triples into doubles this year."

What a great quote. Like I said, even if I wanted to rip Mark Grace, I couldn't. He was too good.

If Mark Grace was good, though, Sammy Sosa was great. Both as a player and a person. And he proved it to me when we had our own one-on-one showdown—where else? in Houston—midway through the 1994 season.

Like Grace, Sosa was upset about something I wrote. But instead of turning the clubhouse into turmoil, Sosa kept his feelings to himself until he found a way to talk about them rationally.

Unlike Grace, Sosa had several glaring flaws in his game, particularly early in his career. He didn't understand the concept of team play at first. His logic was simple and naïvely straightforward: "I try to do my best," he often told me. "If I do my best, I help the Cubs." But Sosa's concept of what was best was swinging for the fences every time, regardless of the situation. He had atrocious discipline at the plate, striking out 493 times in his first 553 games. His teammates thought he sometimes stole bases solely to pad personal statistics. Sosa's defense swung wildly from stupendous to downright stupid. And he was so overanxious with runners in scoring position that he was consistently one of the worst clutch hitters in the game.

But all of Sosa's early flaws were sins of aggression. He almost always hustled. He almost always worked hard. And he almost always listened when coaches and managers tried desperately to harness the amazing raw talent they saw in Sosa.

It is easy to forget that Samuel Peralta Sosa was just 20 years old when he made his major league debut with the Texas Rangers. He was a kid lost in a foreign land, filled with strange customs and a strange language he didn't speak and barely understood. Baseball was his only link to reality and that link was tenuous at best because reality rarely intrudes on Major League Baseball. Growing up is hard to do. It is infinitely more difficult in an alien world under a constant spotlight burdened with incredible pressure to perform amazing feats day in and day out.

Sosa made the adjustment far better than anyone had reason to expect. He never will rival Joey Sewell's record for discipline at the plate (a .312 lifetime average and only 114 strikeouts in 7,132 at bats), but Sosa learned to quit swinging quite so freely and take an occasional base on balls. He learned to take his defense seriously. And, he learned baseball was a team game. "Two, three years ago, I would try to prove something," he told me in a long, rambling, pleasant interview under the Arizona sun after a spring training workout in 1994. "I thought if I didn't get a hit, I wasn't doing my job. Now, I know the good hitters, they take a walk, too. The key is, no matter how good you are, if you don't have a ring on your finger when you retire, it's not the same. I want to see the Chicago Cubs win a world championship."

Before the 1994 season, Jerome Holtzman, the *Tribune*'s senior baseball columnist, wrote: "At [age] 25, [Sosa] is developing into a superstar ... I also have noticed that Sosa seems to have matured, as if he suddenly realizes his potential."

It was true, on every level. Sosa, like all of us, was still prone to the occasional personal lapse. He and several other players had too much to drink on the team plane early in the 1995 season and embarrassed themselves and the club with a flood of crude remarks and obnoxious behavior in front of the flight attendants. But Sosa was properly contrite the next day. He accepted responsibility for his behavior and he never repeated it. As Holtzman noted, Sosa had matured.

The clearest sign I got of that was on a Friday afternoon in the Galleria shopping mall in Houston when Sosa flagged me down. The Cubs stayed at the Westin Galleria for years. It was a decent hotel connected to one of the great shopping malls in the country. The players' wives and girlfriends used to love to make the Houston trip for the shopping. Players' kids loved it too, because the mall had an ice-skating rink. I loved it because it had an acceptable Mexican restaurant and a couple of good coffee bars. I could eat without ever stepping out of the air conditioning.

I was coming back from one of those restaurants, my attention constantly distracted by the seemingly endless parade of beautiful, elegantly dressed, long-legged Texas women, when I heard a loud *hisssss* and looked up to see Sammy Sosa waving at me from behind the wrought-iron bars that blocked off a Chinese restaurant in the middle of the mall. "*Hissss*, compadre. Come here a second."

For once, I didn't have to search the memory banks to figure out what I'd done. I knew Sosa had to be upset with a story I'd written for Wednesday's papers, two days earlier. The Cubs had lost, 6-5, to the Pittsburgh Pirates at Wrigley. Sosa drove in one run with a single to center in the fifth inning to cut Pittsburgh's lead to 5-4, then singled to left to keep another rally going with the Cubs down, 6-4, in the bottom of the seventh. But in the bottom of the ninth, after Kevin Roberson hit a pinch home run to bring the Cubs close at 6-5, Sosa came to the plate with runners on first and third and only one out. It was one of those magnificent weekday afternoons that make Wrigley Field so special. The temperature at game time was 83 degrees with the wind blowing out at 20 miles an hour, gusting to 30. Four home runs had already been hit that day and the crowd of 30,783 was standing, going crazy when Sosa came to the plate to face Alejandro Peña. All Sosa had to do was punch the ball somewhere for a single or loft a lazy flyball into the wind. Even a sacrifice fly would tie the game. It was time to prove he was a team player. Instead, Sosa did what he had done much of his early career. He swung from his heels at everything Peña threw up to the plate and struck out. It was a meaningless loss, dropping the already last-place Cubs to 31-42. But it was frustrating to see Sosa revert to such a mindless approach to the game just when he was showing signs of growing up. I vented my frustrations and those of many Cubs fans with a caustic story the next day that began simply: *"Let Sammy be Sammy."*

I wrote how general manager Larry Himes and his staff had adopted a curious hands-off policy toward Sosa all year—that their thinking was Sosa had such explosive, raw talent he was best left unbridled by any of the usual disciplines imposed on most major league hitters.

"Discipline doesn't suit Sosa's game. Try to rein him in and you risk losing the power and speed that occasionally flash like a bolt of lightening and break open a baseball game."

The story went on from there to admit there was a measure of merit to that thinking. Left alone the previous year, Sosa had exploded for 33 homers and 36 stolen bases. But I also mentioned the rap against Sosa, whispered by his teammates and those outside the Cubs' organization, that many of his statistics were selfish. That he would steal a base in a lopsided game to pad his numbers or that he would swing from his heels for a home run every time, regardless of the game situation. I cited Sosa's free-swinging, ninth-inning performance in the loss to the Pirates as a classic example.

"Hey, why you wanna write that stuff about me?" Sosa asked when I accepted his invitation and sat down opposite three massive, teeming dishes of Chinese food he'd ordered for himself for lunch.

"Because it's true, Sammy."

"I'm not trying to hurt nobody. I'm trying to do my best. Sammy always tries to do his best. I thought you were my friend. How come you write something like that about me?"

For the next 30 minutes, we had a surprisingly frank and enjoyable discussion—both of us trying to come to grips with the confusing concepts of team play, sports journalism, and perception versus reality. Sosa didn't agree with a lot I said about critical writing. I didn't buy into his still-evolving thoughts on winning baseball. But we both talked. And we both listened. And we both came away appreciating each other a little more.

From that day forward, I had newfound respect for Sosa. The players who managed to maintain a sense of perspective—who still saw themselves, the fans, and the writers as flawed, but struggling creatures—were few and far between. Sammy Sosa joined the short list that day he stopped me in the Houston Galleria and wanted to talk about our disagreements. I still went out of my way to keep from being friends with him. But I genuinely liked him. And, now that I'm off the beat, I'm an unabashed Sosa fan. He is a treasure to watch on the baseball field and a pleasure to know off it. Later in that 1994 season, Sosa quietly applied for U.S. citizenship. He started doing charity work for a Chicago children's hospital. He and his wife, Sonia, had their second child. And Sosa's English improved so much that he began to emerge as a loud, bilingual leader in the clubhouse—stepping up to the role Ryne Sandberg refused and Mark Grace never quite filled.

When all is said and done, Sosa could go down as one of the greatest players to wear a Cubs' uniform. He might even lead the Cubs to the promised land of another World Series. But as far as I'm concerned, he's already a winner. He came to a strange land with a strange language when he was still a kid. He was saddled with expectations few could ever hope to meet and was told to exceed them under an unrelenting spotlight. He stumbled along the way, but never for lack of trying.

Mark Grace turned hostile and unforgiving when I wrote something that angered him. Sammy Sosa wanted to sit down and talk. Ryne Sandberg did neither. He just faded away.

I was always a Ryne Sandberg fan. In my office I still have a white pin button with blue letters that reads: "Ryne Sandberg for rookie of the year '82." I was sitting down the third-base line at Wrigley Field the day Sandberg became a legend hitting back-to-back home runs in the ninth and tenth innings to help beat the St. Louis Cardinals and make a division championship suddenly seem real. And I was in the Wrigley Field

Stadium Club that sad and shocking morning almost exactly 10 years later when Sandberg announced he was retiring from the game—temporarily it turned out—because he had lost the will to compete.

That Monday, June 13, 1994, was an off-day for the Cubs. They were scheduled to open a West Coast swing in San Diego the next night. So I was able to cover Sandberg's retirement news conference, write the main story, get a good night's sleep, and fly to San Diego first thing Tuesday morning. But when I checked into the Sheraton Harbor Island the receptionist handed me an urgent message, which said to call the office.

"Joey, we're going to put out a special supplement on Sandberg," associate editor Ed Sherman said when I called. "We want you to have first crack at writing the main piece, but we've got to have it in three hours. If you want to do it—if you *can* do it—it's yours. If not, say so now because we're up against a deadline."

"No, I definitely want to do it. I'll have it for you in three hours."

I sat down at my computer overlooking a marble blue marina and started writing from the heart. The piece began:

"He had the surname of a poet, the soft hands of a surgeon, the mesmerizing looks of a model and the sweet swing of a natural.

"Ryne Sandberg had it all."

All of which was true, of course. But what struck me about Sandberg, and what I wanted to capture in that piece, was how he had taken the gifts of "a natural" and nurtured them with an incredible single-minded devotion; and how he had been genuinely awe-struck when all the hard work and talent exploded into riches and fame. Sandberg honestly never coveted the wealth and glory that came his way. He simply loved the game. And, because of that, it seemed to me he gave back far more than he ever took.

I included a brief description of the shock Sandberg created with his announcement and a modest litany of his accomplishments, then tried to dismiss the inevitable debate over whether he was or wasn't the greatest second baseman of all time. To me, that was irrelevant. As far as I was concerned, Ryne Sandberg's greatest accomplishment was that he never betrayed either the game he loved or the fans who worshipped him.

One unwelcome reality of big-time sports in the late 20th Century—

not only in the United States, but around the world—is that fans are forced to be understanding of the failings of their heroes. Sandberg never needed that understanding. He came into the game as the shy, wholesome boy next door. And he left it that way.

The theme of the piece, the line I was building to, was the old Bob Hope signature song: *"Thanks for the memories."*

"Sandberg's fame can't be measured in statistics. It lies in memories. Memories of Sandberg making a dazzling play in a swirl of dust behind second base. Memories of Sandberg stroking a single to right behind the runner, or turning an inside fastball and launching it onto Waveland.

"Think for a moment of the millions who share some happy memory of Sandberg—mental snapshots of friends and family taken with Sandberg in the background. And every one of them is confined to a baseball stadium somewhere across the country. The sun may be shining. The wind may be howling. But in every one, the real world is on hold and happiness reigns forever."

I have dozens of happy mental snapshots with Sandberg in the background. In one of them, Jimmy Buffett has just sung the national anthem and the Cubs are crushing the San Diego Padres in the first game of the 1984 playoffs. Sandberg is looking into the web of his glove. He is rubbing it lovingly and waiting for Rick Sutcliffe to throw a pitch to Tony Gwynn. In another, my son is hugging me as Sandberg rounds second, head down, after hitting his second game-tying home run in as many innings off the Cardinals.

Two things are common in every Sandberg snapshot: happiness reigns forever; and Ryno never speaks.

Sandberg's reticent ways are well known among Cubs fans. He always had a hard core of close friends—Doug Dascenzo, Dwight Smith, one or two writers, one or two coaches—whom he felt comfortable with. But around everyone else, he was painfully private. I knew that and respected it. I prefer a few select friends, myself, to courting universal amity. So I only bothered Sandberg when it was absolutely necessary. I thought I was doing him a favor. I thought he respected me for it. But Sandberg's excruciating silence indirectly led me to one of my biggest mistakes on the beat—a mistake I'm sorry to say caused Sandberg and his second wife unnecessary pain.

There had been rumors about Sandberg's first marriage for years before his surprise retirement in June 1994. And the rumors only deepened when he quit. Much of his retirement news conference was devoted to his relationship with his two children and his desire to spend more time with them. Sandberg told me in a one-on-one conversation after the news conference about how he had called together his daughter, Lindsey, and son, Justin, and broke the news to them the night before. "It was great. They were both really happy about it. They made me feel good, real good," Sandberg said.

It was clear to me after that brief, moving conversation, that Lindsey and Justin were the focus of Sandberg's marriage, not his wife, Cindy, who was the object of much snickering at the news conference for her dress and demeanor. Cindy Sandberg showed up wearing a tantalizingly short and skin-tight sun dress covered—check the pictures—with giant, phallic yellow corn cobs.

Three months after that news conference, I got a tip from someone in Arizona that Cindy Sandberg had filed for divorce on Monday, June 20, exactly one week after Sandberg's retirement. Until then, I had refused to write about Sandberg's personal life. No puff pieces about him sitting around the pool with his kids or going on camping trips. No idle speculation about the state of his marriage. As far I was concerned, Sandberg was a former Cub and my job was to write about the current Cubs. I didn't go chasing ex-players unless there was a compelling reason, and there rarely was a compelling reason.

But the fact that Cindy Sandberg filed for divorce precisely one week after she stood lovingly by her husband's side at a surprise news conference seemed pretty compelling. Sandberg had walked away from more than $15 million when he quit. Cindy Sandberg would have gotten much of that. One week after the money dried up, Cindy packed up.

At his news conference, Sandberg denied he was quitting because of marital problems. He said he was unhappy with his "mental approach" and performance. "I lost the edge it takes to play—the drive, the motivation, the killer instinct," he said that day. But a year and half later, he would come back to the Cubs and say he'd found the drive again.

Something clearly changed. And the first indication of it came when I got the tip about Cindy filing for divorce just seven days after Sandberg's retirement.

I spent two days on the phones and fax and had to hire a researcher in Arizona to get all the divorce papers from Maricopa County. They showed Cindy Sandberg had, indeed, filed for divorce on June 20, 1994, exactly one week after Sandberg's tear-filled news conference. The papers contended "the marriage of the parties is irretrievably broken and there is no reasonable prospect of reconciliation."

I tried for hours to reach Sandberg. The private number I had for the dream home he had built in Scottsdale, Arizona, had been changed since his retirement. I couldn't find a new one. Finally, I got through to Barry C. Dickerson, the attorney representing Sandberg in the divorce action. Dickerson refused to talk to me or give me Sandberg's number, but agreed to contact Sandberg on my behalf. A few hours later, Dickerson called back and said Sandberg had given him permission to speak with me. "Ryne says you're a good guy and I can talk to you, but he doesn't want to say anything himself," Dickerson told me.

All I got from Dickerson, on the record or off, were sanitized legal quotes that added little to the story. I really needed Sandberg. I wasn't interested in the ins and outs of the divorce proceedings. I wasn't fishing for titillating details. But I did have two concrete facts I thought might add up to a far bigger and more interesting story. I knew from my own conversation with Sandberg the day of his retirement that his two children, Lindsey and Justin, were the light of his life and his primary concern the day he quit baseball. And I knew now that Cindy Sandberg filed for divorce just one week after Sandberg quit. That latter of those two facts told me Ryne and Cindy almost certainly had been having marital problems for a while, which is what Sandberg probably was alluding to when he told the media one of the main reasons he was retiring was because he wasn't happy with his "mental approach."

Putting all the clues together, I got the distinct impression there was an important story here. I believed—and wanted to write—that Sandberg walked away from a Hall-of-Fame baseball career primarily because of custody concerns about his children. If Cindy Sandberg filed for divorce while Ryne was still playing baseball, she would have been in strong position to win custody of the children—at least for most of the year. Sandberg was on the road from late February to October. His children were in school in Arizona much of that time. Sandberg surely would be given liberal visitation rights. But if there was a bitter custody battle, Cindy would have the undisputed upper hand. And even if Cindy agreed to joint custody—as she did after Sandberg's sudden retirement—Sandberg still would have had problems seeing his children apart from their mother during the long baseball season.

If my theory was correct, it was a nice human interest story. A surprising number of major league baseball players are devoted fathers. But how many athletes would, or could, walk away from the kind of fame and fortune Sandberg was surrendering solely to make sure they might spend more time with their kids?

I tried bouncing my theory off Dickerson, hoping it would convince him to let me speak directly to Sandberg. Instead, all I got was a nice comment for the record in which Dickerson said of Sandberg: "He's an excellent father. (Ryne and Cindy) are both very committed to their children. I've been around a lot of sports people and he is one of the best fathers I have seen."

Stonewalled from speaking to Sandberg himself, I did the only other thing I could. I started calling people associated with the team who I knew were close to Sandberg and had stayed in touch with him since his retirement. Several said they thought my theory of the Faithful Father held water, but they couldn't really shed any light on it. I had already talked to the desk about writing a story that essentially insinuated what I thought when I got a call back from someone associated with the team who I knew had been in recent contact with Sandberg.

"Ryno and Cindy are getting back together," this person said. "I was just at their house. Cindy was there. She's moved back in. They're trying to work it out."

Those first-hand comments seemed to fit with some of the innocuous information I'd gotten from Dickerson, the attorney. He had said there had been no legal action on the divorce case since July 1. It was now mid-September. Dickerson went to great lengths to explain that, under Arizona law, a divorce suit becomes "inactive" six months after filing if nothing is done. Three months after that, if nothing further is done, the suit can be dismissed without prejudice to either side— meaning no divorce is granted; the case simply ends.

None of what I'd found out necessarily ruined my nice little tear-jerking story of fatherly love. But nothing backed it up, either. The only "hard" evidence I had was from Sandberg's friend, who assured me the couple was trying to get back together. So that's what I had to go with. My lede on a brief story in the *Chicago Tribune* of September 16, 1994, read: *"Former Cub Ryne Sandberg and his wife, Cindy, are trying to reconcile their marriage while a divorce suit remains pending, but dormant, in an Arizona court."*

After months of trying to stay away from writing about Sandberg's personal life, I'd blundered my way into doing a worthless story because I was looking for a better one. Ironically, I felt good about the piece. I thought Sandberg would appreciate the fact I'd gone to such lengths to seek out his friends and lawyer to get the real story that he and Cindy were trying to get back together without forcing him to come right out and say it. Coupled with the warm one-on-one chat we'd had the day of his retirement and the quiet, respectful relationship we'd had through the years, I was confident Sandberg would have a big smile and a hearty handshake waiting for me the next time we met on the base paths of life.

Imagine my shock, then, when I read an excerpt from Sandberg's biography, *Second to Home,* written by Barry Rozner. In the excerpt, Sandberg talked about how disappointed and angry he was at the Chicago media at times. One incident he singled out was when the media falsely reported he was trying to reconcile his marriage. That never happened, Sandberg said. And the story caused him serious personal problems. He didn't elaborate. And he graciously avoided naming the reporter in question. But it wasn't until I read that excerpt from the book that I pieced together what happened. Sandberg and Cindy really weren't reconciling. The source I'd gotten to was simply wrong—had simply been trying to put the best possible spin on the divorce story in hopes of making Sandberg happy. And the quotes from Dickerson, the attorney, only misled me because I, too, wanted to put the best possible light on the story for Sandberg. All Dickerson did was spell out the legal realities. He wasn't implying anything one way or the other about the marriage or the divorce. I'd gotten one bit of bad information, compounded it through my own unfounded inferences, and whipped it all into a story that a) wasn't very interesting or timely, b) was wrong, and c) caused Ryne Sandberg a lot of headaches. I didn't know it at the time, but it became clear later, that my unnecessary and uninformed story trumpeting the supposed cuddly reconciliation attempt was published just as Sandberg was getting his life back together with another woman, Margaret Koehnemann, who became his second wife in 1995.

Sandberg's passion for privacy in retirement was understandable. But even when he was the best player in baseball, a superstar, Sandberg always was more comfortable being a hermit than a hero.

"We didn't have no relationship. No relationship," says Shawon Dunston, who played shortstop alongside Sandberg for all or parts of 10 seasons before going to the San Francisco Giants in 1996, the year Sandberg made his comeback. The two were reunited in the twilight of their careers with the Cubs in 1997.

Dunston was one of my favorites, as a player and a person. He and Ozzie Guillen. Two great shortstops playing in the same city for more than a decade—two magnificent players who enjoyed the game, excelled at it, got rich and famous from it and usually kept it in perspective. The ultimate compliment a writer, a scout, or anyone in the game of baseball can give a player is to say simply: "I'd pay to the see that guy." I'd pay to see Ozzie Guillen play any day, anywhere. Nobody has more fun in a major league uniform than Guillen. Dunston doesn't quite have Guillen's unbridled Latin flair on the field. But in the clubhouse, Dunston could often hold his own even with Guillen, the undisputed master of mirth.

After Dunston signed with San Francisco and thought his days with the Cubs were over, I sat down with him in the home dugout of one of the most beautiful ballparks in America, tiny Scottsdale Stadium, spring training home of the Giants. We talked for more than an hour with the tape recorder running and covered everything from Dunston's own image with the fans to his relationships with Ryne Sandberg, Mark Grace, and the Cubs. Dunston doesn't smoke, doesn't drink, and idolizes his father and his own children. He has a loud mouth and a Brooklyn temper, both of which he uses to shield a soft heart. We talked about all of that. But what struck me most in our conversation were his candid confessions about Sandberg.

"Ryno's good. Ryno was the best player on that team. He could hit, run throw, field, hit with power. He had range. He just didn't dive. That's the only thing he didn't do. That was the only flaw in his game that he had. Oh, yeah, another flaw was he didn't talk much. But he was the best player. ... I really like him. I wouldn't tell him that. I wouldn't want him to know it, but I really like him."

Dunston paused and I said simply: "Why is that?"

"I wouldn't want him to know. But I really respect him."

"Did you guys have a bad relationship?

"No. We didn't have no relationship. No relationship. I knew what kind of player he was. He knows what kind of player I was. I was wild. He was calm, under control. He taught me a lot about being under control. He goes 4-for-4, he won't say a word. He goes 0-for-4 he won't say a word. I respect that."

Dunston started rambling, as was his wont. He tended to take a shotgun approach to conversation. Blast away with a big wad of birdshot and maybe you'll hit something. Don't waste time trying to hit a target with one tiny bullet.

In the next five minutes, Dunston talked about two errors Sandberg made against the Cardinals back in some forgotten season. He talked about the media, television commercials, longevity among shortstops and second basemen, and half a dozen other things. Then he came back to his relationship with Sandberg.

"I mean, I respect him. I wouldn't tell him I like him. I still won't tell him today. Me and Robby Thompson are closer [after one month of spring training] than me and Ryno ... [But] if Ryno makes the Hall of Fame, I was his shortstop for eight years. I was his shortstop for eight years. Not Larry Bowa. Not Rey Sanchez. It was Asshole Dunston. That's my nickname: Asshole Dunston.

"Ryno's personal and I respect him. I mean, he was having problems with his family and you wouldn't know. I mean, I couldn't play if that was me. He's a good guy. I would not tell him because everybody kisses his ass and I will not kiss his ass. I will respect him. And I'm very happy that I played with him because he was the best player in baseball for three years that I was there. Then he lost it a little bit, but in 1990 he came back to be the best player. He never, ever complained. I knew Ryno was hurt some days. There was days when he was hurt. But when he did take a day off, he looked stupid on the bench. He looked like he didn't even belong there."

I asked Dunston again, as I had several times before, whether he bought in to the commonly held perception that the Cubs could have been a better team if Sandberg—the superstar on the field—had been more of a leader in the clubhouse.

"Oh, yeah, Oh, yeah." And then Dunston was firing the other barrel, going back to his relationship with Sandberg. "He won't open up to me. But he called me [when I left the Cubs], which I thought was very nice. But it hurt. I didn't want him to call me. After the Cubs let me go, he called me three weeks later. I said, 'Who's this?' He said: 'Ryne.' I don't know him by Ryne. I know him by Ryno. And he goes, 'This is Ryne. I was just calling to see how ya doin? You know, man, we're gonna miss you and I wish you the best of luck.'

"I got mad. After I hung up, I was upset. I didn't want him to call me. When he opened up to me, I went: 'Oh, I wish he'd a just left me alone.' … Ryno don't think I like him and I won't tell him. Keep it that way."

Dunston, in his prime, was like Sosa in the early years he was emerging as a superstar. Both were overshadowed by cherub-cheeked white players. In both cases, the players who stole the hearts of most Cubs fans were Ryne Sandberg and Mark Grace. Dunston and Sosa both took it in stride and won more than their share of adulation. But Dunston admits it bothered him a little.

"We were playing against Ramon Martinez in 1991," Dunston said in a typical meandering attempt at illustration. "I hit a home run off Martinez and I think we beat 'em, 2-1. Frank [Castillo] beat 'em. [Some time during the game] there was a pop up that was Ryno's ball and he didn't get it. Grace had to go over and catch it and Gracie got mad. After the game, Gracie gets Ryno in the showers and yells: 'Why don't you catch a fucking pop up once in a while instead of leaving them all to me and Shawon?'

"They was ready to duke it out. I'm like: 'Damn, look at these two. If they kick each others' ass and they go down, then I'll be The Franchise.' I'm going, like: 'Go get him, Gracie. Yeah, beat the shit out of each other. I wanna be The Franchise.' Then they both look at me and told me: 'Shut the fuck up.' I go: 'Whoah, when you start cursing, Ryno? When you start being so ...' Then I see he had this strict look. He was serious. I shut up. Grace told me to shut up. I shut up and just looked. I said: 'Wow. I was trying to make a joke.' But they were serious.

"There was this competitiveness. I like that. That made me feel good that Ryno did that. I mean, Grace didn't surprise me. But, Ryno. He shudda done that a lot more. We wouldn't a said a word. We wouldn't a said one word. I like that, that was one time he stood up. That's a true story."

It's nice to know sometimes even the silent lambs go on the war path.

Chapter 8

Tribulations

The subject of *Oktoberfest* came up. We brought it up. My wife and I were thinking of driving to Munich from Vienna and wanted the advice of Ferry Wimmer, a friend who was director of sales for United Press International in Austria. If central casting called over for a character to play a distinguished Austrian gentleman, Ferry would be the model all applicants would be measured against. He had just enough girth to attest to a generous income, but not quite enough to be dubbed portly. Pleasingly plump would be the best description. He had that healthy, bizarre burnt-orange tan unique to Alpine dwellers. And, though much of his hair was gone, what he had left was brilliant silver, carefully coifed, and thoroughly distinguished. Ferry spoke impeccably, dressed impeccably, and behaved impeccably. He actually wore—even preferred—those green-trimmed gray suits and coarse *loden* hats festooned with boar feathers that most Americans only see in tourist posters or re-runs of *The Sound of Music*. As he said proudly to me one day: "Yah, with these clothes, you don't need a passport."

Ferry was an Austrian's Austrian. And proud of it. He was quick to volunteer, as many older Austrian men will, that he had been conscripted against his military and moral wishes into Hitler's armed forces during World War II. But Ferry would add, with a twinkle in his eye, that he had the presence of mind to get captured so he could spend most of the war practicing his English and putting out the newspaper at a POW camp in Scotland.

Maybe it was compensation for the hardships of youth, or maybe it was a contentment born of his wife's scrumptious baking skills, but Ferry always preferred a laugh to a frown. In fact, when I think of him now, the only time I remember even a hint of a scowl on his face was when we asked him about *Oktoberfest*. His smile melted away. His eyes narrowed. And he was silent for half a dozen heart beats before he finally broke into a slow staccato imitation of Sgt. Schultz, the prison guard from the old "Hogan's Heroes" television series:

"There is nuthh-thinkk quite as frightening as a hahppp-pee German."

For an awkward few seconds, we didn't know what to say or do. Then Ferry's familiar twinkle returned and he gave a silly giggle that told us it was O.K. to laugh. It was a joke. There clearly was a hint of truth to the line in Ferry's mind, but it was a joke.

Lynne and I went to *Oktoberfest* and whispered Ferry's words time and again as we watched drunken Bavarians quaff two-liter steins of beer that we couldn't lift off the table. From that day on, every time we saw a group of beer-guzzling German tourists anywhere in the world, we would look at each other and mouth the first six words of the gospel according to Ferry: "There is nuthh-thinkk quite as frightening ..."

The happy Germans held the gold medal until I came home and started working the baseball beat. Then I discovered the frightening, petty world of big-time "sports journalism." There are few things quite as frightening as a bunch of major league baseball writers feuding amongst themselves or an ambitious sports editor manipulating news coverage for personal gain. We're not talking plague, pestilence, or poverty here. But we are talking Politics with a capital 'P.'

The question I was asked most frequently by knowledgeable fans, fellow journalists, and insightful friends was whether the *Tribune* ever interfered with my coverage of the Cubs—since Tribune Co. owned both the team and the newspaper. For most of my tenure, I honestly could say no. But not always.

On a day-to-day basis, the fact that my bosses owned the franchise rarely had any impact. The only time I can remember a club official even acknowledging the fact we worked for the same company was when Cubs manager Jim Lefebvre boasted that he had gone "to the highest levels of the *Tribune*" to get me fired. That was an aberration spawned by Lefebvre's quick temper and naïveté. Aside from that, the issue never came up. The team's public relations representatives certainly treated me the same as other beat writers. The front office never did me any particular favors. And the players—those who even bothered to read—could care less who signed my paycheck.

Within the *Tribune*, particularly at the senior levels, there was deep and constant concern about the perception of fairness. Those concerns often worked to my advantage, allowing me to rip the Cubs unmercifully when they deserved it—which was almost always—and rarely requiring me to do some puff feature that an underworked assignment editor dreamed up. But I ran into a major problem in the fall of 1994 when the long-overdue ax finally fell on Larry Himes. He was relieved of his general manager duties on October 4, almost one month after Tribune Co. lured Andy MacPhail away as general manager of the Minnesota Twins to become president and chief executive officer of the Cubs. The ouster of Himes was expected. The hiring of MacPhail wasn't—at least if you subscribed to the *Chicago Tribune*. The *Trib* was the last of the sports section paper in Chicago to report the most-important personnel decision its parent company would make all year; the only personnel decision most readers of the sports section cared about.

It should have been the other way around. The *Tribune* should have broken the story that Andy MacPhail was being brought in to sweep up the ashes of a burned-out franchise. But corporate politics, personal ambition, and naked conflict of interest stopped it from happening.

When it became clear the Major League Baseball strike was going to be a prolonged affair, the *Tribune* decided to send me off to write features on some of the prospects the Cubs and White Sox had working their way up through their minor-league systems. The minors, of course, were still playing. And the *Tribune's* senior baseball writer, Jerome Holtzman, was covering the ins and outs of the major league strike for the paper. I jumped at the chance to ignore a maddening labor dispute and go back to watching baseball—real baseball in beautiful little band-box parks. I flew to Nashville, Tennessee, where the White Sox had their Triple-A farm club at the time and spent a few days watching them before getting in a rental car and going across the state to catch the Cubs' Double-A Orlando affiliate for a series against Toronto's Class AA farm team, the Knoxville Smokies. From there, I drove down to Alabama to watch an overmatched outfielder named Michael Jordan play out the waning days of a puzzling self-imposed suspension from basketball with the Birmingham Barons, Class AA affiliates of the White Sox.

That trip, and another a few months later to watch winter ball in Puerto Rico, kept the beauty of baseball alive for me during the Dark Ages when greed and insanity ruled the game. I wished every baseball fan could have been in the car with me driving from Nashville to Knoxville or from Ponce to Mayaguez. The strike could have gone on forever if we'd have all had real baseball to watch.

The junket to the minors wasn't all scam, though. I had to keep working. Besides the feature stories, I had to make sure I didn't get beat on anything important the Cubs might be doing during the strike. Himes was on the hot seat and everybody knew something would happen eventually.

I was in Chicago, getting ready to leave for the swing through the minors in mid-August, when I made a routine call to one of my sources, who tipped me the Cubs were hot after Andy MacPhail. "He's the guy they want. Nobody else," said the voice that had never led me astray. "You can write it. This one is solid."

Naturally, I tried to get more details—other people I could call to confirm the tip; when it would happen; who knew; how my source knew? "Sorry, Joe. I can't tell you anything else. The lid is on tight. But I'm telling ya, you can go with this. It's 100 percent right."

During the next few days, I made scores of phone calls. I had to be careful who I called and what I said for fear of leaking a good tip myself. A few discreet fishing expeditions among media contacts in Minnesota convinced me they had no idea anything was up. Similar guarded conversations with other writers around the country and with a half dozen executives in various franchises produced nothing more than mundane gossip. The one person I had to get to was James C. Dowdle, a senior Tribune Co. honcho whose duties as executive vice president of media operations had been quietly expanded in July to include responsibility for cleaning up the sorry mess of the Cubs. But Dowdle was having nothing to do with me. I couldn't even get him to come to the phone to tell me he wouldn't talk.

I called Dowdle's office every day for a week. At first, I left polite messages with the Keeper of the Castle who answered his phone. She was pleasant enough and promised to pass on my requests to take "about two minutes of Mr. Dowdle's time on a personal issue" regarding the Cubs. What I wanted was for Dowdle to confirm or deny on deep background what I already knew was true. At the very least, I merely wanted Dowdle to give me a knowing silence.

As the week wore on, it became apparent this Tribune Co. vice president wasn't merely busy, he was busy avoiding the *Tribune*. I grew more and more frustrated. And my conversations with Kremlin Katie—as I privately dubbed his unyielding assistant—grew less and less pleasant. By the second week of phone calls, we had degenerated to daily shouting matches and I still wasn't getting any closer to having the Great and Powerful Dowdle step out from behind his curtain.

As usual, when I thought I might be on to a good story, I made a point of talking it over with Ed Sherman, an associate sports editor, who provided one of the few refreshingly sane links between the weird world of baseball and the equally bizarre *commune d'Tribune*. I told Ed I was sure the MacPhail tip was accurate and was confident we were the only ones in the media who knew. I told him I thought we had a few days, at least, to try to get another source and I'd keep him posted. Sherman was one of the best and brightest sports reporters in the country for years and had only recently moved into editing. His reporting instincts flared and he wanted to get the story as quickly as possible. So did I. But I was running up against stone walls. And the thickest and highest of them were right there in Tribune Tower.

Sherman and I talked daily about the story. I knew it was true and Sherman believed me. But he, understandably, wanted additional attribution I was simply unable to provide. In my frustration, and fearing the tip surely must leak somewhere else soon, I drafted a carefully worded story I hoped Sherman could shepherd into print. I detailed my difficulties with Dowdle and confided to Ed the name of my source. It was someone Sherman knew to be both reliable and privy to such a well-guarded secret. Sherman agreed to look the story over and try to get it into the paper. But it had to go through Margaret Holt, the associate managing editor for sports. And Holt turned out to be better at stonewalling than Kremlin Katie.

Margaret Holt was built like a 5-foot-6 bowling ball and rolled through the sports department like one. She was only around a short while, but she cut quite a swath. One of the first things she did after being hired from the business desk of a Florida newspaper to head the sports department at the *Tribune* was to announce her "goal in life." She was determined, she publicly told several people, to become publisher of the *Chicago Tribune*. Not managing editor. Not editor. But publisher. Margaret Holt was barely in the front door and she was already scoping out the private elevator to the 24th floor. Not exactly the best way to win over a staff that was already dubious about her sports background. She had played collegiate golf, we were told. She also was a short-fielder for the *Arlington Heights Daily Herald* slow-pitch softball team when she worked at the suburban Chicago paper before going off to Florida. At a season-ending party, the players jokingly bandied about songs they thought summed up each other's personalities. Sort of lyrical nicknames. Holt wasn't at all pleased when she heard the one her teammates picked for her. The chorus went: *"Lord, it's hard to be humble, when you're perfect in every way."*

Considering her extensive sports background, Margaret Holt had as many strikes against her with the staff as I had when I came home from Warsaw to take over the Cubs' beat. I empathized with her. We were both outsiders to the good-ole-boy (and good-ole-gal) sports department. We were both determined to operate in, without being co-opted by, a strange clannish world.

It never occurred to me when I wrote the first draft of the Andy MacPhail story and passed it on to Ed Sherman that I might be threatening Margaret Holt's career ambitions. But I found out soon enough. Sherman called me back to say Holt had put the *kibosh* on the story. I wasn't surprised until I heard the reason. Sherman told me Holt didn't want to offend Stanton Cook, chairman of the board of the Cubs. If my story was correct, Cook clearly was going to be ousted. The only way MacPhail would leave the Minnesota Twins, where he had enjoyed great success and been treated with both class and affection by owner Carl Pohlad, was if the Cubs made him an offer he couldn't refuse. And the only offer he couldn't refuse was to be made supreme commander of the Cubs, which would mean the demise of Stanton R. Cook.

When Sherman told me the reason the story wouldn't run, I was flabbergasted. I couldn't believe until I heard it directly from Holt. "We can't run this unless someone goes on the record and says what it means for Mr. Cook," she said.

I screamed and hollered but got nowhere. I assured Holt my source was unimpeachable and had been unfailingly accurate through several years of tips and confidences. Stanton Cook wasn't the story. He was part of it—a big part of it. But he was merely the flip side of the real story, which was that Tribune Co. was finally getting around to dealing with the mess of the Cubs and we knew the guy who was going to get the shovel and broom.

The more we argued, the more Holt made it clear—in my mind anyway—that her priority was to protect "Mr. Cook" from being embarrassed. And the only reason that made any sense was if one of her priorities was protecting her grandiose career goals. It would be difficult to become publisher of the *Chicago Tribune* if you played a role too often in embarrassing members of the Tribune Co. board. The fact that the board members might have brought down the embarrassment on themselves through a series of flawed decisions would hardly matter.

Only later did I remember this wasn't the first time Holt had stepped in to intervene on a story about upper management. In July, the *Tribune* ran a perfunctory announcement about new titles for different senior executives. Dowdle's name was mentioned in connection with the Cubs. My competitors on the beat, Barry Rozner of the *Arlington Heights Daily Herald* and Joe Goddard of the *Sun-Times*, were in a panic to find out what it all meant. So was I and I called the desk to see how we were handling the story. Holt said the press-release-of-a-story in the business section would suffice. She assured me that she knew, as an insider, the changes were merely cosmetic. There was no reason to bother with a more critical look at Dowdle's role with the Cubs. It was much ado about nothing.

We were on the road playing a night game and both my colleagues were in a frenzy, working the phones to uncover what they could about the Machiavellian politics of Tribune Co. while trying to keep up with the game in front of them and write a notes column, a game story, and the all-important "How They Scored." In an effort to ease the pressure, I volunteered Holt's declaration and assured them they wouldn't be scooped by the *Tribune* the next morning. I actually believed Holt. I thought I was doing my colleagues a favor, steering them in the right direction and saving them needless panic. Fortunately for them and their readers, they ignored my help and kept working the phones. It wasn't until I read Rozner's story the next day that I knew what was going on. Dowdle had effectively been dubbed King Cub in a Palace Coup.

Fortunately for my sanity, that earlier ominous incident slipped my mind as I was arguing the case for the MacPhail story. I was too stunned and frustrated by Holt's adamant refusal to run the story. Holt never asked me the name, title, credibility, or motive of my source. She never questioned whether the MacPhail part of the story was true; never asked for a second source to confirm his involvement or future role with the Cubs. Instead, she focused entirely on Cook and his feelings. I kept trying to argue that we needed to find a way to report about Andy MacPhail. I was willing to consider any avenue, including a commentary that might simply say the best way to fix the Cubs would be to hire somebody like Andy MacPhail. At least that way, we would be in print linking MacPhail's name with the Cubs and when the real story finally broke some of our readers and the rest of the media would remember where they first heard it.

It would, of course, have been better to publish a hard news story.

And I kept hammering away at the argument that it would be my reputation on the line. I wouldn't risk that reputation if I weren't supremely confident. But Margaret Holt dismissed my pleas and kept coming back to Cook. Then she would demand the impossible. She wanted one of the inner circle of Tribune Co. to go on record saying Stanton Cook was being bounced. Short of that, she didn't want Mr. Cook's name mentioned. And short of that, she wouldn't run the story. What Margaret Holt was asking was the equivalent of the *Washington Post* refusing to run some of its best Watergate stories until a member of Richard Nixon's inner circle at the White House went on record, by name and title, saying the president was a crook. I'm not comparing the events surrounding the hiring of a new chief executive for the Chicago Cubs with the impeachment of a president of the United States. But the likelihood a member of Tribune Co.'s inner sanctum would discuss—on the record—Cook's lynching was about the same as a member of Nixon's White House calling in Peter Jennings and going live with all the dirt about a massive, illegal cover-up.

The silver-haired Cook may have looked like everybody's favorite uncle, but he didn't get to the top of the corporate world by being cuddly and avuncular. He could be ruthlessly cut throat. And his fellow blue bloods weren't going to risk alienating him even if he was on his way out the door. Dowdle, who was coordinating Cook's ouster, certainly didn't want any advance publicity of the impending execution. The clique of insiders who knew what was going on was particularly small and guarded. Getting one source to leak the news was a major coup. Getting another, who would agree to be quoted by name about Cook, was impossible. I contacted Cook directly, cashing in a few chits with an old friend to get the private number of Cook's weekend cabin in Michigan. He was fire-and-ice in our brief talk. Surprised and clearly a little peeved at first that I had his number, Cook tried to adopt an air of politeness. But he quickly shed it to sputter increasingly angry machine-gun responses my every question. "I am not going to comment ... I really have no comment ... I have no comment to make on it at all ... I'm just not going to add any commentary. Good-bye."

Nearly two weeks after I submitted the article that was spiked, and three weeks after I first got what proved to be an accurate tip, Steve

Rosenbloom, then of *Chicago Sun-Times* and later to join the *Tribune*, "broke" the MacPhail story. I was in a grimy little airport hotel in Nashville polishing up a Sunday feature story on Brooks Kieschnick, a former No. 1 draft pick of the Cubs, when Sherman called.

"I've got some bad news," he said.

"Uh, oh," I said, my heart sinking and wondering what in the world this could be?

"You're not gonna be happy."

For God's sake, I wanted to scream. Did my dog get run over? Had the *Trib* abolished profit-sharing? Was the National League going to start using the designated hitter?

"What?!!!"

"The MacPhail thing is in Rosenbloom's column this morning."

Oh, that was all. For a while there, I thought it was something serious. I was secretly happy. Hey, I'd done my job. I knew it. Sherman knew it. Somebody had to get hold of the story sooner or later and Steve Rosenbloom was a better choice than most. Rosenbloom was a hard-working columnist, who often got overshadowed at his paper because he wasn't in the habit of writing rants. I was glad he got the story. I found out later Barry Rozner also mentioned MacPhail's name in print that same day. But I made note that neither Rozner nor Rosenbloom identified a source.

I suppose it could be argued that if I were a good enough reporter, I could have pinned down the story. But, in the process of chasing down a second, named source to confirm what I already knew, I was stonewalled by executives at my own company—the same company that owned both the team and the newspaper. Dowdle routinely answered calls from my competitors in the print and electronic media, but pointedly refused to talk to me even when I rounded up his unlisted home number. He finally gave his first comment to the *Tribune* on Saturday, September 3, days after he had gone on record with both the *Sun-Times* and *Daily Herald* and still refused to answer my calls. I only got a comment then because the story was all over Chicago and because I was lucky enough to catch Dowdle at home as he was heading out the door to watch his alma mater, Notre Dame, roll to a 42-15 win over Northwestern at Soldier Field.

The first quote I got from Dowdle that afternoon was about Cook and his status. The *Tribune* was already badly beaten on the MacPhail angle. Now I had to deal with Margaret Holt's nesting instincts. So I asked Dowdle about Cook. "It's been reported that we are looking for a president," Dowdle said, and we both knew it wasn't the *Trib* he was talking about. "That president would really have the power and at some time on down the road would also represent us in the league meetings. Not immediately, naturally, with Mr. Cook there. But down the line."

Margaret Holt got what she wanted. The first *Tribune* story on the search for a new Cubs' president started with eight paragraphs dedicated to Stanton Cook, an incumbent board member who didn't even have the title of president. It wasn't until the ninth paragraph that I was able to get down to the real news and write: "The leading candidate for the new position is Andy MacPhail, executive vice president and general manager of the Minnesota Twins." I deliberately didn't attribute that statement to any source. I just wrote it as fact. It sailed through unedited.

MacPhail finally was anointed one week later at a Saturday press conference in the Wrigley Field Stadium Club, where a great many significant chapters in Cubs' history begin and end. The club is reserved for season ticket holders during the season and is a delight for Cub fans to visit any time. From the Louisville Slugger bats that serve as handles on the doors to framed tickets from the 1908 World Series, everything in the place spurs a smile. Almost every memory I have of the place, though, is bad. The Stadium Club is where Greg Maddux came to say how happy he was to win his first Cy Young and how likely he was to be leaving Chicago. It was where Ryne Sandberg stunned everyone by confirming the wacky rumors one June morning that he was quitting baseball. It was where Larry Himes loved to hold court and where a dizzying parade of four presidents, five general managers, and 13 field managers promised pennants and produced penance in the first 14 years Tribune Co. owned the Cubs.

The coronation of MacPhail was one of the few happy memories I have of the Stadium Club. But I was still seething that Saturday morning when I spotted Dowdle lingering like a proud puppet master on the fringes of the crowd at the press conference. I waited until I could get him aside and let him know I was upset. I said I understood his delicate position—not wanting to give even a hint of favoritism to the *Tribune* correspondent on a highly competitive and sensitive story. But I felt he had bent over backward in the other direction. "I don't expect any favors, but I do expect a level playing field," I told Dowdle, using what for me was an out-of-character, politically correct cliché.

Two days later, Dowdle called and invited me to a breakfast meeting at the Tribune Co. Media Services headquarters in suburban Oak Brook, Illinois. Over coffee, he admitted his handling of the situation had been wrong and unfair. Dowdle told me he had made the same confession to Jack Fuller, publisher of the *Chicago Tribune*, and hoped we could put the unfortunate situation behind us. I respected Dowdle for that. I came to respect him more as I watched the impressive job he did helping resurrect the Cubs.

Still, the bottom line on the MacPhail story was that the *Tribune* had been beaten on news one of its reporters had for weeks because an ambitious editor was concerned with coddling her higher ups and because an overcautious executive deliberately put an employee of his own company at a disadvantage. It was a blatant conflict of interest and I never again felt comfortable when anyone asked me if the *Tribune* ever interfered with my coverage of the Cubs.

I never really felt comfortable about a lot of things on the baseball beat. One simple and trivial example was the use of quotes from players and managers.

When I came in for the obligatory "Go-Out-There-And-Knock-'Em-Dead" speech just before my first season, managing editor Dick Ciccone said something that was music to my ears. "I don't care if you ever use a single quote from a player in your game stories," Ciccone said. "You're the writer. Tell us what happened. We don't need to read another quote from some guy who says: 'I hit a hanging curveball' or 'Boy, I'm seeing the ball well.'"

Ciccone, like most journalists, was prone to sweeping generalizations. And, because he was the boss, reporters and editors treated his words as edicts from the emperor instead of merely helpful hints from an old hack. I knew Ciccone well enough to understand that if I started turning in game stories without any quotes from players he would be just as upset as most fans. But I definitely agreed with his point and made a sustained effort to minimize the use of inane quotes in my copy.

Pick up any baseball story and read the quotes. Really read them. Here are a couple in front of me right now:

"I like the guy," manager Terry Bevington said. "He's got good stuff and he hangs in there."

"I felt good. I had my pitches going," said John Smoltz.

"A lot can happen in this park, especially when the wind is blowing out like today," said Marlins manager Rene Lacheman.

And, no disrespect to Terry Collins, who is one of the best managers in baseball, but how about these scintillating words of wisdom from the Anaheim manager when he was working in Houston? "One thing you find out at this level is that what happened yesterday is over. You can't get it back. You can't change it. You just have to get ready for tomorrow."

Those quotes aren't from some carefully kept collection. They were chosen at random from the papers in front of me. If somebody really wanted to do a search of the most inane quotes in a season, they could easily come up with far worse. But the point is: Ciccone was right. And I agreed with him even before he spoke the words. Most baseball quotes are a waste of the everyone's time—the player who has to give them, the writer who has to take them down and put them in the paper, and the fans who have to read them. Quotes have become a crutch for weak writing in sports stories in the United States.

Barry Rozner of the *Arlington Heights Daily Herald* used to talk about this occasionally. He disagreed with me. He was younger and insisted that fans today want to hear what the players are thinking every day, after every game, and about every play. I know that's true to an extent. Just look at the proliferation of sports talk shows on radio. There's no limit to the appetite for inanities. I once asked Andy MacPhail what he thought about the explosion of sports talk shows. "I'll get myself in trouble for saying this, but I've never really listened to all-sports radio. I just can't lead myself to believe that is really your core group of fans. That is not really the group you are playing to."

I felt the same about readers who wanted pointless quotes merely because they came out of the mouths of player or managers. If the player or manager had something worthwhile to say, fine. Otherwise, put the space to better use. No hanging curveballs.

The problems with that, of course, are enormous. In the age of SportsCenter and the Internet, fans already know what happened in a game long before they open the newspaper. So conventional wisdom is they turn to the papers hoping to find something they haven't seen or heard already. Hence: give 'em quotes. Lots of quotes that are hastily stuffed into and around chunks of chronological play-by-play at deadline. But what does that really add? I was a baseball fan before I became a baseball writer. I'm still a baseball fan. I can go to a game, keep score, listen to the post-game show on the radio, come home, and watch the highlights on television, and still want to pick up the paper over coffee the next morning and read what happened and why—especially if its crafted into a nice narrative tale. I don't want to read a wire service story with the score in the lede and a quick breakdown of who had the most home runs or who gave up the fewest hits. I know the score. I know the stats. But I wouldn't mind reliving the story of the game.

Dick Ciccone only half jokingly told me in our rah-rah meeting that he wanted my stories to read like Ring Lardner. We both would have loved it if that were possible. But what Ciccone really was doing, in his typical way, was trying to make a point. He wanted good writing. He wanted game "stories," not game recitals. And certainly not game recitals stuffed with sawdust quotes.

Lardner was a sportswriter for the *South Bend* [Indiana] *Times* and the *Chicago Tribune* before becoming a novelist in his mid-'30s. By the time he died in 1933, he was considered one of the finest satirists in American literature. His son was a noted writer, too, who helped produce the script for the classic movie *M*A*S*H*. The senior Lardner loved baseball and used it as the backdrop for much of his best writing, including the book-turned-movie, *Alibi Ike*, where one of his characters writes: "Be home real soon, Mom, they're beginning to throw the curve."

Now, there's a quote worth printing. There is never a shortage of great quotes in baseball. But the enormous pressure of ever-looming deadlines and relentless competition from the ever-expanding broadcast media have led far too many baseball writers astray. They slam quotes into stories with the same unthinking reflex that players and managers spout them. And that sin of laziness is compounded by the constantly shrinking space most papers allocate for game stories. It is a Catch-22. The perception among editors, certainly at the *Tribune*, is that readers don't care about game stories. Readers already know what happened. They want something else. Nobody really knows what readers want, but the perception is they don't want to read what they already know. That perception combined with the constant battle for space made precious by newsprint costs convince gatekeepers at most newspapers to trim game stories. Then, faced with already shrinking space, too many writers waste more by running banal quotes. It is far easier to run something, anything, that Mark Grace mumbles in a locker room after a game than it is to work up a sweat painting a word-picture of something that happened—particularly if a deadline is looming or if it's Monday in mid-July and you're writing about the 48th loss of the season. So game stories become less creative. They become less read. Space is more easily slashed. And the downward spiral continues.

I found it all incredibly frightening and frustrating. But, then, maybe Terry Collins was right after all: "One thing you find out at this level is that what happened yesterday is over. You can't get it back. You can't change it. You just have to get ready for tomorrow."

Sawdust quotes are rarely a problem for foreign correspondents. If Lech Walesa mumbled something inane or uninformed, it may not have been unexpected, but it was news in itself because he was a world leader. He should know better. And it was a reflection on his abilities. If Albert Belle says something mindless and caustic, who expected anything else? Why waste ink?

Foreign correspondents, though, have the handicap of grappling with translations. Sometimes a pointless quote gets turned into something far better just because it goes through a linguistically challenged reporter or a woefully inept translator.

Lech Walesa won a richly deserved Nobel Peace Prize for leading the Solidarity movement, but he was a former electrician who often found himself out of his depth when he became president of Poland. During this interview with me at the Polish White House, Walesa admitted he spent 45 minutes a day playing ping pong and bragged he could whip U.S. President Bush at the game any time. "Also in boxing," he said. "I can face every president in boxing. In the case of other issues, I don't know."

Many foreign correspondents are like me: they rotate through a dizzying variety of assignments. No one expects even the brightest foreign correspondent to be able to master Putonghua, Tagalog, German, Italian, Cantonese, Visayan, Polish, Russian, Arabic, a half-dozen Slavic languages, and two or three score regional dialects—all of which I could have used in my tours abroad. There are, to be sure, some incredible linguists among the foreign correspondents' corps. One of my closest friends, Edward Gargan of the *New York Times*, could speak, read, and write classical Mandarin, was fluent in French and Italian, and, despite his protestations, was capable in Cantonese and Spanish. I, on the other hand, was a general practitioner muddling along in a ward filled with brain surgeons. I could order beer in 97 languages. I could say: "Don't shoot. I'm a journalist" in a half dozen. And it was always wise to learn to recognize the phrase "My friend will pay," because, invariably, some hack would stick you with an unwanted tab when all you thought he was doing was pointing to you with his thumb and telling the bartender you were a good guy.

My language skills were usually good enough to get a decent meal in most places. Usually. Once, when we first moved to Vienna, I was feeling so confident with my grade-school German—and was so enamored with the meat-and-gravy specialties featured prominently in every restaurant—that I boldly picked out a dish based on the few words I understood on the menu describing it. My wife was stunned, and proud, that my language skills had advanced so rapidly and I blushed appropriately at the well-deserved praise. Until our orders arrived. She got exactly what she wanted: a delicately breaded *Wienerschnitzel* with fresh lemons and mashed potatoes on the side. I got a single head of cauliflower about the size of a bowling ball smothered in melted cheese. Not exactly the blood sausage with brown gravy, melted cheese, and Hungarian dumplings I'd been salivating over in my mind. I did get the cheese right, though.

Several months later, my confidence had just begun to rebound and my German had improved enough that I was getting adventurous again. And, with a little homework, I was managing to avoid embarrassment until I walked into the supermarket across from the UPI office and catty-corner from the Vienna Opera House. I wanted a quick sandwich, but was determined to play it safe. I'd go with something nice and easy like a ham sandwich. I was addicted to the fresh ham on hard rolls that many Viennese gobbled down hungrily as mid-afternoon snacks. How hard could that be to order? I confidently told the smiling, round *Fräulein* behind the deli counter I'd like a: *"Schinkenrolle, bitte."* Pretty simple. *Schinken*: ham. *Rolle*: roll. *Bitte*, please. Hey, there's nothing to this German stuff. Imagine my surprise when the lovely *Fräulein* walked away and returned huffing and puffing with a humongous chunk of pig carcass slung over her shoulder. She wiped her brow and demanded to know how many kilograms she should slice off and wrap up. I raised my right index finger, furrowed my brow, and muttered that I had forgotten. I pretended I was going to find my wife to get the answer. Instead, I walked out the front door and never looked back. For the rest of my stay in Vienna, I used to walk four blocks to the next-nearest deli counter because I was too mortified to face my friendly and confused *Fräulein* again. Rick Hornik, then *Time* magazine's East European correspondent and later chief of correspondents for *Time*, howled when he heard the story and spent the better part of one enjoyable evening at the *Prater* in

Vienna patiently trying to explain the difference between *Schinkenrolle* and *Schinkenbrötchen*. Rick taught me that German stuff wasn't so easy after all.

I'm not sure, though, I went about polishing my German in the best of all manners. UPI picked up the tab for language lessons. But the company couldn't afford a private tutor so I went to a language school filled mostly with tourists and spouses of business executives who were in Austria for relatively short stays. Those kinds of schools rarely provide the language skills a correspondent needs. I should have known it wasn't going to be a particularly productive investment when one of the first phrases they taught us was: *"Wieviele Aale fasst Ihr Schweib-eschiff?,"* which, roughly translated, means: "How many eels does your Hovercraft hold?"

What goes around, comes around. Years later, my wife, who laughed so hard at the giant head of cauliflower I ordered in Vienna, took a linguistic tumble of her own in Italy. We lived on the Aventine, one of the seven hills of Rome, just past the Circus Maximus and down the slope from Santa Sabina, a magnificent Fifth Century church overlooking the slow-moving Tiber. It was a stunning location, one I will always associate with the sickly sweet smell of orange trees in bloom.

With our world-traveling Labrador, Havoc, packing up to leave the Philippines for Rome in December 1988.

But it was miles from the nearest supermarket. My son, Kelly, was a senior in high school then. He and our dog, Havoc, used to guzzle milk by the gallon and the only place to buy milk nearby was in a bar. The first week we moved into the neighborhood, my wife went into the bar in the middle of the afternoon and sidled past three leering old men sipping *grappa*, the jet-fuel derivative that Italians extol as a *digestívo*—an after-meal digestive aid. In her best newly acquired Italian, she politely asked for four milks. Or, at least, that's what she thought she requested. The howls of laughter and the old men slapping each others backs to stop from choking were the first clues she'd done something wrong. Instead of four milks, she'd asked the bartender to provide her four beds. When things quieted down, she straightened out the *faux pas* and got the four milks—along with a standing invitation to visit the boys in the bar any afternoon.

Fortunately, when it came to work overseas, I always had a translator—often two. And most of them were excellent. But even the best translators can struggle with the nuances of language. A perfect example was the transcript *Time* magazine published in 1996 of an interview between Madonna and the Hungarian newspaper *Blikk* during filming of the movie version of *Evita*. The "transcript" actually was a parody written by humorist Gary Trudeau. In it, Trudeau described a typical process in which the original interview questions were posed in Hungarian, translated to English for Madonna, then re-translated into Hungarian for *Blikk*. *USA Today* paid to have the *Blikk* version re-translated one more time back into English for its own amusing article, then Trudeau let his fertile imagination loose to produce a satire that was frighteningly real for anyone who ever has worked and writen with a language handicap.

Blikk: *Madonna, let's cut toward the hunt: are you a bold hussy-woman that feats on men who are tops?*

Madonna: *Yes, yes, this is certainly something that brings to the surface my longings. In America it is not considered to be mentally ill when a woman advances on her prey in a discotheque setting with hardy cocktails present. And there is a more normal attitude toward leather play-toys that also makes my day.*

Blikk: *Is this how you met Carlos, your love-servant who is reputed?*

Did you know he was heaven-sent right off the stick. Or were you dating many other people in your bed at the same time?

Madonna: *No, he was the only one I was dating in my bed then, so it is a scientific fact that the baby was made in my womb using him. But as regards these questions, enough! I am a woman and not a test-mouse! Carlos is an everyday person who is in the orbit of a star who is being muscle-trained by him, not a sex machine."*

The transcript went on like that for several more side-splitting questions. I read it all carefully quite a few times. As far as I could tell, *Blikk* never got around to asking Madonna how many eels her Hovercraft held.

Class isn't a word that leaps to mind when I think of baseball writers. Hard workers, yes. Dedicated, yes. Self-consumed, yes. But class? That was something too many baseball writers skipped in college.

One notable exception was Joe Durso of the *New York Times*. Durso was a beat writer for 27 years, covering the Yankees and Mets and every World Series game during that span. He wrote 13 books, including full-length biographies of Casey Stengel and John McGraw, a 50-year-history of Yankee Stadium and as-told-to books with Mickey Mantle, Whitey Ford, Tug McGraw, and Eleanor Gehrig.

Durso was a gentleman, a scholar, and a nice writer, who, quite rightly, was enshrined in the Baseball Hall of Fame in 1996. But he almost never made it. Durso nearly had his place in the Hall stolen from him by a small group of fellow writers, including one of his colleagues for more than two decades on the *New York Times*.

The most prestigious honor a baseball writer can win is the J.G. Taylor Spink Award, established in 1962 in the name of the former publisher of *The Sporting News*. Winners of the award are enshrined in the Baseball Hall of Fame in Cooperstown, New York. Among the recipients are Ring Lardner, Damon Runyon, Grantland Rice, Jerome Holtzman, Leonard Koppett, and John Derbinger, the Cal Ripken of baseball writers who covered the game for 37 years and wrote the lead story in the *New York Times* on 203 consecutive World Series games from 1929 to 1963.

The Baseball Writers' Association of America nominates its own members for the award annually through a committee made up of former Spink Award winners. The committee voted in the winter of 1994-95 to nominate Joe Durso for his outstanding career. Normally, such nominations are tantamount to election. They are routinely approved and Durso had no reason to expect otherwise. But shortly after he was nominated by the committee, Durso was challenged by six colleagues, including Murray Chass of the *New York Times*. Chass and Durso were baseball writers on the same paper for 22 of the 27 seasons Durso covered the sport. Despite the longevity, Chass clearly had no love lost for Durso.

I could understand that because I was in a similar position with Alan Solomon, my fellow baseball writer at the *Chicago Tribune*. But Solomon and I didn't have to work side-by-side for long because he gracelessly self-destructed. He was yanked off the baseball beat in the middle of the 1994 season when he lost a showdown with his boss, Margaret Holt, over one of many changes she made to the sports department. The particular incident involved Holt's decision to remove a television set that sat on the sports desk in the newsroom at night so copy editors could keep up with late-breaking events and scores and help the beat writers by rushing in crucial details on deadline. Holt thought the editors were spending too much time watching TV and ordered the set taken away. That wasn't a particularly productive decision on any level. But it only enflamed an ugly morale-killing rage that had been simmering for months because Holt was: a) a newcomer recruited from outside Mother Trib, b) not a dyed-in-the-wool, up-from-preps sportswriter, c) someone with new ideas, d) the boss, and e) a woman.

Removing the TV set had nothing to do with Solomon's job covering the White Sox. But he apparently thought it was a good time to show solidarity with his friends on the desk. He was in Pittsburgh covering the All-Star Game when he wired flowers to Holt with an accompanying note that said: put back the television, everybody is laughing at you.

Sending flowers and a condescending note to a female boss isn't a particularly bright move for a short, round, cigar-smoking, middle-aged sports hack. Solomon didn't recognize that immediately. But he got the message soon enough. Holt seethed for a day, telling everyone who would listen that she wanted to give Solomon a chance to apologize. She didn't want to be accused of making any rash decisions.

A day later, the White Sox came home for the first series after the All-Star break. Solomon was in his regular front-row seat in the New Comiskey press box when Margaret Holt showed up and sat one row behind him. Even if he didn't intend to apologize, which he clearly didn't, common courtesy called for Solomon to at least acknowledge his boss and start a conversation. Apparently, though, Solomon was flushed with the encouragement he had gotten from the other Holt-haters for sending the flowers. He never deigned to enter into conversation and Holt made a silent exit several innings later. The next day, she called him at home, ordered him into her office, and told him his baseball writing career at the *Tribune* was over.

Solomon's actions were so laughably tragic that he coined a new word for baseball writers. From then on, whenever anyone did something particularly asinine, we would simply say they "pulled a Sol."

What Solomon did was the dumbest thing I saw a baseball writer do. But what Chass and his co-conspirators did to Durso was the ugliest. They very nearly deprived Durso of one of the greatest honors of his life. The pathetic controversy lasted for months and spilled vats of venom. Chass and five colleagues forced the four-member Spink Award nominating committee to vote three times on Durso's nomination. An accompanying letter-writing campaign was so nasty there was open talk of slander suits. And, for nearly a year, it seemed as if Chass would win out over class. Only a determined crusade by Jerome Holtzman, president of the Baseball Writers' Association of America, prevented it from happening.

Murray Chass and his co-conspirators claimed they only organized their campaign for the good of the Spink Award. They contended they simply didn't feel Durso was a Hall-of-Fame writer and they felt it their moral obligation to stop his induction if possible. "Most of us consider carefully our Hall of Fame ballots, holding former players to high stands. We must apply similar standards to the election of our own people," they wrote in a two-page, single-spaced elite type letter explaining their stance.

I don't question their sincerity. But the danger is that same noble stance could be used to cloak any number of villainous sentiments from petty jealousy to outright vindictiveness.

With all due respect to Ferry Wimmer and the happy Germans of this world, and admitting that I am proud to know a few exceptions, I have to agree with my distinguished predecessor on the beat at the *Tribune*, Ring Lardner, who said in his own epitaph:

"Nothing on earth is more depressing than an old baseball writer."

Chapter 9

Ahhhh, One of Life's Great Moments

J. Chew's is a tiny jazz bar on the edge of Civic Center Plaza in Scottsdale, Arizona, a few miles up the road from where the Cubs train every spring. There is just enough room inside for an upright electronic piano along the wall closest to the bathrooms, five postage-stamp-sized tables, and a bar shaped like the missing piece of a jigsaw puzzle that meanders to and fro seating a dozen determined disciples elbow to elbow.

Perched on the barstool next to me, looking like a pet bullfrog with dirty glasses, is just what I came home to find: the closest thing to the heart and soul of Middle America. Harry Caray.

Harry is telling stories about Elvis Presley and what a nice kid he was; what a great baseball fan. The stories started about an hour ago and Harry is only half-way through his second one—the one about how he was in Memphis to do a St. Louis Hawks NBA game and the "The King" calls his hotel room to talk baseball and Harry doesn't realize who it is. He's just at the part where Elvis is saying: "Really, Harry, it's me. I'll prove it …" when he has to stop yet again. The noise is too loud to ignore any more.

"Hey, Harrr-rreeeee!" someone is shouting from outside through the long, low window that opens onto another typically perfect desert night. Harry Caray swings his barstool around to home-in on the sound and the voice outside downshifts to a stage whisper for just a second. *"See. I told you it was him."* Then shouting again: *"Hey, Harrr-rreeeee. Harrr-rreeeee, we love ya. You're the best, Harrr-rreeeee."*

The source of all this frantic wailing is a beanpole of a man in his early 20s wearing a dark blue Nike baseball cap. He is practically a relay throw from the bar, standing on an elevated concrete walkway that runs alongside and six feet above the street-level entrance to J. Chew's. The young man has to bend his knees and fold himself in half to peer down into the bar. But he seems perfectly content with his contortions now that he's caught Harry Caray's attention.

"Hey, Harrr-rreeeee! We love ya, Harrr-rreeeee!"

If Harry Caray can see the young man out there in the darkness, then he ought to be playing left field for the Cubs instead of sitting in the broadcast booth. He can't. But that doesn't matter. Harry gives a web-fingered wave and croaks in that familiar phlegm-coated voice: "Thank you, son. Thank you, very much. Now let these good people enjoy themselves."

Harry laughs like a lawnmower sputtering to a stop after a hot afternoon's work and sweeps the room with a smile. "Sorry, folks. Go on. Enjoy yourselves."

There have been plenty of times in Harry Caray's life when he's needed to apologize. But this isn't one of them. Everybody in J. Chew's is happy he's there; happy to be sharing one night of their lives with him—if only by being in the same cozy bar for a few hours.

Before Harry can get back to Elvis, a vague notion that has been fermenting in the back of my brain for a long, long while suddenly slams into fractured focus. The reason so many people love Harry Caray is because he is what so many of them want to be. He is good-hearted, fun-loving, and happy. Incredibly generous and outgoing. A winner. A dreamer. A rags-to-riches success, fashioned from a little luck and a lot of hard work. He is devoted, loyal, justifiably proud, properly grateful, supremely confident, and all-too-forgiving. He is the Ronald McDonald of the American spirit—the slightly goofy, yet somehow, comforting cartoon corporate symbol of everything happy in a magic land.

But Harry has all the faults of the great American soul, too. He is self-centered, argumentative, occasionally narrow-minded, and almost always naïve. His vision is limited, his patience swiftly strained, and his resolve quickly crumbled. He knew agony and hardship, but they were so distant he can only vaguely recall—despite what he says and believes. His world is a pampered and protected place now. And he thinks it's so because he made it so; and because it should be so. All, just like America.

Watching him wave to that distant shadow in the night, I realize Harry Caray is the America I came home to find. He could mask a world of shortcomings with a good heart and a wide smile. He is hopelessly bumbling and wondrously irrepressible. But, then again, so is America.

This is an All-American evening. At the bar with Harry, taking a break from the piano, is Ike Cole, twice-a-week back-up star attraction of J. Chew's and brother of the late Nat "King" Cole. Next to him is Ned Colletti, assistant general manager of the San Francisco Giants. A few feet away, content, but bored with stories they've heard a hundred times, are Harry's son, Chris, and one of Harry's oldest friends, Jack Leahy, nephew of legendary Notre Dame coach Frank Leahy.

And, of course, Elvis is here—conjured in denim, not sequins, from Harry's memory.

"Awh-right. Where was I? Oh, yeah. We're in Memphis and this guy on the phone keeps insisting he's Elvis. 'Really, Harry, it's me,' he says. 'I'll prove it. Be down in front of your hotel in 10 minutes.' So I figure, what the heck? And 10 minutes later this huge limousine pulls up and the driver says: 'Mr. Caray. Would you come with me?'"

Harry Caray cranks up his lawnmower laugh again, smacks his lips, and takes a long sip of alcohol-free beer.

"Listen, Joe, I know I've told you this before. But if anybody tries to tell ya you can have as much fun _NOT_ drinking as you do when you're drinking, they're a goddam liar."

Harry's right. He has told me that before. A few dozen times, at least. Harry hasn't had a sip of alcohol since June 23, 1994, the day he collapsed face-first onto some concrete steps near the visitor's dugout at Joe Robbie Stadium in Miami. He was on his way to the field to tape a pre-game show with manager Tom Trebelhorn and had just come from the air-conditioned clubhouse into the 90-degree heat and 70-percent humidity of a South Florida afternoon. The change in temperature had something to do with it, but what really knocked Harry down for the eight count was a lifetime of hard, hard living. Everyone's heard Harry Caray stories. Most of them are true.

The first year I covered the Cubs, the team media guide listed Harry Caray's age as 72. That was in 1992. Nobody believed it. Most of us assumed 72 was simply a realistic starting point. So I wasn't worried about being able to keep pace when Harry invited me and my wife to join him and some friends for "dinner and a few cocktails" at his favorite restaurant early in spring training. Most of my fellow hacks hadn't even bothered to ask me out socially yet. That Harry was one of the first to extend a welcome hand was typical. He was orphaned early in life and raised by an aunt in St. Louis. He knew what it was like to be the outsider looking in. From the moment I met him, Harry Caray always went out of his way to make me feel part of his baseball family.

"The reservations are for 8 o'clock at Avanti's," said Harry. "Come whenever you can. Just ask for my table."

A wiser soul, more-experienced in Caray Custom, would have known immediately what lay ahead. In one breath, Harry had said the reservations were for 8. In the next, he said come when you can. The two were perfectly compatible in his mind, as I soon discovered. My wife and I made the mistake of showing up at 8 o'clock. About 1 A.M., Harry said: *"Heyyyy, I think we oughtta get something to eat."* Sometime between 3 and 4, we finally stumbled blindly out the door. In between, we engaged in one of Harry's favorite pastimes: arguing about baseball. He threw out the bait early and I took it hook, line, and sinker. The topic Harry started trawling that evening was Pete Rose and whether he should be in the Hall of Fame. My opinion was Rose forfeited his rights to Cooperstown when he bet on baseball games.

"Awh, Joe, what are you talkin' about? I thought you were smarter than that. How can you keep the guy with the most hits in the history of the game out of the Hall of Fame? How can you even call it a Hall of Fame if you don't let Pete Rose in?"

I reminded Harry they'd kept "Shoeless Joe" Jackson out of the Hall for his part in the Black Sox scandal. And Jackson's contributions to throwing the 1919 World Series were far more dubious than the evidence against Rose. Jackson led all batters in the 1919 World Series with 12 base hits, including the only home run of the Series. He led the Sox with five runs scored and six batted in. And he only struck out twice. Those don't sound like the stats of a player who was going in the tank. On top of that, Jackson finished his 13-year career with a .356 life-time batting average—third-best of all time behind Ty Cobb and Rogers Hornsby. He had the 13th-best career on-base average in the history of the game (.423) and his .517 slugging percentage put him 35th on the all-time list. Pete Rose had Hall-of-Fame numbers. But he wasn't even among the Top 100 all-time leaders with a .303 batting average, 377 on-base percentage, and .409 slugging percentage.

Harry and I could have avoided the entire discussion if only base-ball had followed the advice of one of my old colleagues, Fred McMane of United Press International, who advocated two Halls—the Hall of Fame and the Hall of Very, Very Good. During a similar long dinner debate with my old friend Pat Benic and me at the 1993 National League playoffs in Atlanta, McMane insisted the Hall of Fame should be reserved for the tiny few "who illuminated the game." The other stars, McMane said, tongue firmly in cheek, should be inducted into the Hall of Very, Very Good. In The World According to Fred, Babe Ruth would be in the Hall of Fame, Reggie Jackson would be in the Hall of Fame. But Bill Mazerowski, Orlando Cepeda, Tony Oliva, and players like them would be in the Hall of Very, Very Good.

Unfortunately, the Hall of Very, Very Good wasn't an option. But I did offer Harry another compromise.

"I'll give you this, Harry," I said. "If they let 'Shoeless Joe' in the Hall, then they can let Pete in."

"Awh, come on, Joe. Don't be ridiculous," Harry moaned, almost spitting his drink across the table in his rush to express disgust. The only thing Harry liked more than a pretty girl, a cold beer, or a Cubs' win was a good argument. He was having a ball and he kept on having a ball for hours. By the time Harry got around to asking for the dinner menus, he was arguing solo. I was so tired and had so much to drink I couldn't have spelled Pete Rose with cue cards. I was feeling like Pete Rose him-self, which isn't a pretty state. Pete was a great hitter, but he wasn't the brightest bulb on the Christmas tree. There's the old Joe Nuxhall line about how dumb Pete Rose was: He was so dumb, he got stuck on an escalator for 12 hours during the New York blackout. The way I felt when Harry got through entertaining me that night, Petey and I would have been standing on that escalator together waiting patiently for the power to come back on.

The first televised Cubs game of spring training was the next day—actually, later that same day. And Harry was in peak form, obviously enthralled to be starting another season doing what he loved best. It was a magnificent spring afternoon with cloudless blue skies and the sun glinting off Red Mountain beyond the center-field fence. But I was in too much agony to appreciate it. I had the worst hangover of my life. The same sun that was shimmering so beautifully on Red Mountain was beating down mercilessly on the galvanized shelf that doubled as a desk in the old HoHoKam press box. The heat and glare were so intense, and the knife pain was buried so deep in my brain, that I couldn't bear to open my eyes for more than a few seconds at a time. I sat in a metal folding chair with my forehead pressed against the soothing cool plastic of my closed laptop computer, just praying for survival. Harry was 10 feet away, laughing, cutting up, enjoying himself like a 22-year-old kid at a company softball game.

Sometime between innings, Harry got up to make a quick run to the rest room. As he passed my seat, he slapped me hard on the back, startling me and nearly causing an ugly mess. Then in a voice loud enough to be heard five rows into the stands, he growled: "Hey, Joe, you don't have another one of those Jack Daniels stuffed in your pocket, do you? I could sure use one right about now."

If Harry Caray was 72 that spring, I pity the friends who had to run with him when he was 22.

Harry in New York was something to behold. He used to fidget in his seat on the team flights into LaGuardia. He couldn't wait to get started. Once, when he didn't have his limousine for some reason, he had the team bus stop on the way from the airport to the hotel and drop him off near a favorite watering hole. The sight of Harry Caray waddling purposefully down a dark Manhattan street on a mission of merriment is enough to rekindle anybody's zest for life.

Like all true hedonists, when Harry got started, he didn't know when to stop. And he was particularly dangerous in Manhattan where there's always a friendly tavern open any hour of the day or night. The Cubs were in New York early in the 1994 season, about two months before Harry collapsed. They had a rare Monday afternoon game at Shea followed by a off-day Tuesday and a night game Wednesday, which made for a most-unusual—and welcome—mid-week break. Typically, the team is traveling on days when there isn't a game. But this time, we had almost 48 hours free in New York City from Monday night 'til late Wednesday afternoon without having to board a plane, train, or bus. It was as if the teachers had just blessed us with a bonus recess.

Joe Goddard of the *Sun-Times* invited me to make the most of our rare freedom by joining him for dinner at his favorite restaurant, Cristo's. We had a superb meal, a nice bottle of wine, and a couple of after-dinner drinks at the tiny stand-up bar before moving on to the original Runyon's on East 50th Street for what we promised would be one last nightcap. Unfortunately, the realization that all we had to do on Tuesday was produce a relatively simple "off-day feature" was too much to resist. We kept going long into the night and morning. Sometime around 3 A.M., we spotted a little piano bar on Second Avenue and decided it looked like the perfect place to have the "one last nightcap" that had been just a step ahead of us all evening. We walked through the doors and were closing in on the bar when we heard a familiar voice shout from a table in the corner. "Hey, Joe and Joe. C'mon over here." It was Harry. Apparently, he'd been on his own hunt for an equally elusive nightcap. He was, uncharacteristically, alone. He'd outlasted the usual party of friends and hangers-on and told his limousine driver to pull up to the curb on Second Avenue for one last stop on the way home. The three of us sat there laughing, telling stories, and having a great time for another half hour before Harry announced he was going back to the hotel. Goddard and I were still sipping and decided to stay the course. But Goddard gallantly volunteered to walk Harry to his car. Apparently, when they got there, Harry had second thoughts. For the next five minutes, I roared laughing, and the bartender across the room joined me, as we watched through the window at a scene right out of a W.C. Fields movie. An obviously bored and weary chauffeur stood at attention holding the long door of his stretch white limousine open while Joe Goddard tried haplessly to fold Harry Caray into the rear seat. Goddard would get him halfway in and all of a sudden here would come Harry's other half right back out. It was like trying to shove a 25-foot balloon into a five-foot hole. Every time Goddard pushed one part of the balloon in, another part would squirt out. The younger man finally prevailed in a split decision, but the fight took too much out of him. Goddard and I never finished that last nightcap. He was suddenly exhausted.

Then there was the story Harry loves to tell about himself—about how lecherous he could be and how much he appreciated a pretty, young woman. He was at home in Palm Springs, California, during one off-season with Dutchie, his third wife. Harry was divorced twice before getting it right with Dutchie. "So I'm sitting by my pool in Palm Springs one morning and Muffy, that's Dutchie's daughter from a previous marriage, is prancing around the pool in a very small bikini. Well, I'm reading the paper and sipping a Budweiser. And I keep looking around at 22-year-old Muffy in her very small bikini. Dutchie catches me and tells me I'm awful for peeking and I tell her: 'Heeeeaayyyy, it wouldn't exactly be incest, you know.'"

Ah, Harry. Hopelessly bumbling and wondrously irrepressible.

It's fun to remember what a rogue, rake, and raconteur Harry was. His reputation was hard-earned and richly deserved. But he also deserved a reputation for working as hard as he played. Harry did more homework than any broadcaster I came across. And his homework didn't stop—or necessarily start—with baseball. Or even sports. He was a voracious reader. Rarely did he have time for books during the season, but he would devour newspapers and magazines by the hour on team flights.

As a kid growing up in St. Louis, Harry earned 40 cents a day selling newspapers near a library that he loved to visit in his spare time.

"I'd rent a book for three cents and go to a soda fountain," Harry told Curt Smith, author of *Voices of The Game,* a history of baseball broadcasting. "I'd pay 10 cents for a big chocolate marshmallow sundae. Before the sundae was finished, I was halfway through the book. I read a lot and always felt that my career began there."

On game days, Harry would be in the broadcast booth filling out his scorecards and skimming notes long before his colleagues. It never guaranteed a flawless performance, of course. Harry's foul-ups on and off the air are legendary. A personal favorite, one Barry Rozner of the *Arlington Heights Daily Herald* and I used to resurrect and laugh about for hours every season, was the time one of baseball's greatest hitters, Eddie Murray, came to bat in crucial situation against the Cubs.

"Boy, oh boy," Harry said, the worry thickening his tongue. "There's danger here, Chéri. Here comes Sol Murray."

Sol Murray? Rozner was convinced Harry must have known a guy named Sol Murray who ran a deli somewhere. Every time we went to a new city, I'd check the phone book to see if I could find a listing for Sol's Deli. Never found one owned by Sol Murray.

Hispanic names were the bane of Harry's career. That a "J" could sound like an "H" was beyond him. But those mispronunciations became routine after a while. The real joy was listening him to grapple with new classics that came along. Names like: Grudzielanek, Konuszewski, or Isringhausen. He would dutifully ask around for the proper pronunciations, practice them a few times off the air, then mangle them mercilessly during a game.

"Here's Gru … Gru … Gruds … Grudsell … Awh, for Pete's sake. What kinda name is that."

Harry, though, was a shrewd veteran and born entertainer. He always had a fail-safe fallback when he couldn't spit out a player's name. He'd turn to Steve Stone, his longtime broadcasting partner, and say: "You know, Steeeee-uhvvvh. This guy's name spelled backwards would be K-E-N-A-L-E-I-Z …"

Steve Stone and Harry Caray made a wonderfully entertaining pair.

They were the Odd Couple of broadcasting. Steve was Felix Unger, the witty, urbane, neurotic clothes horse. Harry was Oscar Madison, the disheveled, fun-loving, endearing scoundrel. The big difference between the real-life broadcast Odd Couple and Neil Simon's fictional characters was a role reversal when it came to smoking cigars. Oscar puffed away on cheap stogies in the play. Harry didn't smoke. But Stone made up for it by lighting up $10 cigars.

Harry used to complain constantly about Steve's cigars—both on and off the air. One of his classic put-downs came in the middle of a game in St. Louis on a typically miserable hot, muggy afternoon.

"Heyyy! A great big cock-a-roach just crawled across the desk," Harry screamed into the microphone, teetering between panic and hilarity. A few seconds later, after the thuds of palms and scorebooks being smacked against the desk finally died down, Harry chirped in: "You know, Steeeee-uhvvvh, I think that cock-a-roach musta come out of your cigar."

Off the air, between innings, the classic lines kept coming, often involving Mandy Cohen, a skillful, hard-working assistant director who stayed in the broadcast booth and was a vital link between Harry and Steve and Arne Harris, the legendary producer down in the production truck.

In addition to running the show in the booth, Mandy waited on Harry hand and foot. She was 50 years younger than Harry, but like most of us, she loved him and would do anything for him, including fetching hot dogs, coffee, or whatever Harry needed between innings.

"Heyyy, Mannnn-deee. What did you put in this coffee?" Harry said one day after taking a sip from a freshly deposited mug.

Steve Stone, in a calm, bemused voice said: "Uh, I think that's tea, Harry."

Without hesitating, Harry said: "That explains it." And went on with his business.

Harry's most famous line, of course, was "Holy Cow!" which was a popular slang expression among teens in the 1940s, back when Harry was still a young man. But "Holy Cow!" was popular even before that. My grandfather, who passed his passion for baseball on to me, was a lifelong New Orleans Pelicans fan—even after the Pelicans were nothing but a memory in New Orleans. One of my treasured possessions is a picture he gave me of the Pelicans and Fort Worth Cats standing on the baselines before the first pitch of the Dixie League World Series. And my grandfather always insisted he called me Joey— instead of Joe like my father and his father—in honor of Joey Sewell, his favorite player on the Pelicans. Joseph Wheeler Sewell was named for a confederate calvary officer, attended the University of Alabama and got his start on a Hall-of-Fame career with the Cleveland Indians when he was called up as a late-season replacement for Ray Chapman, the last major leaguer to be killed by a pitch on August 16, 1920.

When I first became a Harry Caray fan listening to the distant strains of KMOX at night in my teens, my grandfather was quick to tell me it was an old Pelicans' announcer who originally made "Holy Cow!" popular. He never told me the name of the broadcaster—or, if he did, I never remembered it. But I read years later that it was Jack Holiday on a New Orleans radio station called WTPS. My grandfather wasn't trying to take anything away from Harry Caray. He loved Harry, too. He just thought his grandson should know the Pelicans contributed more to baseball than Joey Sewell and Jim Riggleman.

The only other broadcaster famous for saying Holy Cow was Phil Rizzuto, the former Yankee infielder-turned-announcer. Rizzuto liked to claim he was the first to use the expression, but Harry Caray started broadcasting major league baseball games in 1945 with the St. Louis Cardinals. Rizzuto didn't retire from the Yankees until 1956. As Harry says: "If Rizzuto was saying it before me, then he was saying it from shortstop, not the booth."

There are a hundred other favorite Harry-isms—phrases instantly identifiable with Caray. "It might be. It could be. It is!" ... "Pohhpppppp-dit-upp" ... "Ohhh, for a hit" ... "Boy, ohhh, boyyy" ... "How in the worrlddd???" ... "Now, Steeeee-uhvvvh" .... "Ya knowww. I just don't understand" ... and dozens more, including Barry Rozner's favorite that Harry moaned into a microphone when the Cubs were on their way to finishing 20 games out of first place in 1991: "Boy, ohhh, boyyy. What a lousy team."

One of the great things about Harry—one of the things that caused him occasional trouble with players and the front office—was that he always told it like it was. That 1991 Cubs' team *was* lousy. And so was White Sox shortstop Bee Bee Richard in a game Harry was broadcasting in the early 1970s. Richard had already made two errors early in the game when Harry saw him bend down on the infield. "Bee Bee Richard just picked up a hot-dog wrapper at shortstop," Harry told his listeners. "It's the first thing he's picked up all night."

But the one Harry-ism I loved most was when a foul ball would arc into the stands during a particularly uneventful point of a particularly uneventful game and Harry would watch a youngster scurry through people's legs, under iron railings, and over empty seats to snag the souvenir. Or when Arne Harris would have his camera operators focus on a father who'd just snared a foul and was proudly presenting the ball to his elated daughter. Harry would watch the scene along with the rest of us and then sum it up beautifully with a heartfelt sigh: "Ahhhh. One of life's great moments."

It sounds incredibly corny, but I felt that way every time I went out with Harry and his wife Dutchie. *"Ahhhh. One of life's great moments."* There were a million surprises and nearly as many disappointments about coming home to the United States after all those years abroad. But Harry Caray was neither. He was the same Ole Harry I'd listened to and watched for years before I left; the same Ole Harry who made 1984 more magical than it had a right to be. Only for me, the same Ole Harry was even better. Instead of merely being an amusing, distant codger, Harry became a real, live friend—an occasional dinner companion, a frequent traveling partner and a daily fixture in my life. And, unlike some other people and things, Harry wore well under prolonged exposure.

Harry Caray wasn't a saint. You don't live a life as hard and full and high-profiled as his without making your share of enemies and attracting more than your share of critics. And I can't attest to Harry's behavior in his younger years when all men are prone to their greatest mistakes. But I do know that by the time he rounded third and was heading for home, Harry brought a lot more happiness than hurt into the world.

That isn't to say Harry didn't have a penchant for getting into trouble and causing controversy. He did. And one troubling incident came during my final days on the beat at the end of the 1995 season. It was the case of the "slanty eyes" and it was another reminder to me of how much things had changed while I was away. It was a reminder, too, that even after a few years back, I was still lost in the world of "sports journalism."

The Cubs were in San Diego for the start of their final road trip of the season. They were $14\frac{1}{2}$ games out of first place with 17 to play. A division title was out of the question. They still had a remote shot at the new wildcard playoff berth, but they were four games back in that race with three teams still ahead of them. The Cubs eventually made it exciting, hanging on until the last weekend of the season two weeks later before finally being mathematically eliminated. But, as much fun as it was, even manager Jim Riggleman admitted those two weeks were like a dream. The reality was, the Cubs were out of the race when they flew out to California. A sure sign of that was the fact the other two Chicago newspapers—the *Sun-Times* and *Arlington Heights Daily Herald*—opted to save money by keeping their beat reporters home. They hired local stringers to cover the team in San Diego and, then, in Houston for the final three road games of the year.

Knowing I was the only reporter with the team on that last road trip took a lot of pressure off me. I never actually noticed the strain until it was gone. But I suddenly realized on that road trip just how much time I spent worrying every day of every season about missing something or being badly beaten on a story. With Barry Rozner and Joe Goddard back in Chicago, I didn't have to worry nearly as much. There was, of course, the odd chance that one of the local stringers would stumble onto something of significance. But it wasn't very likely. And it was even less likely that much time would go by without me finding out about it on my own or being told about it by someone in the organization.

So I was feeling incredibly relaxed and happy when my phone rang in the San Diego Marina Marriott on Friday morning. I'd just come from a long walk along the bay and a marathon session reading newspapers and sipping coffee in a little bookstore I loved that had a half-dozen tables and chairs tucked in among the overflowing shelves. I was past-ing the major league standings from the morning paper into my stat book when the phone rang.

"Hey, Joey, this is Ed. What are ya doin'?"

It was Ed Sherman, associate sports editor of the *Tribune*—a good guy, a tireless worker, and one of the best journalists I dealt with in sports. Sherman had covered national collegiate sports for years and done a simply astounding job melding the complex business, emotions, and politics of big-time amateur athletics into a readable package that everyone could understand and enjoy. Nobody in the country did it better.

I almost always enjoyed talking to Ed. But this was one of two or three times I didn't.

"You know about the Harry thing, right?" Sherman said after exchanging a few perfunctory pleasantries.

"What Harry thing?"

"He's gone and done it, again."

Sherman filled me in on the details of a brief story written by Steve Nidetz in that morning's *Chicago Tribune*. Nidetz was the *Trib*'s "Media Columnist" and his 12-paragraph story ran in the sports section under the headline: "WGN Apologizes for Caray's Remark in Interview." Nidetz had gotten as far as the start of the second paragraph before making his first factual error. Writing for Friday's newspapers, he said WGN radio had apologized for remarks Caray made Tuesday during a taped radio interview with manager Jim Riggleman about Los Angeles Dodgers pitcher Hideo Nomo, the then-rookie from Japan who was scheduled to pitch that night against the Cubs. Actually, the incident took place on Wednesday afternoon, the day *after* Nomo held the Cubs to just one run over eight innings in a 7-1 win. Amazed at how well Nomo had pitched the night before, Harry opened his daily pre-game interview with Riggleman by saying: "Well, my eyes are slanty enough, how 'bout yours?" Harry could be heard sputtering his loud lawnmower laugh as he passed the microphone, and what he thought was a good-natured opening line, to the manager.

Riggleman, to his credit, knew a land mine when he saw one. Like most good managers, and all good politicians, Riggleman could talk for 10 minutes without saying anything if the situation called for it. And this situation definitely called for it. After a moment's hesitation, Riggleman had the interview back on track to baseball inanities.

The interview was taped more than an hour before the 1:20 P.M. game and fed by a WGN assistant from the broadcast booth back to the studios in Tribune Tower a few minutes later. Neither the assistant nor anyone back at WGN edited the tape or thought to question Harry's obviously controversial opening comment. The interview ran intact on the "Jim Riggleman Show" and Tisa LaSorte, WGN's program director, said she didn't receive a single complaint or phone call until Nidetz followed up on Thursday—a day after the actual incident and two days after Nidetz thought it occurred. The Cubs had left for the West Coast after Wednesday's game. Harry stayed behind in Chicago, as usual. He'd quit doing most road games since his collapse in Florida in 1994.

Nidetz called WGN after talking to Bill Yoshino, who was identified in the story as a member of the Japanese-American Citizens League. Yoshino was quoted in the story as saying it was "not the first incident of this nature" and recalling Caray had used the term "Jap" on the air several years earlier. "We'll send a letter to station management issuing some concern on our part that that type of phraseology is allowed to go out," said Yoshino. "Because it is disparaging and something we try to guard against. We'll ask the station to issue an apology at the very least."

The seventh paragraph of Nidetz's story said: "Attempts to contact Caray for comment were unsuccessful."

And that was why Sherman was calling me in San Diego on what, until then, had been a perfect Southern California morning. Sherman wanted me to do a follow-up for the Saturday paper with Harry's reaction.

"What a minute. Why should I get involved?" I asked Sherman. "First of all, it's not my story. I don't cover the media. That's what Nidetz does. Secondly, Harry's in Chicago. I'm in California. Get Nidetz to do it. It's his story and he's in Chicago."

"He says he doesn't have Harry's number."

"*What?*" I couldn't stop myself from an incredulous shriek. "You're telling me the *Tribune's* media columnist doesn't have Harry Caray's phone number? And he doesn't know how to get it? Gimme a break. It doesn't sound Nidetz is doing his job if you ask me."

Sherman hadn't asked me. And he wasn't real pleased with my re-action. He was caught in the middle of something and trying to find the best way out by dragging me into the middle of it with him.

I always liked Nidetz and never had a reason to think he was any-thing but professionally competent. Until that day. But something wasn't right about the whole set up. And I didn't want any part of it. I told Sherman I'd give him Harry's number. He could pass it along to Nidetz. But I wasn't going to do a follow-up on what I personally thought was a nonsense story that wasn't mine in the first place—par-ticularly since I was 1,700 miles away and the reporter who started it was sitting right there in the same city with Harry Caray.

Sherman took Harry's phone number and said he'd see what he could do. But he made a point of asking if I would be in my room for a while. I told him yes and wasn't shocked when the phone rang again a half hour later. In a calm, pleading voice, Sherman asked me politely to do the story. "Apparently Nidetz doesn't get along with Harry for some reason. He says Harry hates him. Can you, please, do me a favor and get to Harry for us? We need his reaction."

So that was it. At least it made more sense than the lame excuse that the *Tribune's* media critic didn't have Harry Caray's phone number and didn't know how to find it. I repeated my strong objections, both in the volume and composition of my words, but finally told Sherman I'd do it. We agreed we would make Harry's reaction the lead item in the daily Cubs' notes column rather than a separate story and let it go at that.

"Hey, Harry, this is Joe Reaves. How ya doin'? You're missing some great weather out here."

It was mid-afternoon Chicago time and Harry was just back from lunch at his own restaurant where one of the Chicago television stations had already cornered him and gotten his humorous reaction to the morning's story.

"Listen, Harry, I hate to do this. But I need you to say something about the story Nidetz had in today's paper."

The receiver exploded in my ear. The next five minutes of that long-distance phone conversation were filled with a stutteringly obscene recap of Harry's history of complaints against Steve Nidetz. I never got a word in edgewise. The gist of the rant was that Harry felt Nidetz had been taking cheap shots at him for years. He didn't use the exact words, but Harry made it plain he thought Nidetz belonged to the "Knee-the-Gorilla" school of journalism, which basically says the best way a columnist can make a name real quick is to pick out the biggest gorilla in town, walk up to him, and kick him in the groin.

When Harry finally vented his spleen enough to draw breath, I jumped in and told him I appreciated his feelings, but what I really needed was his reaction to the story. "Awh, come on, Joe. What did I say? If he was a boxer with a cauliflower ear, I'd say he had a cauliflower ear. All I said was he had slanty eyes. He does have slanty eyes. What's the big deal?"

The big deal was that in the politically correct '90s you couldn't say those things anymore. Especially if you were working for a company that amassed unspeakable fortunes publishing a right-wing newspaper for generations and now was committed to parading its penance. Political correctness may have been in vogue at other media outlets in the United States, but Tribune Co. embraced it with excruciating blind zealotry. Incredibly outrageous and illogical decisions were made in the guise of sensitivity and social consciousness. And all the while, such seemingly sacrosanct principles as individual rights, corporate morale, and even freedom of speech were swept aside.

The first real insight I had from afar into the troubles on the home front was when I picked up the *International Herald-Tribune* one afternoon in Warsaw and read a *Washington Post* story about an ugly cat fight between columnist Mike Royko and Howard Tyner, who two years later would be named editor of the *Chicago Tribune*. Royko had written a typical tongue-in-cheek column that some young members of the staff found offensive. It tweaked their cultural sensitivity, which, of course, was precisely what Royko had in mind—and precisely why Royko was so good. The young staffers stewed in their umbrage before deciding to deputize themselves moral enforcement officers for the evening. They fretted and fumed together until they got the courage to go to Tyner, who, as deputy managing editor, was ranking editorial officer in the news room that night. Tyner was possessed of what the poet John Keats called "thick-sighted" ambition. It impaired his judgment time and again at varying cost to the *Tribune*. This time it nearly cost the newspaper one of the best columnists in the country.

Tyner heard the complaints and decided the politically correct thing to do was to pull the column from the next day's paper. He planned to run a small notice advising readers that Mike Royko had taken the day off. A friendly staff member, however, alerted Royko about the attempted book burning. Royko called managing editor Dick Ciccone at home and told him if the column was pulled the *Tribune* better change the notice in the paper to read: Mike Royko has resigned. Without even having read the column, Ciccone overrode Tyner's panicked decision and ordered it run in the paper.

The fact that a Pulitzer Prize-winning columnist nearly had an article censored by his own newspaper in a squabble over political correctness was big enough news to attract the attention of many media in the United States, including the *Washington Post*. It was a reprint of the *Post* article by staff writer Howard Kurtz that ran in *International Herald-Tribune*, which plopped on my doorstep on Podbipiety Street in Warsaw.

In the article, Royko, typically, went straight to the heart of the conflict: "What disturbs me about it is it was an attempt at censorship by newspaper people." Ciccone, too, saw immediately what Tyner failed to grasp: "My own philosophy is we don't censor columns and cartoons unless there's an unequivocal threat of blatant libel or universal offensiveness."

I couldn't agree with Royko and Ciccone more. In fact, my stance on freedom of speech is even more radical. I worked in too many countries—Singapore, China, Vietnam, and dozens more—where governments decided what people could say or write and what they could see or hear. I agree wholeheartedly with the late Supreme Court Justice Hugo Black, who took an uncompromising stance: "My view is, without deviation, without exception, without any ifs, buts, or whereases, that freedom of speech means that you shall not do something to people either for the views they have or the views they express or the words they speak or write ... I am for the First Amendment from the first word to the last. I believe it means what it says." And what it says is: "Congress shall make NO LAW ... abridging the freedom of speech, or of the press."

To me, and to Justice Black, that meant no libel laws; no slander laws; no laws about yelling fire in a crowded theater. In his opinion in the landmark case *New York Times Company v. Sullivan* in 1964, Justice Black wrote: "An unconditional right to say what one pleases about public affairs is what I consider to be the minimum guarantee of the First Amendment."

The majority of Congress and the Supreme Court, representing the majority of people in the United States, have chipped away at what seems an unequivocal stance in the United States Constitution. So be it. Majority rules in a democracy. But it was disturbing to see young professional journalists set themselves up as moral police intent on censoring a column—a personal opinion column—that happened to offend their constantly changing stanchions of political correctness. It was worse than disturbing to see a veteran journalist who would eventually become editor of the *Tribune* meekly pander to such pups.

The Kinder Coup against Royko, and Tyner's role in it, were clear harbingers to me in Poland of the atmosphere that awaited at the *Trib*, in particular, and the country in general. I didn't like it—certainly not in the extreme. But, at least I recognized the new climate and knew how to work and behave within it. Harry Caray never had a chance.

"Harry, just give me a quote saying you didn't mean any harm. You're sorry. And you don't hate the Japanese."

"Awh, Joe. Anybody who knows me, even my detractors, will tell you I love everybody. As a matter of fact, that's why I'm in the restaurant business. I can't go anywhere without saying hello to everybody. I don't care whether they're white, yellow, pink, brown, Oriental, or whatever. I love everybody."

"That's great, Harry. I know that. And that's what you need to say if anybody else calls about the interview. Just apologize, tell them you're not prejudiced and get this thing behind you."

"All right, but I don't understand it. If a boxer's got a cauliflower ear ..."

I didn't know the specifics at the time, but Harry had already given his reaction to a couple of people. One was the local television station, which had video of Harry Caray pulling the corners of his eyes back and laughing at himself. The other was Joe Goddard of the *Sun-Times,* who apparently had gotten the same quotes I had from Harry and ran with them. He had a front-page story—front page of the paper; not the sports section—that said Harry refused to apologize. The cauliflower ear comment figured prominently. My nine-paragraph story, in contrast, ran atop the Cubs' notes deep inside the sports section of the Saturday paper and began: "Hall of Fame broadcaster Harry Caray said Friday he was stunned and embarrassed by criticism that he was insensitive in remarks about the Japanese people during a pre-game discussion of Los Angeles Dodgers pitcher Hideo Nomo this week."

Both stories were accurate. Goddard's was news. Mine was a feeble PR release.

I knew I didn't want to get involved in that story from the first.

My friendship with Harry prevented me from being objective. I could have written the same story Goddard had and made just as big a splash. Instead, I coached Harry on what to say and what not to say, then wrote a puff piece that made him look as good as possible. I was covering the circus and sleeping with the elephants.

I've thought about that story a lot. I was forced to do something I didn't want to do and then did a bad job doing it. That was unprofessional and embarrassing. It was the main reason I had gone out of my way for years to keep from being friends with the players I covered. Harry was different. He was part of the Cubs, but not really part of my beat. The *Chicago Tribune* had a full-time media columnist for that. So I can't feel bad about developing a friendship with someone as thoroughly enjoyable as Harry Caray. Journalists are human—despite occasional evidence to the contrary. They can't cut off all social contact on the remote chance they might some day unexpectedly have to write about a friend.

Once I was thrown into that unwanted situation, though, I should have behaved more professionally. Or should I? Where was the rule book on professionalism in "sports journalism?" Whenever I tried to wrestle with the notion—even after four years on the baseball beat—I still couldn't quite seem to grasp it. I was like Joe Goddard trying to stuff Harry Caray into the back seat of that limo. As soon as I got hold of one end, another part would pop up to look entirely different. Was it journalism? Or was it entertainment? Was it some bizarre mix? Or was it neither? Maybe it was O.K. to sleep with the elephants after all. A lot of my colleagues sure seemed to have peanut breath.

Forty-eight hours after that anemic Harry Caray story ran, I quit the *Tribune*. The two events were unrelated. I was in the new Denver International Airport on my way from San Diego to Houston when I checked my voice mail and had a message to call Anne Marie Lipinski, who had succeeded Dick Ciccone as managing editor. It was the first time she had ever graced me with a conversation. She seemed nervous and hesitant— never a good sign in a boss—when she told me Howard Tyner had received my letter asking for a leave of absence from the *Tribune*. She said Tyner had asked her to call me and tell me he couldn't grant the request.

I had known Tyner for nearly 20 years. Our careers paralleled each other for more than a decade. He, too, had been a UPI correspondent in Eastern Europe, been hired by the *Tribune,* and gone back overseas for the paper. We both worked extensively in Warsaw. I was the *Trib*'s Beijing correspondent when he was the Moscow correspondent. And we once sat about 50 feet apart in the *Trib* newsroom in the early 1980s when Tyner was renowned for decorating his desk and filing cabinets with an impressive, god-awful army of pink flamingoes in every size and shape.

I hadn't intended to ask for a leave of absence from the *Tribune*. I simply planned to quit when I learned in early August 1995 that my wife was being hired by a British public relations firm, Shandwick Ltd., to be second-in-command of their Asia headquarters in Hong Kong. It was a high-powered job with the pay and perks to match. And since we had been scheming to get back to Asia for several years, there never was any question of turning down the offer. I planned to finish out the season and quit after the playoffs and World Series so the paper would have the entire off-season to find a replacement and get her or him up to speed. But, as I had always done in my career at the *Tribune*, I decided to touch base with Dick Ciccone before I did anything. I called him from Florida the last week of August when the Cubs were in the middle of a three-game series with the Marlins. Ciccone was out of power by then—kicked upstairs to the post of associate editor. But I still wanted him to know what I was doing.

"Why don't you ask for a leave of absence?" Ciccone suggested. "You probably won't get it, but it won't hurt to ask. And it's better than just quitting."

I hadn't thought of asking for a leave, but when Ciccone suggested it, I remembered my predecessor, Andy Bagnato, had gotten a six-month leave of absence to move to Scotland and decompress after he finished three grueling years on the baseball beat. I was about to finish my fourth season—longer than any baseball writer had survived on the beat at the *Tribune* since Fred Mitchell in the early 1980s. And I'd been jumping on and off planes all around the world for the *Tribune* for a decade before that. Maybe it would make sense to ask for a leave of absence. The precedent was there. And after a year off, I'd be in Hong Kong in 1997 when the Communists took over the last jewel in Britain's once mighty empire. The *Tribune* already had a correspondent moving to Hong Kong to cover the story, but perhaps I could serve as a backup at minimal cost.

I took Ciccone's advice and wrote Tyner, asking for a leave of absence and telling him I was moving to Hong Kong to follow my wife's career for a change. I mentioned that he, of all people, could appreciate that since his talented wife, like mine, had been forced to pack up and follow him for years with UPI and the *Tribune*. I told him I intended to enroll at Hong Kong University the first year to complete an already half-finished degree in Asian Studies, but that Lynne's contract called for her to be abroad two years. I could be available to help with coverage of the Hong Kong handover in 1997. I reminded him that the first story I wrote out of China when I went there for the *Tribune* in 1984 was Margaret Thatcher's visit to sign of the instruments of handover for

Hong Kong at the Great Hall of the People in Beijing. I would be one of the few journalists around to have seen both the beginning and end of an historic story 13 years in the making.

"The *Tribune* has been great to me. And I believe I have rewarded the company's commitment to me with an exceptional effort for nearly 14 years. I don't want to leave the paper, but I certainly understand if nothing can be done," I wrote.

The letter was marked "Personal and Confidential" and sent only to Tyner. I didn't carbon my supervisors in the sports department. My reasoning was simple: 1) I'd known Tyner for nearly two decades, 2) he was the boss; the one who would make the final decision, and 3) as I spelled out clearly in the latter, I wasn't planning to quit for another few months—after I'd finished the baseball season and taken vacation and time-due. There was plenty of time to notify my supervisors in sports once the leave of absence issue was settled.

When Anne Marie Lipinski told me on the phone the leave of absence had been denied, I wasn't shocked. I never really expected one and wouldn't even have bothered if Ciccone hadn't suggested it. I told Lipinski that was fine. But I also let her know I was tremendously upset that Howard Tyner hadn't seen fit to call me personally. I had written to him, not to her. I thought he owed me the courtesy of a call.

It was about 10 A.M. in Denver. I'd been up since 5 A.M. California time to check out of my hotel, get to the airport, return my rental car, and board the first of two flights that would take me to Houston, where I would have to hit the ground running to cover a game that night. I had another 18-hour work day stretching in front of me—just one of many I'd stumbled through in four years on the beat. And, with a prolonged spring training because of the strike, I had been away from home 151 of the last 212 days. I never complained because I was doing something I loved. And I thought my bosses appreciated it. But here I was standing in an airport in Denver and hearing from an underling that my own boss didn't think enough of me to respond personally about one of the most momentous career decisions I ever had to make.

"Anne Marie, I wish you would convey to Mr. Tyner that I think this complete lack of class is all-too typical of the way things are done at the *Tribune* lately and I don't appreciate it," I said in the same surprisingly calm voice I'd found that day Steve Sax attacked me at Comiskey. "I don't particularly see any reason to keep busting my butt for people who lack even the most basic common decency. If I were you, I'd send some-body to Houston right away to cover the game tonight because I'm not going to be there. I quit. I'm changing my flight reservations right now and going back home."

There was a silence for several seconds and then the nervous, hesi-tant voice that I will forever associate with Anne Marie Lipinksi. "What are you saying? That you quit?"

"Yes," I said, wondering where I might have been unclear. "If I were you ..." and I repeated, slowly and precisely, word for word, the last three sentences I'd just said to her.

Unbelievably, when I finished, there was another awkward pause and Lipinski stammered: "So, let me get this straight: you're quitting?"

Arghhhh!! It was maddening, but wonderful. Most people wait a lifetime and never get the chance to tell their bosses to take this job and shove it. Thanks to Anne Marie Lipinski, I got to do it three times in three minutes. And each one was better than the last.

As soon as I got back to Chicago, I went to my desk at home and telephoned the team hotel in Houston. Both Cubs president Andy MacPhail and general manager Ed Lynch were on the road trip. With the other beat reporters gone, I'd been able to enjoy several leisurely, personal conversations with the two bosses during the weekend in San Diego. I knew the rumor mill would crank into full gear when I didn't show up in Houston and I thought I owed them the courtesy of letting them know first-hand what had happened, as well as to let them know how much I enjoyed working with them. I had a typically thoughtful and enjoyable conversation with MacPhail. Lynch was out, but called back the next day and thanked me for letting him know what happened.

One of the last calls I made was to track down Mike Hirsley, an old friend and the reporter who had to jump on a plane and fly to Houston to cover for me. I caught him in the press box at the Astrodome and apolo-gized for getting him involved in an ugly situation. I offered any help he needed—statistics, contacts, phone numbers, anything—and explained exactly what happened. I told him to feel free to tell anyone who asked. There was nothing to hide.

With the phone call to Hirsley, I figured my duty was done. I sat back with my wife and reflected on what a great career I'd had at the *Tribune* and how glad I was that it was over. "I can tell," she said. "You look 10 years younger."

"I feel 10 years younger," I said, lying. I really felt 20 years younger.

Four days later, the phone rang in my kitchen. It was a Friday night and I'd just watched Kevin Foster beat the Pirates, 6-3, in the first of what would be an exciting eight-game winning streak for the Cubs down the closing days of the season. As soon as I picked up the receiver, I had the bizarre sense of *déjà vu*—or, as former Cub manager Don Zimmer, once called it: *"Ron-jih-voo."*

"Hey, Joe. What the hell is going on?"

It was Harry Caray. He hadn't made the trip to Houston, so he missed my sudden exit. The first he knew about it was when he got to Wrigley Field for Thursday night's game against the Pirates. That ended late and with the quick turnaround for a Friday afternoon game, this was the first chance Harry had to call.

"I missed your stuff in the paper the past few days, but I just figured you were taking some time off. Holy Cow! I just found out what happened."

Once again, just as he had that first spring training, Harry Caray was going out of his way to make me feel part of his baseball family. There was no reason in the world Harry had to call me. I hadn't called him earlier in the week. But here he was listening to me explain that I was moving to Hong Kong to follow my wife, who was going to make me a "kept man" for the next few years.

"Jesus Christ, Joe. I never figured you for a gih … a gig … a gig'-ah-low."

"Yeah, Harry, that's me. I'm just an old gigolo."

"Hey, maybe you should take me with ya. They got a lotta people with slanty eyes over there. I'm real good with slanty-eyed people."

Dozens of people called in the days just after I quit. Many wanted to congratulate me on going back overseas. A few were fishing for gossip that wasn't there. Most called to express awe at the way I walked away. One high-profile columnist sent me an e-mail on CompuServe—outside the *Tribune's* easily tapped and ridiculously archaic computer network—that ended: "I know you will prosper and even though I am in a position right now where I utterly enjoy what I am doing, I envy you the pleasure of making that call from Denver."

It was, indeed, a pleasure. One of life's great moments. And I forever will be grateful that I was in position to make it. As my nephew, Cory Brock, had said: covering the Cubs for the *Chicago Tribune* "is one of the five greatest jobs in the world." But no job is worth it if the people you are working for don't treat you with simple common decency. And that was one of most glaring sins that hit me during my four years back in the States. Corporate America had alienated its greatest asset, the American workers. They were treated more like disposable razors than the cutting edge employees they had always been, and still were. And the cost of that treatment was staggering. Almost no one I knew was truly happy in their work and, hence, truly happy in their lives. Almost everyone I knew envied me the opportunity to walk away from even what they realized was a terrific job.

I watched from across the Pacific Ocean as Patrick Buchannan tapped that national disenchantment during the 1996 Republican presidential primaries. I found it frightening to see such right-wing venom gain popular acceptance. But I understood why it was happening. There was a malaise about the land back home. And everybody was looking for a cure—except the only people who had it in their power to make things better: the Howard Tyners and Anne Marie Lipinskis of the world.

One very American theme emerged almost without exception among those who called in the days after I quit. "Let's get together for dinner before you leave," the caller would say shortly before hanging up. It was almost as if the phrase good-bye had been renovated and expanded from two words to ten. Nobody could hang up without holding out the hazy promise of getting together at some unspoken place at some nebulous time in the future. Good-bye was just too final. Harry Caray echoed the All-American Farewell. Only, for him, it wasn't a crutch. He meant it. Three weeks later, in the final mad rush as we were packing for our now happily accelerated departure to Hong Kong, the kitchen phone rang again.

"Hey, Joey, when the hell are we gonna get together for that dinner?"

"Awh, Harry, I thought you'd be back in Palm Springs by now. I never figured you had time to get together."

"What the hell do you mean? We gotta date. When can we do it?"

We agreed on a time and Harry asked where we wanted to go. My wife and I always enjoyed Harry Caray's restaurant and I suggested that.

"Nawh, we don't want to go there. We'll never have a chance to talk. People will be coming up to me all the time. How's about ..." and he suggested a favorite Italian restaurant near his condominium just off the Gold Coast. That sounded even better and Harry said: "I'll make the reservations for 8 o'clock. Come whenever you can. Just ask for my table."

Those words had an ominous ring. *"Ron-jih-voo"* all over again. But I was wiser in Caray Custom than I had been four years earlier. Besides, Harry wasn't drinking anymore. How bad could it be?

We got to the restaurant a little before 8 and the maitre 'd escorted us to Harry's table. There, already chilling, was a bottle of wine. I worried it was for us. But I quickly learned it was for Harry. He wasn't drinking anymore, but he wasn't drinking any less either. The only difference was that now the wine was alcohol free.

A few minutes later, promptly at 8 o'clock, Harry and his wife, Dutchie, showed up. Harry had to thread his way through several groups of well-wishers, who recognized him immediately. So Dutchie was already seated when he walked up to the table. The first thing he did was lean over in front of me, put his two index fingers just below his temples, and pull back the folds of skin on his face.

"Hey, Joe, you gonna take me to Hong Kong? You know how good I am with those slanty-eyed people." And he nearly choked laughing at himself.

Ah, America: hopelessly bumbling and wondrously irrepressible.

The waiter came over and opened the first of two bottles of alcohol-free wine Harry would drink that night. When it was uncorked, Harry made a touching toast and Dutchie, Lynne, and I raised our cocktails to join him. As soon as we finished, Harry smacked his lips, looked at his wine glass, and said: "Listen, Joe, I know I've told you this before. But if anybody tries to tell ya you can have as much fun _NOT_ drinking as you do when you're drinking ..."

Five months later, I was sitting on the barstool next to Harry at J. Chew's in Scottsdale. I used this book as the excuse to fly from Hong Kong to Arizona. But next time there will be another one. What I really wanted was to wallow in spring training again. I love it. I hope I never miss another one, no matter how far I have to fly.

Ned Colletti of the San Francisco Giants had begged me to ask Harry about Elvis. Colletti was in the Cubs' front office under Dallas Green, Jim Frey, and Larry Himes. He'd known Harry for more than a decade and heard all his stories a hundred times. But he never tired of them. Like most everyone who got the chance to know Harry, Ned loved him and cherishes their friendship.

"Hey, Harry, what about that time in Vegas when Elvis had you paged at the crap table?"

"Oh, yeah. I almost didn't recognize him when he came down to meet me. Here's this good-looking guy walking up to me and he's wearing those blue jean shorts and dark glasses. It takes me a minute and then I realize it's Elvis. He says: 'Harry, why didn't you let me know you were in town? Come on up to my room so we can talk.' He loved to talk baseball. I remember he said to me ... "

Harry doesn't get to finish the Elvis story. From outside J. Chew's,

Hard at work on this book poolside in Scottsdale, Arizona, at spring training 1996. (Photo by Patrick T. Benic)

another fan has spotted him. This time it's a woman who's put on the extra pounds she'll need to carry her through middle age. She's wearing a cheap nylon wind breaker with the red, white, and blue Cubs logo painted like a target over her heart.

"Harrr-rreeeee!" she shouts in an out-of-tune voice that makes Ike Cole shudder. Harry Caray swings around on his barstool and the woman's voice downshifts to a stage whisper for just a second. *"See. I told you it was him."* Then shouting again: *"Hey, Harrr-rreeeee. We love ya, Harrr-rreeeee."*

Colletti and I look at each other and exchange smiles. We're both thinking the same thing: "Ahhhh, one of life's great moments."

Harry isn't tired, but he's considerate. Jack Leahy is his guest and Jack is obviously ready to go home. Ike Cole has to get back to work. The other patrons of the bar haven't heard a song for an hour because Ike has been quietly enjoying the conversation at the bar. Harry reaches into his pocket and asks for the tab. He always pays the tab. And he always tips generously. One night after a dinner at El Charro's in Phoenix, I watched Harry hand out $110 worth of tips in the walk from the table to his car. He tipped waitresses who worked his table the *last* time he had been in the restaurant. He gave $10 to busboys who happened to be passing through the dining room as he left. This time, at J. Chew's, Harry drops a pair of twenties on the bar for $24 worth of beer and says to the bartender: "Keep the change. I had a nice time."

We offer our good-byes. Harry stays true to the All-American ritual and says he and Dutchie just might come to Hong Kong some day. Then he heads off toward another perfect Arizona spring night. Jack Leahy is leading the way, followed by Chris Caray. Harry tries to follow, but stops every five feet to flirt with a beautiful, young women—or a woman he makes feel beautiful and young just by saying hello.

When he finally reaches the door, Harry turns and gives a final web-fingered wave. Everyone in the room is smiling. I feel like turning to Colletti and saying: "Hey, Nehhhhh-uhd. You know how to spell America backward?"

Chapter 10

Wrigley to Wanchai

A thick, milky cloud just drifted in off the South China Sea and covers half of Victoria Peak. I can just see the vague outline of the new Peak Tram station, an appropriately gaudy piece of architecture that looks like a bowling trophy turned upside down and stuck into the mountainside. A welder is working near the base of the trophy, which is really the top of the building. The flicker of his torch could be angry lightning churning in the bowels of the cloud, but there are no other signs of storm. The skies below and around the gossamer veil are a perfect Cubbie blue. The shrub-shrouded hillside out my window overlooking the Wanchai district of Hong Kong is lush and green as the ivy walls of Wrigley Field in July.

It is, to quote my favorite troubadour, Jimmy Buffett: "a beautiful day—the kind you want to toast."

And it just got better. Scott Servais hit a solo home run in the top of the 10th inning to beat the Florida Marlins, 5-4. Turk Wendell struck out the side in the home half of the inning to get the win. And Luis Gonzalez, one of the nicest men I had the pleasure of meeting in baseball, stroked a pinch double to spark the Cubbie comeback.

Best of all, I got to watch it live on the radio. Right here in Hong Kong.

The world and I have changed a lot since I first went overseas in 1979. Back then, my strongest link to home was a clunky suitcase-sized Grundig shortwave radio that still sits on my window sill and still brings the comforting drone of the BBC news every day. But now, too, I can turn on my computer, dial a local phone number, click a few buttons and listen to a country-and-western station in Phoenix. I can tune in National

Public Radio in the States or KLSU, the campus radio station at my alma mater in Baton Rouge. Most importantly, I can pick up a Major League Baseball game every day of the season, anywhere in the world.

The Internet. Personal computers. Satellite television. AIDS. Soft-porn aerobics. The split-fingered fastball. Wildcard playoffs. Oprah Winfrey. Cell phones. All-sports radio. Drive-through daiquiri stands. Drive-by shootings ...

So much change in so little time.

Nathaniel Hawthorne, the 19th Century American author, spent a long stretch abroad in the 1850s when he wrote *The Marble Faun*. In it, he talked of going home to New England "because the years have a kind of emptiness when we spend too many of them on a foreign shore." But he talked, too, of the dilemma of going home. "If we do return, we find that the native air has lost its invigorating quality and that life has shifted its reality to the spot where we have deemed ourselves only temporary residents. Thus, between two countries, we have none at all."

I often felt that way. I was comfortable anywhere, and at home no-where. People would come up to me at cocktail parties and baffle me with the simplest, most straight-forward, ice-breaking question: "So, where are you from?" Or: "Where's home?" Sometimes I would say Chicago, since I worked for the *Chicago Tribune*. But Chicago really wasn't home. I never went there until I was 30 years old. And when I did go, it was only for brief interludes between foreign postings. Sometimes I would say New Orleans because that's where I was born. But I left the Big Easy to go the LSU when I was 17 years old and never planted roots there again.

Hawthorne had an either-or solution for expatriates like himself and me who wander in homeless purgatory: "It is wise," he wrote, "...to come back betimes, or never."

Betimes were long overdue when I finally came home from Warsaw. I wonder, now, if I should have chosen never. My four years back in the States were comforting, confusing, exciting, enlightening, frustrating, and only marginally fulfilling.

Baseball was the perfect road map back to America in almost every way. Despite its many failings, despite the popularity of more sprightly sports, baseball remains the quintessential American game. It mirrors

On deadline in the press box at Candlestick Park in San Francisco the weekend of O.J. Simpson's weird freeway chase. (Photo by Nancy Wong)

the national psyche. It unfolds slowly and irrevocably, like our lives, on different fields of different shapes in different cities at different times. Yet, it is the same beautiful game in Chavez Ravine as it is in the SkyDome. Baseball, like our lives, is a quilt of interminable routine interrupted by moments of delirious joy or unspeakable heartache. There are winners and losers, just as in life. But, like life, baseball is cumulative. It plays itself out over a prolonged period. Every game, like every life, can end any time or last longer than anyone expects. Each season lingers from the childhood of spring to the funeral of fall. Losers can always become winners. And winners can never coast.

When I left the States, people pasted their proudest, and sometimes deepest, thoughts on bumper stickers. When I returned, T-shirts held sway. And one of the first that caught my attention read simply: "Baseball is Life." I found out later "Water Polo is Life." So is ice fishing, lacrosse, hockey, poker, macramé, mahjong, and bowling. But, at the time, I chuckled remembering an old friend who once broke up with his girlfriend partly because she refused to accept his cardinal tenet—still proudly posted on his home page on the Internet—that "Life is a Baseball Game." For more than 20 years, my friend was a cliché waiting to be copied.

In the two decades it took for that gospel to become hallowed, though, both life and baseball changed.

Andy MacPhail, president of the Cubs and one of the most thoughtful people I met, inside baseball or out, during my four years back home, appreciated some of the things I felt about the country and saw parallels in the game.

"Baseball is very reflective of where the country is going. It might even be ahead of it. And it's not exactly the prettiest picture in the world," MacPhail said one day in his office at the Cubs' spring training complex in Arizona. "There is something innate about baseball in the American character that makes the game popular. It makes the game unique. With all our troubles in 1995 [the year of the last strike], we still had 50 million people in the turnstiles. What other labor disputes in other sports have caused the interdiction of the president of the United States and Congress and all the things that baseball has? President Clinton never got up there and started talking about the hockey strike. Baseball is a big part of our culture, and as society changes and as technology and other changes affect our society, the same things happen in baseball."

But just as I wasn't enthralled with all the changes I found when I came home, MacPhail wasn't overjoyed with some of the changes in baseball.

"I've seen things this spring that I've never seen before. You know, you go to a game in Phoenix where you have people twirling around bats between innings, and they'll be throwing bean bags between innings and they'll be running bingo numbers on the scoreboard. On the one hand, you've got clubs who don't have to do any discounting and they're still drawing. And on the other hand, you've got clubs giving away tickets and they're not getting anybody in the stands. I don't understand it. I've seen fireworks, Disney characters, The Chicken. What's going on? I don't like the Hollywoodization of the sport because, to me, people respect the sport. That's what we're selling. It's not Arnold Schwarzenegger. It's not one name on the marquee. Ken

Griffey, as good as he is, cannot win alone. Nor can Randy Johnson. What people, in my view, celebrate in baseball is the team concept.

"Part of the unfortunate thing about baseball is there aren't many people—there aren't enough people in the game—that, in my view, truly understand what makes the game popular. They take things from other sports that don't apply. Baseball is a different pace. Yeah, we might lose some 14-year-olds who want laser lights and computer effects. But to make radical changes to appeal to a group that may not like the game anyway under any circumstances and risk losing your core makes me concerned. People come to games not to see The Chicken, not to twirl around the bat three times and then run to third base and get a free Hooters' sweatshirt. They come to see baseball.

"It's like a society that loses track of its past a little bit—you know, loses track of who they are. We can't afford to lose track of where we've been and who we are. That doesn't mean you don't promote the game and that you don't try to come up with new things that are popular for the fans. But that has to be tempered with an understanding of what you're selling in the first place, what it is that makes you special."

The very things MacPhail felt about baseball, I felt about America. "It's like a society that loses track of its past a little bit—loses track of who they are. We can't afford to lose track of where we've been and who we are" ... what makes us special. It's not one name on the marquee. It's the team concept.

Just when technology, dwindling resources and common concerns are combining to shrink the world and make McLuhan's "Global Village" a reality, Americans, it seems, have reverted to an island mentality. Forget about Poland. Forget about "the village." How 'bout dem Cubs? What's happening with O.J.? What about me?

One of the pivotal events that influenced my thinking about America, its people, and our priorities came the day Orenthal James Simpson, a fugitive from justice, climbed into a white Ford Bronco with his passport, a gun, and thousands of dollars in cash and led a fleet of police cars on a long, leisurely, globally televised drive up and down the southern California coast. The Cubs were playing the Giants at Candlestick Park that day and I was hoping desperately the game would move along. I enjoy even the most-boring baseball game, but I begrudged every lost hour in San Francisco. It is one of the great cities of the world and I was chafing to get back in it when suddenly there was a huge hubbub and every TV set in the press box switched to live coverage of O.J. Simpson's Bronco ride. I missed whole innings for the next hour as I sat in stunned silence watching thousands of Californians line the highways and flock to overpasses just to cheer on O.J.

I've seen Mao Zedong's carcass turn orange in a glass mausoleum over the years. I once stood in the Casino du Liban with my dear friend Cathy Booth tossing purple-and-gold chips worth 10 dollars apiece onto a roulette table while we looked down a mountainside onto a grisly nighttime bombardment of Beirut. And I used to drink in a bar in Manila where all the waiters were dwarves and the main attraction was a 3-foot-7-inch, hip-swishing dynamo who did such a terrific Elvis impersonation you thought you'd stepped back 30 years and were watching the real thing through the wrong end of a telescope. But I can't honestly say I've seen many things weirder than O.J. Simpson's little sunset spin. The really weird part was just how quickly most people quit thinking it was weird.

An even more-astounding O.J. moment came months later when I watched, again on live television, as a group of inner-city women living in a shelter for abused wives jumped out of their chairs in jubilation at news of Simpson's acquittal. Battered wives were cheering a confessed wife beater. They cheered, of course, not for him but for themselves. They cheered because the system they felt had beaten them down had finally itself been beaten. The reaction those women had to the O.J. Simpson verdict had nothing to do with truth. It had nothing to do with justice. But it had everything to do with the American way—with Americans losing their way.

I didn't have to come home to learn the American system is flawed. Everyone knows that. I did have to come home, however, to be reminded it is far less-flawed than any other system I've seen. Or it was. And it still can be, if we follow MacPhail's recipe for baseball and don't lose track of who we are. Don't lose track of where we've been and what makes us special.

Of all the places I've lived and worked, the one where I left most of my heart has to be the Philippines. Whenever I think of that land of 7,000 islands, a flood of passion and pain bathes me. The honeyed perfume of sampagita flowers wilting in an air-conditioned car ... mud-caked carabaos slogging through a forest of emerald rice paddies ... tantalizingly beautiful women ... tar pitch and kerosene ... corruption ... incompetence ... gunfire ... more gunfire ... mortars ... mangoes ... communism ... colonialism ... horny American sailors ... German pedophiles ... tireless nuns ... courageous priests ... a million people singing ... a thousand people dying.

The Philippines was a muddle of giddy highs and desolate lows. Twice in one night, my wife and I narrowly escaped being shot reporting a coup. The eerie pre-dawn silence outside Malacañan Palace was broken only by the ominous sounds of our own shoes slapping the pavement of an empty street followed by the heart-panging thud of a bullet just a few feet away. My panicked wife suddenly ran toward the sniper, instead of away, until I could catch her and throw her against a wall. During another coup, a New Zealand photographer who was pinned down near me for half an hour in no-man's land between the opposing forces had his head blown off because he was being macho and refused to hug the ground like the rest of us.

When normalcy intervened, we would host catered dinners for Filipino senators or comical costume parties for diplomats from half a dozen countries and journalists from around the world. The president, Corazon Aquino, personally came to visit when the *Chicago Tribune* and the Foreign Correspondents' Association opened joint offices in Manila. But there were times, too, when I ate bananas and cold rice with communist guerrillas in the jungle. Once I sipped fine red wine with a missionary in the hills of Mindanao, a thousand miles from Manila and a half day's hike from the nearest highway.

On every level, the Philippines was a maelstrom of emotions. But

Hugging the ground during one of the coup attempts in the Philippines. We are pinned down between anti-government forces and loyalist troops. The photographer grinning and refusing to take cover was from New Zealand. He was shot in the head and killed minutes later.

when I think of the Philippines today, one image—one memory—transcends everything. It is the face of a filthy, frail waif dashing desperately from one car to the next in the middle of Manila's ever-stalled traffic. She, he—it doesn't matter, there are armies of both—has the chilling black eyes of caged cur. Sad, scared, and surrendering all at once. The waif brings the fingers of one hand together and uses muddy nails to tap once, twice, three times on the rear window of a car. Then the fingers fan out momentarily, come back together and move slowly to the mouth in a pitiful plea for Pesos and food. The plea always comes to the rear window. Money rides in the back in Manila. Almost everyone who can afford a car, can afford a driver. And almost everyone who can afford a car, can afford one with tinted windows. Black tinted windows. They shut out two tribulations of life in the Philippines: searing sun and peering eyes. All a beggar sees when she looks for hope in the Philippines is darkness and her own, forsaken reflection.

The Philippine Islands are so lush you could push a year-old

Dreamsicle stick into the soil and grow a dream. Still, the land is littered with starving children, emaciated women, and broken men. Americans know poverty, but few have ever known it on this scale. Few can comprehend it on this scale. Generations of colonial oppression, endemic corruption, and unfettered population growth have turned a tropical paradise into a breeding ground for killers, Communists, and crooks.

And the Philippines is hardly the most-impoverished place on the planet. It's problems pale to the misery in Bangladesh, Africa, parts of China, and a hundred other places. A World Bank study in the summer of 1996 found one in five people on the planet were struggling to survive on less than $1 per day.

Most Americans enjoy a level of comfort in their daily lives that is simply inconceivable in much of the world. Yet, few realize it—let alone put it in perspective. We have our own problems. Our jobs are increasingly unrewarding and unfulfilling. Our ambitions are needlessly stifled. Our frustrations are magnified and spawn a frightening web of crime and violence.

The murder of Michael Jordan's father was another telling moment in my return to the States. The fact that Robert Jordan was dragged from his luxury car and shot to death at a rest stop along an interstate highway was appalling. Terrible. But it was hardly worse than anything that happens on a regular basis in the Philippines—or outside Miami airport. It certainly can't compare to the everyday horrors in places like Sabrah and Shatilla, the refugee camps outside Beirut, where I saw women and children massacred. What was particularly appalling about Robert Jordan's murder to me, though, was his son's reaction. Michael Jordan took a year off. He tried baseball. He marketed his success and even did some publicity work for his charity, the Michael Jordan Foundation. But he did little publicly to bring about substantive change. Michael Jordan was probably the most-recognized athlete of his time. He was adored. Imagine if Michael Jordan had summoned the same charisma and flare he had for peddling Chevy Blazers, Nike shoes, or McDonald's hamburgers and focused it on a televised plea for hand gun control—or even some less-controversial social reform? He had the power to make a difference.

The single biggest change I saw after nearly 14 years abroad was what Rick Hornik, my old friend from *Time* magazine, constantly referred to as "the dumbing of America." I prefer to think of it as the "numbing of America." Almost everybody I met was ready to talk about O.J. or M.J., but there seemed an almost universal commitment to avoid anything even vaguely resembling serious thought or discussion. Was there ever anything else besides O.J. and Michael? Had I changed? Or had America?

My last day on the beat, I was sitting in the lunch room at Jack Murphy Stadium in San Diego with Cubs president Andy MacPhail having one of the most interesting conversations of my four years in baseball. We talked about Shelby Foote's book, *Stars in their Courses,* which MacPhail had just finished and I was just beginning. We were going back and forth about the incomprehensible courage it must have taken for those men and boys to march across that mile-wide open field under a torrent of cannon fire and fusillade to their deaths at Gettysburg on July 3, 1863. I mentioned my favorite passage from *Intruder in the Dust,* where Faulkner talks about the frozen moments just before Pickett's charge when "the brigades are in position behind the rail fence, the guns are laid and ready in the woods and the furled flags are already loosened to break out ... (when) it hasn't happened yet, it hasn't even begun yet." I loved that passage because Pickett's charge at Gettysburg was one of the rare moments in history where you can point to the exact hour, the precise moment, when a civilization died, and wonder what it must have felt like to be there.

Caught in the enjoyment of the conversation, and, frankly, frustrated at how rare such moments were on the baseball beat, I—like Lee—pressed on foolishly. I talked about how, in general, I was disappointed that few people in America seemed to read anymore; that so few people seemed to care what was going on in the outside world. I said most of the players I met—not all, but definitely most—had reinforced the stereotype of the one-dimensional jock. But I knew MacPhail had been around the game far longer. I asked him who was the brightest player he ever knew?

It was a moronic, mood-killing question. MacPhail spent several long minutes in genuine embarrassed silence trying to think of a player he considered truly bright. He quickly threw out names of a few players he respected, then paused again and backtracked, trying to define precisely what "bright" meant. Cultural literacy? Sheer intellect? Street smarts? Finally, we both did ourselves a favor and politely steered the conversation in another direction.

Nothing epitomized the numbing and dumbing of America more than the staggering success of the movie *Forrest Gump* with its paean to passivity. Just show up, have a good heart, and fate will take care of everything. It drove me crazy.

Maybe I made too much of Forrest Gump. Then again, I caught a glimpse of Oprah Winfrey and Ricki Lake. I watched all-sports radio stations sprouting like weeds and heard them fill endless hours with mindless gibberish. Everywhere I turned, emotionalism and sensationalism seemed to have taken reign over intellectualism.

Some will say that was mainly because I was immersed in the weird world of sports. They will say that has always been the case in sports. But I disagree. Especially with baseball. The game holds special sway over both scholars and scoundrels. It evokes the same passion from Bart Giamatti, Vin Scully, George Will, Bob Costas, and Lee MacPhail as it did from Yogi Berra, Casey Stengel, Dizzy Dean, Jim Lefebvre, and Harry Caray. It is possible to love Faulkner and appreciate a forkball; to cherish Monet and Maddux. It is possible, too, to follow the Cubs and care about curbing violence and curing illiteracy; care about what happens in Krakow, Croatia, and Cebu.

One thing, I think, changed drastically while I was gone. And I think it had a lot to do with the numbing of America. Sports—baseball included—has become more a vent for frustration and less an avenue for jubilation. Frustration comes easily to those who refuse to think. Jubilation is one of the many gifts of an active imagination.

Along with the late Bart Giamatti, one of my baseball heroes is Lee MacPhail, father of Cubs' president Andy MacPhail, and son of the late Larry MacPhail, once president of the Cincinnati Reds and owner, at different times, of the Brooklyn Dodgers and New York Yankees. Larry

MacPhail was a flamboyant, hard-drinking, fast-living innovator, who introduced night baseball and live radio and television to the game. His son, Lee, was a staid, scholarly conservative, who flourished as a prep schoolmaster before becoming general manager of the Yankees and president of the American League.

"Lee MacPhail holds three big league records that may never be broken," author Thomas Boswell wrote for the *Washington Post* Writers' Group in March 1986. "He has visited at least two art museums in every major league city. He has been to the symphony in all of them. And, while on airplanes between those towns, he has read at least one biography of every American president, two on most."

I came home to America hoping to find a few Lee MacPhails. And I did. But I also ran into a frightening number of Forrest Gumps.

In a Plexiglas cube, resting atop my computer monitor, is an official National League baseball. Handwritten in blue ink, nestled under the comforting crescent of red stitches on one side, are the words: "To Joey, Welcome Home." Turn the ball over and cradled beneath the twin crescent in the same blue ink is the familiar autograph of Ernie Banks—Mr. Cub.

The ball is one of my most-treasured possessions. It was a surprise gift from a long-lost friend, photographer Michael Theiler, when I returned to the States in 1992. My wife had gotten Ernie Banks' autograph on the brim of a white Cubs' visor when she bumped into him outside Wrigley Field early—very early—the morning of the first game of the 1984 playoffs. I wasn't with her. I'd given my ticket to another friend, Bill Trott. I had to work that day, writing the front-page story of Chicago's deliriously disbelieving reaction to a 13-0 win over the Padres.

Ten years later, though, at spring training 1994, I would sit for hours in the press box at HoHoKam Park in Mesa, Arizona, talking with Ernie Banks. He liked to pull up a chair during games and sit among the writers. Truth be told, it could be a bit of a pain. First of all, Ernie Banks talks better and longer than he ever hit—and he hit well enough to get into the Hall of Fame. He jabbers away nonstop. Secondly, the fans would inevitably spot Ernie and start reaching over the press box rail to hand him balls, hats, bats, programs, umbrellas, bottles of suntan lotion, and anything else to autograph. Rarely does much of great import happen on the field during a spring training game. Still, as long as I was there, I liked to see what was going on. That wasn't always possible with Ernie Banks sitting at your side. But, hey, it was a small price to pay. What do you say, Ernie? Let's play two.

Even though the inscription on my Ernie Banks ball said "welcome home." And even though I constantly talked about "coming home" or "being home," I'm not sure I ever made it. One night, more than two years after returning to the States, my wife and I were standing in the covered courtyard of a hotel in northern Indiana watching men in penny loafers stalk hookers at a bar while their wives filtered away to a Julio Iglesias concert at a nearby auditorium and their children shrieked through games of indoor golf or swam in the giant pool that polluted everything with a nauseating reek of chlorine. The place was Milton's *Pandæmonium* to me. I turned to Lynne and said: "You know, I think I was more at home in Tibet than I am here tonight." We both laughed. And we've regaled friends abroad with that story a hundred times. But, you know, I think I was right.

Two generations ago, Thomas Wolfe wrote: "we are lost here in America." Wolfe's character, George Webber, talked about the cancer of "cureless hates" that had "eaten in one way or another into the private lives of all his friends." And of the realization "that all, alas, was not friends, was not freedom, was not love" in America. But he was quick to add, too, that "the essence of America's hope had not been wholly ruined, it's promise of fulfillment not shattered utterly."

I think it is all true today. Perhaps, it will always be true. What I don't know is if Wolfe was right when he wrote: "You can't go home again." I believe he was right in all the many complex and marvelous dimensions he explained the phrase to mean for him. And I believe in the deepest sense, he speaks a universal truth. But on the most-mundane level, I simply don't know if he was right because I don't know where home is. I fear I will never know.

But I do know I will always feel at home in a ballpark. And I do know the journey from Warsaw to Wrigley was one of the most wondrous in a life filled with wanderings.

The last time I left old HoHoKam Park in Mesa, Arizona, just days

In front of Wrigley in December 1991, the winter I came home to start the Cubs' assignment.

before they started tearing it down to build a new spring training complex for the Cubs, I pulled my rental car into the dusty parking lot to take one final mental snapshot. The heavens that day were as pristine blue as they are this afternoon in Hong Kong. The only difference was the desert sky refused to suffer the flaw of even a single fluffy white cloud.

I stared at that beautiful little ballpark and thought of all the memories I will carry of it, and the people who played in it—both on the field and in the stands—the rest of my life. I remembered I was here the day my mother died. I thought of four years of good times and bad, four years of searching and learning. And I took it all it in without a tear of regret—either for having come, or for moving on.

When I finally started the car and flipped on the radio, I froze for a second, stared down at the speakers, and then laughed so loudly the sound echoed off the red brick facade of the visitor's clubhouse. An old Ronnie Milsap song I hadn't heard in years put words to my very thoughts:

"I wouldn't have missed it for the world."

Chronology

1972 BATON ROUGE, LA/NEW ORLEANS
Named "Outstanding Graduating Senior in Journalism" at Louisiana State University and hired by United Press International in New Orleans.

1975 DALLAS
Transferred to UPI Dallas.

1976 DENVER/NEW ORLEANS
Transferred to UPI Denver; transferred again in July back to UPI New Orleans as Bureau Manager and Louisiana State Editor.

1979 LONDON
Transferred to UPI London; first reporting trips to Middle East.

1980 LONDON
Iraq invades Iran. I become the first Western reporter inside the war zone.

1981 VIENNA
Transferred to UPI Vienna as Chief Eastern European Correspondent.

1982 CHICAGO
Hired by *Chicago Tribune*; return to USA; sent to Beirut in June when Israel invades Lebanon. Spent summer under siege; nominated for Pulitzer for coverage. Won *Chicago Tribune*'s Edward Scott Beck Award for "courageous and sensitive writing under relentlessly adverse conditions during the invasion of Lebanon and siege of Beirut."

1983 CHICAGO
Based in Chicago; sent back to Lebanon to cover Yasser Arafat's last stand in Tripoli. Nominated for Pulitzer for series of stories on impact of illegal immigration on U.S. economy.

1984 CHICAGO/BEIJING
Named Jefferson Fellow of Asian Studies at East-West Center in Honolulu; nominated for Pulitzer for series of stories on lack of progress in Civil Rights in the U.S.; named Asia Correspondent and Beijing Bureau Chief of the *Chicago Tribune*.

1986 BEIJING/MANILA

Established dual residency in Beijing and Manila; nominated for Pulitzer for coverage of the People Power revolution in the Philippines. Won the *Chicago Tribune*'s Edward Scott Beck Award for "highly professional performance in covering the People's Revolution in the Philippines, especially under intense deadline pressure."

1988 MANILA/ROME

Elected president Foreign Correspondents' Association of the Philippines; named Rome Bureau Chief of *Chicago Tribune*.

1989 ROME

Covered collapse of communism in Eastern Europe; also dispatched to cover funeral of Ayatollah Khomeini in Tehran and aftermath of Tiananmen massacre in China.

1990 WARSAW

Moved to Warsaw as East European Correspondent of the *Tribune*.

1992 CHICAGO

Returned to USA to become Cubs' beat writer.

1993 CHICAGO

Covered division-champion White Sox; inducted into LSU Manship School of Communications Hall of Fame.

1994-95 CHICAGO

Returned to Cubs.

1996-97 HONG KONG

Moved to Hong Kong and wrote *Warsaw to Wrigley*. Enrolled at Hong Kong University. Working on a Master's of Philosophy degree in Historical Research. Subject: A History of Baseball in Asia—The rise and fall of America's game from the Arctic through the Pacific.